Contemporary Philosophies and Theories in Education

Volume 17

Contemporary Philosophies and Theories in Education signifies new directions and possibilities out of a traditional field of philosophy and education. Around the globe, exciting scholarship that breaks down and reformulates traditions in the humanities and social sciences is being created in the field of education scholarship. This series provides a venue for publication by education scholars whose work reflect the dynamic and experimental qualities that characterize today's academy. The series associates philosophy and theory not exclusively with a cognitive interest (to know, to define, to order) or an evaluative interest (to judge, to impose criteria of validity) but also with an experimental and attentive attitude which is characteristic for exercises in thought that try to find out how to move in the present and how to deal with the actual spaces and times, the different languages and practices of education and its transformations around the globe. It addresses the need to draw on thought across all sorts of borders and counts amongst its elements the following: the valuing of diverse processes of inquiry; an openness to various forms of communication, knowledge, and understanding; a willingness to always continue experimentation that incorporates debate and critique; and an application of this spirit, as implied above, to the institutions and issues of education. Authors for the series come not only from philosophy of education but also from curriculum studies and critical theory, social sciences theory, and humanities theory in education. The series incorporates volumes that are trans- and inner-disciplinary. The audience for the series includes academics, professionals and students in the fields of educational thought and theory, philosophy and social theory, and critical scholarship.

More information about this series at http://www.springer.com/series/8638

Itay Snir

Education and Thinking in Continental Philosophy

Thinking against the Current in Adorno, Arendt, Deleuze, Derrida and Rancière

Itay Snir
The Open University of Israel
Ra'anana, Israel

The Max Stern Yezreel Valley College
Yezreel Valley, Israel

ISSN 2214-9759 ISSN 2214-9767 (electronic)
Contemporary Philosophies and Theories in Education
ISBN 978-3-030-56528-2 ISBN 978-3-030-56526-8 (eBook)
https://doi.org/10.1007/978-3-030-56526-8

This Springer imprint is published by the registered company Springer Nature Switzerland AG
The registered company address is: Gewerbestrasse 11, 6330 Cham, Switzerland

Acknowledgements

Thinking is a nomadic and lonely activity. Perhaps it is no accident, then, that this book about thinking was not written at a single academic home but rather migrated between several institutions. Being in constant motion poses many difficulties, but also enables to enjoy the company of many friends and the hospitality of various locations. The difficulty of putting thoughts into words, which is one of the themes of this book, is felt acutely when trying to articulate the deep gratitude I feel to all those who helped along the way.

Jan Masschelein hosted me as a Postdoctoral Fellow at the Laboratory of Education, Culture and Society at KU Leuven University, Belgium, where this study made its first steps. The encounter with the brilliance and originality of Jan's thought drew me into the field of philosophy of education, and his guidance and encouragement made it possible for me to pave my own way in it. Jan taught me what a good teacher is – in theory as well as in practice – and I feel privileged to continue being his student to this day, even after my (too short) stay in Leuven is long over. Jan supported this study from its very early stage and invited me to develop it into this book.

Upon returning to Israel, I met with Hanan Alexander, of whose contribution to the philosophy of education I have constantly been hearing about in Europe. Still, Hanan's kindness and generosity went beyond all my expectations. Despite our different philosophical orientations, Hanan was enthusiastic about my work. He hosted me as a Postdoctoral Fellow at the Faculty of Education at the University of Haifa and introduced me to the Anglo-American tradition of education for thinking.

The origins of this book lie in my doctoral dissertation, which, although not bearing directly on educational questions, still contains many of the elements of which the current book is composed. The chapters on Arendt and Deleuze are adapted from the dissertation, written under the supervision of Anat Matar. Yet this is not the only reason for my gratitude to Anat. What I learned from her far exceeds philosophy, and accompanies me within and without academic life.

During the long period of writing the book, the Lexicon Group at the Minerva Humanities Center at Tel Aviv University has been for me a place of study, writing, and intellectual engagement with colleagues who are also close friends. Despite constant shortage of material resources, the group offered support in many other ways, and most importantly proved that even today there is still room in academia for genuine thinking.

The Open University of Israel, where I have been working as a teaching fellow for the last 8 years, has generously supported the publication of the book by financing the language editing. I am grateful to the University's Research Authority and especially Dafna Hirsch, Head of the Department of Political Science, Sociology and Communication, for this support.

Ami Asher is the book's language editor, but his contribution far exceeds English grammar and style. Throughout the process of writing and rewriting, Ami has often been my first reader and interlocutor. His comments and suggestions have improved the book in philosophical, political, and educational aspects as well.

Various friends have contributed in different ways to the book, whether by reading and commenting or less directly. It is my pleasure to thank them all: Adam Aboulafia, Ariel Handel, Chen Misgav, Gal Levy, Hans Schildermans, Keren Sadan, Lavinia Marin, Merav Amir, Michal Givoni, Michal Gleitman, Naveh Frumer, Ori Rotlevy, Ruthie Ginsburg, Samira Alirezabeigi, and Stefan Ramaekers.

An earlier version of Chap. 2 previously appeared as "*Minima Pedagogica*: Education, Thinking and Experience in Adorno" in the *Journal of Philosophy of Education*. I am grateful to John Wiley and Sons for their permission to use it here.

None of this would have been enough without the support and encouragement of my loving family: my mother Nurit Snir, my sister Nitzan Snir-Benyamin, my mother-in-law Tova Ascher, and father-in-law Yoni Ascher. Above all, I owe the most to my wife, Anat Ascher. Anat has read and commented on large parts of the book, and her support and inspiration are present in every word. With her I learn every day anew what wisdom is as well as what love is. While many people do not understand how two philosophers can live together, thanks to Anat I cannot imagine life – or philosophical thinking – any other way. This book is dedicated to our two young thinkers: Noga and Alon.

Contents

Chapter 1
Introduction

1.1 Rethinking Thinking

- What are you thinking about?
- Nothing
- How can this be?
- Because I don't think of anything important.
- Thinking is only about important things?
- I have to think about it later.

This short conversation between a father and his five-year-old daughter is thought provoking. Unintentionally, just by trying to start a conversation, it raised a series of interesting questions: What does thinking mean? Is daydreaming a kind of thinking? Is it possible for someone not to think? Although no clear answers are given and no knowledge is conveyed, this conversation has a definite educational aspect, as it makes the child – as well as her father – ask new questions and start thinking in new directions. The fruits of this educational moment are by no means immediate: as the child indicates, thinking on new questions cannot begin instantaneously and flow smoothly with the stream of consciousness. It must go against the current, interrupt it, and find its own time and place. When it starts, it is able to question the thinker's presuppositions, engage others in thinking and give birth to new insights – and in turn, new questions. Sometimes it can sow the seeds of a new book.

This book deals with five philosophers of the continental tradition – Theodor W. Adorno, Hannah Arendt, Jacques Derrida, Gilles Deleuze and Jacques Rancière – in an attempt to think about thinking and highlight the links between education and thinking. Following in the footsteps of Marx, Nietzsche and Heidegger, twentieth-century continental philosophy challenged the modern tradition of understanding thinking, and offered new, original conceptions thereof. However, although the philosophical alternatives formulated within that tradition realized that thinking was never an isolated individual act, but rather one anchored in a sociopolitical context,

I. Snir, *Education and Thinking in Continental Philosophy*, Contemporary Philosophies and Theories in Education 17,
https://doi.org/10.1007/978-3-030-56526-8_1

it devoted relatively little attention to educational questions per se. The five philosophers discussed in this book rarely tie their views of thinking to the field of education, and even when writing or commenting on that field, their concepts of thinking do not play an essential role or is not properly developed in that discussion.

In recent decades, education for thinking has become a rich and productive field in its own right, with numerous expressions in theory and practice. Various pedagogues and philosophers, most of whom belonging to the analytic philosophical tradition, attempt to provide this field with a proper conception of thinking and to formulate the importance of education for thinking. Despite differences and disputes, some of which are presented below, all agree that unlike education focused on the transmission of knowledge and abstract values, education for thinking emphasizes the intellectual activity of the thinker herself, thereby challenging the asymmetrical, hierarchical relationship between teacher and student. Such education therefore has a clear critical and democratic dimension – it contributes not only to the students' academic abilities but also to their political capacities as citizens. Stressing the ability of each individual to think and the convention-undermining effect of thinking, education for thinking has radical political potential. This makes the apparent neglect of the challenge of education for thinking by the continental philosophers discussed herein even more perplexing, for political concerns are at the heart of their philosophies.

Perhaps it is no coincidence, though, that the contemporary thriving of the field of education for thinking has occurred in tandem with the restoration of thinking to a prominent place in radical political theory. Marxist materialism, as is well known, placed Hegelian idealism on its feet, maintaining: "It is not the consciousness of men that determines their existence, but their social existence that determines their consciousness" (Marx 2000c, p. 425). Unlike the enlightenment philosophers who had believed in the power of rational thinking to lead political change, for Marx thinking was part of the "superstructure", the world of ideas determined by the economic-historical mode of production. For him, thinking merely reflected existing society and it could be transformed only through political activity – itself depending on class-consciousness, but not necessarily on thorough thinking.

In this spirit, Slavoj Žižek, one of the best-known critical theorists today, wrote in 2002 that the liberal demand for freedom of thought should be understood according to Kant's famous call in his 1784 "An Answer to the Question: What is Enlightenment" (2003) to *think freely and obey unconditionally*. Free thought, Žižek argued, is not a means for political freedom but an ideology reproducing social domination: "not only does freedom of thought not undermine actual social servitude, it positively sustains it" (2002, p. 3). However, in 2012, Žižek himself expressed a rather different view on thinking and politics. Looking back on the Occupy Wall Street movement, he said:

> I am, of course, fundamentally anti-capitalist. But… What shocks me is that most of the critics of today's capitalism feel even embarrassed… when you confront them with a simple question, "…what do you really want? What should replace the system?" And then you get one big confusion… This is why,… with all my sympathy for [the] Occupy Wall Street movement… I call it a Bartleby lesson. Bartleby, of course, Herman Melville's Bartleby,

> you know, who always answered his favorite "I would prefer not to"... The message of Occupy Wall Street is, I would prefer not to play the existing game. There is something fundamentally wrong with the system and the existing forms of institutionalized democracy are not strong enough to deal with problems. Beyond this, they don't have an answer and neither do I. For me, Occupy Wall Street is just a signal. It's like clearing the table. Time to start thinking... My advice would be, because I don't have simple answers:... precisely to start thinking. Don't get caught into this pseudo-activist pressure. Do something. Let's do it, and so on. So, no, the time is to think. I even provoked some of the leftist friends when I told them that if the famous Marxist formula was, "Philosophers have only interpreted the world; the time is to change it"... thesis 11 on Feuerbach ... that maybe today we should say, "In the twentieth century, we maybe tried to change the world too quickly. The time is to interpret it again, to start thinking." (2012)

Žižek is being provocative (and perhaps inconsistent) as usual, but he is not alone. In the same context of the 2011 world protests, Israeli scholar Noam Yuran read Marx's 11th thesis as saying, "thinking that does not include revolution is no thinking at all. This interpretation of the thesis is not far-fetched. All it means is that thinking must actually change the world..., or it is no thought at all but only part of the way the world interprets itself. In other words, revolution is an attribute of thought" (2012, p. 167, my translation). To take another example, in "Slow Thought: A Manifesto", Vincenzo Di Nicola (2018) argues that against consumer society, which encourages us to "act now, think later", an appeal to Slow Thought – inspired by the Slow Food movement – can be a real political counter-method.

To be sure, returning thinking to the front does not necessarily mean rejecting or postponing political action. Thinking itself can be understood as a political activity, a kind of refusal or even active resistance to common sense, one that does not remain within the individual mind but influences and challenges others as well. The renewed interest in thinking is therefore at the same time a return and a challenge to the foundations of modern philosophy: it puts thinking, dethroned by Marx, back at the center, while rejecting the simple distinction between intellectual and political activity.

While the rehabilitation of thinking in radical political philosophy has given birth to new conceptions of thinking or renewed interest in old ones, however, these conceptions are rarely present in contemporary educational discourse, which is still dominated by traditional conceptions of thinking. In this introductory chapter, I examine the philosophical and educational background within and against which I posit the encounters between the conceptions of thinking offered by the continental philosophers and the educational field. I begin with discussing the constitutive role of thinking in modern philosophy, and analyze the Cartesian conception of thinking that has become paradigmatic. Next, I present the existing field of education for thinking and trace the trends, controversies and assumptions shared by all who work in it, almost all of whom belong to the analytic tradition. Without committing to any clear difference between the two traditions, I then turn to continental philosophy, to examine how three of its founding fathers – Marx (who is examined also through the psychological work of Lev Vygotsky), Nietzsche and Heidegger – have challenged the Cartesian conception of thinking. Finally, I present the aims of the book and outline its chapters.

1.2 Thinking and Modern Philosophy

Modern philosophy was born in the thought of René Descartes, who made the "I think" the Archimedean point on which philosophy must rely for a solid edifice of knowledge. The entire Western philosophical tradition, of course, understands man in light of his cognitive, intellectual capacities – Greek philosophers such as Plato and Aristotle, to give just two obvious examples, described man as endowed with *logos*, the ability to speak and think rationally. However, Descartes argues that thinking about thinking is the very foundation of philosophy. Let us examine Descartes' conception of thinking, which is the point of reference to practically every consequent philosophical discussion of that concept.

Descartes refused to accept the authority of the philosophical tradition, and after calling all previous knowledge into doubt realized that since doubting is an act of thinking, the one thing one cannot doubt is the existence of one's own thoughts, and therefore one's own existence as a thinker. Even if an evil demon deceives me and distorts the *content* of my thoughts, I still exist as the one thinking them (Descartes 2008, p. 18). Thinking, therefore, is not just an ability of some biological species, but rather man's very essence: "this alone cannot be stripped from me. I am, I exist, this is certain. But for how long? Certainly only for as long as I am thinking; for perhaps if I were to cease from all thinking it might also come to pass that I might immediately cease altogether to exist… I am therefore, speaking precisely, only a thinking thing, that is, a mind, or a soul, or an intellect, or a reason" (2008, p. 19); "I knew I was a substance whose whole essence or nature is simply to think…" (1985b, p. 127). This starting point has important implications for Descartes' conception of thinking, and consequently for the whole of modern philosophy.

First, Descartes understands thinking in terms of representations, ideas, or "images of things" (2008, p. 26); namely, mental pictures of the outside world within subjective consciousness. Ontologically speaking, the thinking subject is essentially distinct from the material object, detached from the extending substance that stands against him. Epistemologically, knowledge is adequate representation, and truth is conceived as correspondence between mental image and external reality (p. 27).

Second, Descartes maintains that every idea that comes to mind, regardless of its truth content and relation to external reality, is a case of thinking: "I am seeing a light, hearing a noise, feeling heat.— But these things are false, since I am asleep!— But certainly I *seem to* be seeing, hearing, getting hot. This cannot be false. This is what is properly meant by speaking of myself as having sensations; and, understood in this precise sense, it is nothing other than thinking" (Descartes 2008, p. 21). For Descartes, then, thought is not defined according to content or quality: all mental events – either true or false, passively representing an object or adding some active relation to it (as when I want this object or judge it to be valuable) – are kinds of thinking (Smith 2015, pp. 116–7; Cottingham 1993, pp. 163–4). I am a thinking being, and as long as I exist, I think all the time, in many different ways; if I stop thinking, I might stop existing.

Third, Descartes insists that the ability to think is *fundamentally equal* in all human beings: all thinking beings are equally capable of exercising that essential capacity. Nevertheless, in reality not everyone makes the same use of their thinking abilities, as many false representations and misjudgments are by no means unusual: "... the power of judging well and of distinguishing the true from the false... is naturally equal in all men, and consequently... the diversity of our opinions does not arise because some of us are more reasonable than others but solely because we direct our thoughts along different paths and do not attend to the same things" (1985b, p. 111). This is why Descartes ascribes great importance to formulating the rules for proper thinking, the "rules for the direction of the mind" (1985a) or the "method" that will lead thought to positive knowledge (1985b, p. 120). Descartes' specific method is of no interest to us here, and it is highly doubtful whether it succeeds in accomplishing its mission. What is important is the ideal it sets for modern philosophy: one according to which proper thinking proceeds according to a clear, rational method, advancing step by step from the most simple to the most complex.

The last point worth mentioning here is the image of the *thinking subject* implied in the Cartesian conception of thinking. Emma Williams argues that understanding thinking as taking place in an inner sphere detached from a material world is tightly connected to "the rational-liberal ideal of the *autonomous* and *self-sufficient* subject, whose representative acts of thinking work to master and dominate the object-world that it stands over and against" (2016, p. 34, emphasis in the original). The world, then, is merely food for thought, the material thought operates on and manipulates at will; the thinking subject is essentially independent from this world, which remains passive in relation to thought. For Descartes, then, thinking itself is a neutral, unproblematic and intuitive notion, willy-nilly present in each mental event, and the difference between good and bad thinking – and consequently the way to proper representation of external reality – can be formulated rationally and methodically so as to guide the rational thinking subject.

This Cartesian conception, which Williams dubs "rationalistic" (2016, p. 11), following Michael Bonnett (1994), has become the cornerstone of modern philosophy. To point to just one important example, it is evident in Kant, who writes that "The *I think* must *be able* to accompany all my representations" (2000, p. 246 [B131], emphasis in the original): for Kant, too, thinking is a general concept, inseparable from all mental activities, which includes both representations and actions such as judging and uniting representations in consciousness (2004, §22). Furthermore, Kant also claims that there are practical rules able to guide proper thinking, which he formulates as the "maxims of the common human understanding" (2004, §40) each person is capable of following. These include thinking consistently, without contradictions; thinking autonomously, without succumbing to prejudices; and "broad-minded way of thinking", namely one in which the thinker is "putting himself into the standpoint of others". Such thinking, for Kant, is the key to liberal citizenship, and man is free as long as his thinking is free of both internal and external constraints (2003, p. 55) – a view whose problems were pointed out by Žižek above.

The Cartesian-Kantian picture of thinking proceeds throughout the mainstream of 19th- and twentieth-century philosophy, and into the 21st. This does not mean it remains unchanged. While Descartes emphasized the thinking individual – recounting how “I was completely free to converse with myself about my own thoughts” only when “shut up alone in a stove-heated room”, and adds that “buildings undertaken and completed by a single architect are usually more attractive and better planned than those which several have tried to patch up” (1985b, p. 116) – subsequent philosophers acknowledged that thinking was essentially tied to its sociopolitical surrounding, and how the thinking subject was influenced by others. John Stuart Mill, for example, argued not only for freedom of opinion and thought but also for freedom of public expression, maintaining that without open public discussion the individual could not think freely and form an informed opinion (2003, pp. 82–3). Nevertheless, the core of the Cartesian worldview, according to which man is essentially a thinking being capable of representing the world in thought and directing it according to rational method, remained largely intact.

This is how things still stand in the contemporary philosophy of mind, in which human thinking is often understood in computational terms which merely replace Cartesian representations with symbols manipulated according to mathematical, algorithmic procedures (Williams 2016, p. 31), and Charles Taylor (1995) stresses the commitment of cognitive psychology and artificial intelligence studies to understanding thinking as an abstract, formal operation. Similar trends are discernable in behavioral studies and linguistics (Fauconnier and Turner 2002). Thus, the essential aspects of Cartesian thought reach even beyond the disciplinary limits of philosophy and determine the outlines of the entire modern discourse on thought.

* * *

The Cartesian conception of thinking contains a significant educational dimension: proper thinking is one that follows a method, and a method is an instrument that can be taught and used to improve the quality of thinking. Although the educational dimension is not always explicit in and often underdeveloped by philosophers who think about thinking, the task of articulating a theory of thinking education has not been neglected by pedagogues and philosophers of education.

First among them is John Dewey, one of the founders of the modern philosophy of education. Dewey vehemently rejected the Cartesian mind-body dualism, understanding the mind as actively engaged in the material world, not only manipulating it but also adapting itself to its demands, growing as a result of the need to cope with the problems it poses. Nevertheless, Dewey’s conception of thinking maintains some essential aspects of the Cartesian one. Most importantly, he relates thinking to the scientific method, arguing that to achieve results – namely, learn how to better interact with the world and solve various problems in it – thinking must proceed according to a predefined method: it is to start with a problem in understanding or acting in the world, and continue with raising hypotheses and examining them until a plausible explanation is found (Dewey 1997, pp. 71–78). Moreover, much like the Cartesian subject, the Deweyan one thinks in order to achieve autonomy and be able to predict future events and master the objective world. Lastly, while for Dewey man is by no means a "thinking being" he wholeheartedly adheres to the Cartesian view that everyone is capable of learning and practicing correct thinking.

Dewey's approach is discussed in detail in the next chapter, which focuses on Adorno, but it is important to mention already now that he not only analyzed thinking and dedicated independent studies to it, but also developed the view that one could learn how to think into a comprehensive theory of education for thinking that is integral to his educational philosophy (2004). Thinking, according to Dewey, cannot be taught theoretically, and it is impossible to abstract the method of correct thinking from the actual material. Rather, thinking arises out of the student's direct interaction with the world and is learned only when practiced. To incite thinking the teacher generates encounters between her students and problematic, perplexing aspects of reality. Dewey, then, calls for teachers to encourage their students to think and help them do so methodically and rationally.

Dewey's enormous influence on the theory and praxis of education is pivotal in that in recent decades, education for thinking has become a central theme in the (Anglo-American) analytic tradition of philosophy of education. Before turning to the continental philosophical tradition on which this book focuses, I examine the former. The aim of the ensuing discussion is by no means to criticize the analytic philosophical tradition or its approach to education and thinking, or even to draw clear boundaries between the two traditions. The aim is rather to outline the existing discourse of education and thinking, which takes place almost exclusively in the Anglo-American context, as a backdrop against which we can think the originality and uniqueness of the continental philosophers discussed in this book.

1.3 Education for Thinking in the Analytic Tradition

Education for thinking is not only a recurring theme in the analytic philosophy of education, but one that has long since become an independent field with its own conferences (Hitchcock 2018, p. 2); edited volumes (Baron and Steinberg 1987; Wegerif et al. 2015a); journals (e.g. *Thinking Skills and Creativity* and *Inquiry: Critical Thinking Across the Disciplines*); and historiographies (Harpaz 1991; Higginsm 2015). Higginsm (2015, p. 23) argues that the growing interest in the field in the second half of the twentieth century was motivated by reluctance to accept claims made in psychology and pedagogy that human intelligence is fixed and unchangeable, and that some students simply cannot think as well as others. Against that, it is argued (Feuerstein et al. 1980) that by using various techniques and methods it is possible to improve thinking abilities and improve students' intellectual achievements. From the very beginning, then, the field of education for thinking has been motivated by a political-egalitarian interest, and oriented towards improving academic performance. For this reason, the conception of thinking prevalent in the field is normatively laden: unlike the prevailing discourses in psychology and cognitive sciences, the focus is not descriptive, and the aim is not only to understand how thinking works; emphasis is put rather on how to improve thinking (Bailin and Siegel 2003, p. 181).

As several authors have pointed out, there is wide consensus regarding the *need* and *possibility* of educating for good thinking, while there are disputes regarding *what* exactly is good thinking – namely how to differentiate it from poor, unsatisfying or "plain" thinking – and consequently, what is the best way to teach thinking (Wegerif 2010, p. 1; Bailin et al. 1999, p. 285). All agree that poor thinking can be remedied by proper teaching of the right method, and debate what this method actually is.

The key term in the contemporary field of education for thinking is *criticism*. Good thinking is primarily critical, namely the rules and standards the thinker applies are supposed to enable her to critically evaluate her own as well as other people's thoughts. Even when other terms are used to characterize good thinking – high-order thinking, decision-making, problem-solving, etc. – they can be subsumed under the notion of critical thinking. This means that critical thinking is not just one kind of good thinking, but also an umbrella term designating the high quality of thinking in any context (Bailin and Siegel 2003, pp. 187–8). The notion of criticism does not originate in the educational discourse, of course, but from other philosophical contexts, most notably epistemology and the philosophy of science: critical thinking is designed to avoid mistakes and unfounded opinions, leading to knowledge of the truth or at least to reasonable opinion given partial information. A qualified thinker, it is assumed, should follow the example of a scientist, constantly reexamining views, theories and explanations in light of the available evidence. The term "critical thinking", in any case, is used today mainly in the educational context, referring to the need and possibility to educate for better thinking – the "Critical Thinking" entry in the Stanford Encyclopedia of Philosophy, for example, is dedicated entirely to *education* for critical thinking (Hitchcock 2018).

Teaching critical thinking requires precise specification of the principles guiding such thinking as well as the skills the thinker should exercise. A crucial step in the formation of the field of education for critical thinking, therefore, is the detailed, systematic taxonomy of critical thinking dispositions and abilities proposed by Robert Ennis (1987). While others (e.g. Hitchcock 2017, p. 485) suggest somewhat different classifications, the general idea that critical thinking is an everyday version of the scientific method – prevailing at least since Dewey or even Descartes – is now practically consensual.

There is a long-lasting debate, however, regarding the *generality* or *specificity* of critical skills and standards. Some argue, following John McPeck (1981), that the meaning of criticism varies contextually (for being critical in mathematics is very different from being critical in history or politics) (Bailin et al. 1999; Butler 2015). Others argue that some principles of critical thinking are applicable across contexts (Higginsm 2015; Butler, 2015). An influential version of the latter approach is Harvey Siegel's "reason conception" of critical thinking (1988), according to which "A critical thinker is one who appreciates and accepts the importance, and convincing force, of reasons. When assessing claims, making judgments, evaluating procedures, or contemplating alternative actions, the critical thinker seeks reasons on which to base her assessments, judgments, and actions" (1988, p. 33). Such a commitment to reasons, argue Bailin and Siegel (2003, p. 185), is relevant in every context and discipline. In any event, the debate between the adherents of specificity and generality has direct curricular implications: adopting the generalizability approach implies opting for the development of courses dedicated to teaching critical thinking, while accepting the specificity of critical thinking leads to implementing or reinforcing critical elements in each discipline (Higginsm 2015, p. 23).

On a different level, most critical thinking scholars agree that acquaintance with theoretical principles and even mastering practical skills are not enough, for knowledge and ability do not automatically lead to execution: one may be able to practice critical thinking without actually engaging with it. Therefore, education for thinking must also include the development of intellectual *virtues* (Hamby 2015; Bailin and Buttersby 2016), namely habits and dispositions to apply critical skills in large variety of relevant contexts (Passmore 1980; Ennis 1991; Zagzebski 1996; Turri et al. 2017). Siegel (1988) argues, accordingly, that education for thinking should work in two parallel dimensions: skill, which he relates to the ability to use and evaluate arguments, and the disposition to apply the arguments. This double-edged approach is common in the contemporary field (Swartz 1987; Bailin et al. 1999, p. 299). Importantly, emphasizing the dimension of dispositions ties the field of education for thinking to the long tradition of character formation. Williams (2015, p. 146) rightly observes that education for critical thinking produces a certain kind of individual: man as an autonomous, reflective subject, as perceived in the tradition of Kantian enlightenment (see also Bailin and Siegel 2003, p. 189; Cuypers 2004, p. 79; Siegel 2017a, p. 208).

An important field that overlaps with education for critical thinking is philosophy for children (P4C). Founded in the 1960s by Matthew Lipman and Ann Margaret Sharp, this field aims not at teaching of philosophical texts but at developing philosophical thinking (Lipman et al. 1980). It is quite indicative that the journal Lipman founded and which operated from 1979–2014 was called *Thinking: The Journal of Philosophy for Children.* Yet P4C's contribution to critical thinking education is not limited to expanding the relevant age range. It has contributed greatly also to the international spread of education for thinking, as well as to the introduction of group interaction as an essential aspect thereof. Lipman and Sharp emphasize the influence of dialogue and cooperative work on the individual thinker, suggesting work in "communities of inquiry" as means of encouraging every individual child to engage in thinking (Lipman 2003, pp. 81–104; Gregory and Loverty 2017). Recent work by Rupert Wegerif (2010) and others (Harpaz and Lefstein 2000; Burden 2015) has contributed further to applying the dialogical dimension in teaching thinking to all ages.

Two recent developments in education for thinking also deserve brief mention. The first concerns the relation of critical thinking to *creative* or *imaginative* thinking. As Bailin and Siegel (2003, pp. 185–7) demonstrate, unlike the common assumption that these are two very different kinds of thinking – critical thinking is linear, rigorous and truth-preserving whereas creative thinking is generative and rule-breaking – they are in fact very close to each other: every good critique has an original, creative aspect, and creativity is no different from mere capriciousness unless it involves some critical reflection (Bailin et al. 1999, p. 288; Wegerif et al. 2015b, p. 2). In the same vein, Wegerif (2010, p. 10) argues that creativity and criticism have the same origin, namely the irreducible tension between positions elaborated in thoughtful dialogue. For this reason, education for thinking should encourage dialogic interactions that give rise to both critical and creative thinking.

The second recent development is the growing interest in the notion of *understanding*: proper thinking processes, it is argued, must be conceived not in terms of formal rules and principles but rather according to how they allow for genuine understanding of the material being thought about (Wiske 1998; Perkins 2014). According to Yoram Harpaz (2015, pp. 38–9), this shift of focus from mere thinking to understanding brings back knowledge and content to the field of education for thinking, as emphasis is placed not on how the thinker thinks but on what the process and products of thinking mean to her and how they are incorporated into her world.

Despite its growing popularity, which increases even more following the development of online tools for teaching thinking and communities of inquiry (Wegerif 2007; Wegerif 2013; Knight and Littleton 2015), the field of education for thinking has also been criticized. One of several lines of criticism is particularly relevant for our purposes: it is argued that critical thinking is in fact political ideology disguised as neutral philosophy or universally valid pedagogy (Harpaz 2015, Thayer-Bacon 1992). The standards of rationality and critique that are being taught, so the argument goes, promote or strengthen a particular worldview. Different commentators understand this ideological bias in different ways – Western, male, bourgeois, etc. (Alston 1995; Bailin 1995; Wheary and Ennis 1995) – but they all maintain that the conception of thinking underlying education for thinking reflects cultural and political hegemony rather than creating the conditions for challenging it.

The common answer of supporters of education for critical thinking to this critique is telling: they argue that critique of critical thinking, like critique of rationality and of its claim for unbiased universality, can only be made by critical thinking itself (Bailin and Siegel 2003, p. 192). There is no other way of evaluating critical arguments – including the ones voiced against critical thinking – except according to the standards developed in the very field of critical thinking. That is to say, critical thinking necessarily involves self-reflection, and must function also as its own mechanism of self-correction. This way, external critique is internalized to become part of the discussion within the field of critical thinking.

Throughout this book, we will see how the continental philosophers address the political-ideological dimension of thinking and the problem of establishing a neutral, universal foundation on which thinking can rely. Nevertheless, it is important to mention now that despite their significant differences, all five philosophers discussed in this book conceptualize thinking as inherently related to the political sphere. While for the analytic philosophers, thinking itself is supposed to either be politically neutral or contribute to strengthening consensual political values like active democratic citizenship (Hitchcock 2018, p. 2; Siegel 1988, pp. 55–61), the continental philosophers I discuss not only think of thinking from a political perspective, but do so as part of an attempt to rethink politics in a new, often radical way. Rather than accept the framework of capitalist liberal democracy as given, they reevaluate the political-historical conditions of human existence and examine the role of thinking within it.

As already mentioned, my aim in this book is not to criticize the Anglo-American analytic tradition of education for critical thinking and present the continental alternatives as superior or more comprehensive. Even without committing to clear-cut differences between the analytic and continental traditions, experience shows that most attempts of engagement across traditions – by way of either dialogue or critique – have led to impasses. Such attempts in the context of education for thinking were recently been made by Williams (2015), who analyzed Siegel's view in an attempt to point to the inadequacy of his position and indicate a way of thinking beyond it through Martin Heidegger's conception of thinking. Williams' arguments were carefully structured, and the differences between Siegel and Heidegger's views were lucidly portrayed. And yet, in his response to Williams Siegel clung to his original position, admitting Williams and himself were probably talking across each other and that she was likely to say he did not understand her argument (2017b, p. 209). For this reason, I will mostly refrain from explicitly criticizing the analytic field of education for thinking and allow any differences and critiques to emerge from my discussion of continental philosophy.

1.4 Thinking in Continental Philosophy

The term continental philosophy is as controversial as the intellectual sphere it designates. Not only is it difficult to describe the common denominators shared by all philosophical theories normally subsumed under this category – so that there is actually not one but many different continental philosophies – but its geographic connection to continental Europe (just like that of the analytic tradition to the US and Britain) is also not unproblematic. While some of the frontrunners of analytic philosophy, like Gottlob Frege, Ludwig Wittgenstein, and Karl Popper have at least originated in central Europe, a significant part of continental philosophy has actually been written in English-speaking countries. Among the philosophers discussed in this book, Hannah Arendt immigrated to the US in 1941, while Adorno and Derrida spent significant years there (for very different reasons, to be sure).

Even where philosophical contents are concerned, it is highly difficult, maybe even unproductive, to determine exactly what makes some philosophical view (or philosopher) continental rather than analytic. It seems that there is no one significant view shared by all philosophers considered continental as opposed to their analytic colleagues. Perhaps it is all about writing style: while most continental philosophers opt for a complex, hyperbolic style, the analytic ones usually prefer stylistic clarity. Maybe the difference lies in the continental insistence on the impossibility of detaching style from content. Still another option is, to borrow the famous expression by Wittgenstein – the Viennese who moved to England to become the one of the most important analytic philosophers – that we can speak of "family resemblance" (1973, §66) also between philosophies: similarities between family members are more or less visible to all observers although there are no discernable features shared by all family members. Thus, although it is probably possible to identify resemblances between texts belonging to each tradition – and more importantly, philosophers identified with one tend to ignore if not denounce those belonging to the other[1] – adhering too simplistically to the distinction might cause us to miss surprising points of resemblance, limiting our ways of thinking rather than opening up new ones.

The present focus on five continental philosophers is therefore not meant to contribute to separating between the two traditions or to argue for the superiority of one over the other. Rather, it aims to outline an important tendency in continental philosophy, whose expressions vary from one philosopher to the other and which may have some parallels with the analytic tradition. This tendency can be thought of as philosophy's self-reflection: continental philosophy, perhaps due to its constant need to defend itself and establish its place in the academic world, is preoccupied with self-examination, asking what philosophical thinking is and examining how it is related to other forms of thinking. As a result, this tradition is also preoccupied with tradition: it understands that philosophy is inseparable from the historical and cultural contexts in which it operates, and often appeals to texts from the past as a means of inquiring into its own conditions of possibility. That is to say, continental philosophy thinks of itself as one kind of human thinking, and views such thinking as a sphere of activity that cannot be understood apart from other, more mundane spheres. An important aspect of this reexamination of the history of philosophy is rethinking and proposing alternatives to the Cartesian conception of thinking. Although the relation between the philosophers discussed in the following chapters and Descartes' philosophy is complex and can by no means be reduced to simple rejection, they all put question marks on his conception of thinking. Such reluctance to accept the Cartesian "I think" is not uncommon in continental philosophy. Three of its founding fathers – Marx, Nietzsche and Heidegger – challenged Descartes' philosophy, including his conception of thinking and of the thinking subject. I turn now to examining their views, as the backdrop against which Adorno, Arendt, Deleuze, Derrida and Rancière develop their own conceptions of thinking.

* * *

Marx does not address Descartes' philosophy explicitly, but his conception of man, according to which human consciousness is determined by sociohistorical development, itself determined by that of the means of production (Fromm 2004), implies obvious critique of the Cartesian "I think". This critique is clearly present

[1] A clear example of such denunciation is the reaction of many analytic philosophers to Cambridge University's decision to award Derrida an honorary Doctor of Letters in 1992. A list of distinguished academics, mostly philosophers, published a public letter of protest, arguing that his writings include "tricks and gimmicks" unworthy of the academic sphere, and do not meet academic standards.

already in Marx's dispute with the "idealism" of the young Hegelians who prioritize mind over matter, as well as in the early formulations of historical materialism. In *The German Ideology*, we read: "The production of ideas, of conceptions, of consciousness, is at first directly interwoven with the material activity and the material intercourse of men, the language of real life. Conceiving, thinking, the mental intercourse of men, appear at this stage as the direct efflux of their material behavior" (2000b, p. 180). Marx's materialism, then, does not ignore the phenomenon of thinking but insists that the language it speaks, which determines the terms and meanings it can conceive and understand, is that of "real life", of activity in the actual world. The subject indeed thinks, but his thoughts are not the essence that determines and enables his other actions – they derive from the latter. This relation between thought and world has weighty implications for Marx's conception of truth, which is addressed in the second of the *Theses on Feuerbach*: "The question whether objective truth can be attributed to human thinking is not a question of theory but is a practical question. Man must prove the truth, i.e. the reality and power, the this-sidedness of his thinking in practice" (2000a, p. 171). That is to say, denying the independence of subjective thinking from the objective world means rejecting the conception of truth as correspondence between representation and reality. Thinking is now understood as an active, productive power in the world and its truth is a function of its correspondence with this activity, not a reflection of one medium in a categorically different one.

To better understand the implications of Marx's concept of man for human thinking and its relation to education let us take a short look at Vygotsky. Unlike many other Soviet scientists and intellectuals who used to weave citations of Marx and Engels in their writings as lip service to the communist party, Vygotsky's views demonstrate thorough understanding and genuine commitment to Marxism (Cole and Scribner 1978, p. 1; John-Steiner and Souberman 1978, p. 126). At the foundation of Vygotsky's understanding of the human psyche lies the claim that society and culture shape the individual's psychological mechanisms, including the higher cognitive functions such as thinking: "All the higher functions originate as actual relations between human individuals" (Vygotsky 1978, p. 57). Rather than conceiving of man as a thinking atom who meets similar atoms to form society, Vygotsky maintains, in line with Marx's historical materialism, that psychological functions are first and foremost social patterns of interaction that are internalized to become part of man's "nature" (Vygotsky and Luria 1994).

Furthermore, Vygotsky adopts Marx's insight, developed also by Engels (1940), that *tools* – material means of production – are of crucial influence on the organization of society and individual behavior. He applies this insight to cognitive structures: people who live in societies that use different tools develop different thinking patterns (Vygotsky and Luria 2013). But Vygotsky expands Marx and Engels' notion of the tool, arguing that mental functions must also be understood according to "psychological tools", which are the systems of signs used to control and direct cognitive and behavioral processes (Vygotsky 1978, chs. 1–4; Kozulin 2004, p. 16). Like material means of production, these tools are the result of social activity, and hence develop historically, thereby changing thinking itself, creating new mental structures (John-Steiner and Souberman 1978, p. 132). Psychological tools are like the mind's prostheses, artificial technological addenda to thinking – which means that a significant part of our thinking exists outside us, activated as we interact with other people and tools (Zellermayer 2004, p. 173).

The most important tool in Vygotsky's writings is language. In his 1934 *Thought and Language* (2012), he describes how the child internalizes social language, making it an inseparable part of his thought. The point, once again, is not only that language, which originates in society, influences thought; it is rather that thought is social through and through. Unlike Jean Piaget's theory according to which children's thinking is initially self-centered, idiosyncratic, and becomes comprehensible to others only following interaction with adults (2001), Vygotsky argues that the child's "inner speech" is always already an internalization of communicative speech, however primitive (Kozulin 2004, pp. 22–3). Inner speech mediates between cultural sign systems on the one hand and idiosyncratic images and forms of thought characteristic of individual thinking on the other. As Alex Kozulin points out (2004, p. 25), this approach implies that human thinking has a dialogic, discursive nature, and that the human subject is an agent executing the act of thinking within the conditions determined by the tools at his disposal.

Vygotsky's Marxist conception of thinking obviously has important educational implications. Against the prevailing claim that learning must be made to fit the spontaneous cognitive development the child naturally undergoes, he argues that cognitive development is conditioned by interaction with the surrounding, namely by learning processes. That is to say, education cannot provide knowledge and rules to be implemented by existing cognitive functions; it rather brings about the development of such functions, which are never merely parts of some natural cognitive equipment. Hence, the role of teaching is not only to transmit knowledge but first and foremost to contribute to the child's cognitive development by providing sociocultural tools with which the learner develops his capacity for thinking (Vygotsky 1978, ch. 6; Zellermayer 2004, p. 176). This view leads Vygotsky to reject any kind of intelligence tests meant to measure and evaluate intellectual capacity as if it were naturally given (Cole and Scribner, p. 9). In that, he approaches the analytic tradition of education for thinking that also objects to intelligence tests. We must not overlook the crucial difference, however: while analytic philosophers usually focus on the individual and conceive of the principles of critical thinking as ahistorical, Vygotsky always looks at the connections between the individual thinker and his surrounding, emphasizing the interdependence between thought structures and society.

* * *

Unlike Marx, Nietzsche and Heidegger both put Descartes' "I think" at the heart of an explicit critique that is integral to their philosophy. In *Beyond Good and Evil*, Nietzsche attacks the Cartesian *cogito*, according to which I cannot doubt that I think and I therefore exist as a thinking being:

> the philosopher has to say: "When I dissect the process expressed in the proposition "I think", I get a whole set of bold claims that are difficult, perhaps impossible, to establish, – for instance, that *I* am the one who is thinking, that there must be something that is thinking in the first place, that thinking is an activity and the effect of a being who is considered the cause, that there is an "I", and finally, that it has already been determined what is meant by thinking, – that I *know* what thinking is… In place of that "immediate certainty" which may, in this case, win the faith of the people, the philosopher gets handed a whole assortment of metaphysical questions, genuinely probing intellectual questions of conscience, such as: "Where do I get the concept of thinking from? Why do I believe in causes and effects? What gives me the right to speak about an I, and, for that matter, about an I as cause, and, finally, about an I as the cause of thoughts?" (2002, pp. 16–17).

Descartes' move, which is supposed to be beyond any doubt and provide philosophy with a solid foundation free from scholastic prejudices, rests according to Nietzsche on a series of unfounded assumptions, which may be unavoidable in everyday life – for who can live without believing he is an "I"? – but must be questioned by philosophy. The nature of the relation between thinking and the thinker, the validity of the inference from thought to the existence of a thinking subject, and consequently the very meaning of thinking activity, all call for further thinking.

Nietzsche does not hesitate to take on this challenge and offer an alternative perspective for thinking about thinking – one, to be sure, that does not claim the kind of indubitability presumed by Descartes, but rather remains an assumption: "Assuming that our world of desires and passions is the only thing 'given' as real, that we cannot get down or up to any 'reality' except the reality of our drives (since thinking is only a relation between these drives)…" (Nietzsche 2002, p. 35). Thinking is here a byproduct, an effect of something more essential that is affectual in nature. Man is but a collection of drives, of various expressions of what Nietzsche calls "the will to power", and thinking is not an independent essence or primary given of mental life but merely an expression of the dynamic of the drives. Elsewhere, Nietzsche relates the process through which the rational, self-conscious "I think" is formed to the unavoidable need of man, that assemblage of asocial wills and desires, to be "enclosed within the walls of society and of peace" (1989, p. 84). The transition into society, which Nietzsche probably understands not as a historical event but as a necessary moment in every person's life, is likened to what happens to sea creatures that find themselves on land and are forced to adjust to their new, terrible condition in order to survive: "From now on they had to walk on their feet and 'bear themselves' whereas hitherto they had been borne by the water: a dreadful heaviness lay upon them. They felt unable to cope with the simplest undertakings; in this new world they no longer possessed their former guides, their regulating, unconscious and infallible drives: they were reduced to thinking, inferring, reckoning, coordinating cause and effect, these unfortunate creatures; they were reduced to their 'consciousness', their weakest and most fallible organ!" (1989, p. 84). Conscious, rational thought, then, is a kind of degeneration, forced weakening of healthy drives that can no longer be satisfied. The traditional view according to which rational thinking must rule over the passions – stretching back beyond Descartes, at least to Plato – is presented here as an illness in need of cure.

Another striking point in Nietzsche's critique of Descartes, present already in the above quotation, is put in even sharper terms in the following one:

> As far as the superstitions of the logicians are concerned: I will not stop emphasizing a tiny little fact that these superstitious men are loath to admit: that a thought comes when "it" wants, and not when "I" want. It is, therefore, a *falsification* of the facts to say that the subject "I" is the condition of the predicate "think." It thinks: but to say the "it" is just that famous old "I" – well that is just an assumption or opinion, to put it mildly, and by no means an "immediate certainty."... People are following grammatical habits here in drawing conclusions, reasoning that "thinking is an activity, behind every activity something is active, therefore –." (2002, p. 17).

Not only does thought not rule over the passions, argues Nietzsche, the thinker does not rule over his own thoughts. We tend to believe, following an old prejudice originating in the structure of European languages, that thoughts cannot exist without a subject who summons and commands them; that I can think whatever and whenever I want. But Nietzsche appeals to the experience of being unable to control thinking and severs the causal link, which was obvious even to Vygotsky, between the thinker's will and his thoughts.

At first sight, it seems that Nietzsche's view defies any connection between education and thinking. What is the point of educating for thinking if thinking is an illness? How can we teach thinking if thought does not even obey the student's will, but rather comes "when it wants"? However, on second thought, it is possible that Nietzsche only calls for a different kind of relation between education and thinking: not one in which the student learns how to control the distractions originating in the passions and organize thought rationally, but rather one in which the student learns to ask precisely about the traditional assumptions regarding the nature of thinking – to rethink thinking itself. Moreover, it may also be that education can take into consideration the independence of thoughts and ask how new thoughts can be made to appear – how to summon them and be attentive to their appearance.

* * *

While Nietzsche's discussions of thinking are scattered in different places throughout his writings, Heidegger is much more systematic. Thinking had concerned him already in *Being and Time* (2010), as part of his critique of the Western philosophical tradition's "forgetfulness of Being", but this interest grew stronger with the "turn" his thought underwent from Man, *Dasein*, to Being itself – culminating in the 1950s and 60s in lectures and essays dedicated to thinking about thinking. Much like Nietzsche, Marx and Vygotsky, Heidegger rejects both the traditional conception of thinking and the conception of man it entails. Thinking, for him, is not a sequence of ideas or a process whereby external objects are represented in the mind of an observing subject. It is distinguished also from logical reasoning and scientific inquiry aimed at attaining knowledge of the world, although it is not unconnected to them (Gray 1976, p. x; Lee 2019). Heidegger attempts an independent understanding of thinking, of thinking *as such*, distinguished from other mental activities that may *make use of* thinking and therefore depend on it.

Still, saying what thinking is not is one thing; saying what it is quite another. Heidegger cannot simply present an alternative conception of thinking in the form of a new theory explaining what thinking is; such representation of thinking would betray thinking's non-representational nature. To know what it means to think, argues Heidegger, one has to engage in thinking, or rather *try* to, for he insists that not only do we not yet know what exactly it means to think – we are also *not yet capable of thinking*. He famously says, "Most thought-provoking in our thought-provoking time is that we are still not thinking" (1976, p. 6). Therefore, he opens his 1951 lectures on thinking by saying that "we must be ready to learn thinking" (p. 3). Heidegger's discussion of thinking, therefore, has an explicit historical and educational dimension. Education is needed for being able to cope with the highest task of the modern age, namely to start thinking. But what is so thought provoking in "our time" and why are we not yet capable of thinking?

An important characteristic of the present time, in the context of Heidegger's discussion of thinking, is what he calls "the end of philosophy". This "end" does not mean, of course, that people have ceased doing and studying philosophy. It means rather that philosophy has been completed, having attained its uttermost possibility as the metaphysical questions originating in Plato's philosophy have been incorporated into the empirical sciences (2008, p. 433). Since these sciences approach their objects, including man, through an experiential-technological perspective, Heidegger writes, "The operational and model-based character of representational-calculative thinking becomes dominant" (p. 435). Our age is a scientific-technological one, and precisely because technical knowledge and the ability to calculate have reached unprecedented heights it is an age in which we are not engaged with *genuine* thinking.

For this reason, the end of philosophy, which goes hand in hand with the thriving of empirical science, implies an important task for thinking: it is to find its own way, one independent of traditional metaphysics as well as modern science. To be sure, this task is not new – it is an attempt to return to what has already been there at the beginning of philosophy, before metaphysics and science evolved into their familiar forms, but has not been explicitly thought. But what thinking is looking for is more primordial than philosophy not only in the temporal sense: while philosophy deals with beings and asks about their relation to subjectivity, thinking tries to approach that which allows beings to appear, the condition without which metaphysics would not have been possible. Beings, according to Heidegger, are not simply given to us, waiting for us out there to be observed and recognized; in order to appear, they have to come out, as if through an opening, and light has to reach them for them to radiate towards the one attempting to perceive them. Heidegger refers to this opening that provides the possibility of appearing as a "clearing" (2008, p. 441), a term that originally designates a place in the woods where the trees have been diluted and light can enter the forest: "The clearing grants first of all the possibility of the path to presence, and grants the possible presencing of that presence itself" (p. 445). Without the clearing, things remain in the darkness, hidden behind the thicket of woods. Hence, Heidegger calls the contact with what appears in the clearing *alētheia*, which does not mean truth in the sense of correspondence between knowledge and beings but rather unveiling, disclosure. Through clearing and *alētheia*, the connection between thinking and Being is exposed: "We must think *alētheia*, unconcealment, as the clearing that first grants Being and thinking and their presencing to and for each other" (p. 445).

That is to say, Heidegger agrees with the tradition that views man as the only being capable of thinking, but insists that fulfilling this capacity does not depend on man alone. Like Nietzsche, he claims that man is not in full control of his thoughts: "Man can think in the sense that he possesses the possibility to do so. This possibility alone, however, is no guarantee to us that we are capable of thinking. For we are capable of doing only what we are inclined to do. And again, we truly incline only toward something that in turn inclines toward us, toward our essential being" (Heidegger 1976, p. 3). In other words, while rejecting the conception of truth as correspondence between representation and object, Heidegger thinks there should be some other kind of connection, more intimate and essential, between the thinker and the thing being thought. Thinking means forming a strong connection with something, reaching for its essential being. To be sure, this has nothing to do with personal interest; while different people find different things interesting and worthy of attention, Heidegger insists that some things are food for thought *in themselves*: "some things make an appeal to us to give them thought, to turn toward them in thought: to think them" (p. 6).

What is thought provoking, however, does not simply offer itself up for examination or use. Heidegger writes that "What must be thought about turns away from man. It withdraws from him" (p. 8). Such withdrawal is very different from mere concealment, no less than from simple presence. Withdrawal is an event, and this event concerns and claims man, draws him towards that which withdraws, towards withdrawal itself, like draft wind: "What withdraws from us, draws us along by its very withdrawal, whether or not we become aware of it immediately, or at all… And once we, being so attracted, are drawing toward what draws us, our essential nature already bears the stamp of 'drawing toward'" (p. 9). That is to say, withdrawal creates infinite distance, which makes thought an infinite movement toward that which withdraws; yet the distance between what withdraws and the one drawn to it is by no means infinite. By drawing, withdrawal develops "incomparable nearness" (p. 17) between man and that which withdraws from him and provokes his thought: "Once we are so related and drawn to what withdraws, we are drawing into what withdraws, into the enigmatic and therefore mutable nearness of its appeal. Whenever man is properly drawing that way, he is thinking – even though he may still be far away from what withdraws, even though the withdrawal may remain as veiled as ever" (p. 17).

This point, which might seem enigmatic, is further developed by asking the question, "What is called thinking?" (*Was heißt Denken?*). This question, Heidegger says, can be interpreted in different ways: it can be understood as asking what the thing we call thinking is, as asking how traditional philosophy conceives of thinking, or as asking what the prerequisites for correct thinking are. All these questions, however, derive their meaning and validity from a more primordial question implied by the same phrasing: "What is it that calls us into thinking?" (1976, pp. 113–4).

The question, then, is what commands us to start thinking, what directs us toward a thoughtful relation with something. However, this command or direction, as Heidegger makes clear, does not involve coercion. When something calls us into thinking it stretches toward us, reaches out to us, thereby inviting, instructing, getting thinking underway (p. 117).

Heidegger further explains this relation by adding that "What calls on us to think, demands for itself that it be tended, cared for, husbanded in its own essential nature, by thought" (1976, p. 121). Thinking, then, is not complete unveiling, which would have been no more than using and abusing the thing that is thought; concealment is an essential part of *alētheia* (2008, p. 448), and the thinker is called to provide shelter and preserve the object being thought. This means that for Heidegger, thinking is very different from abstract, "theoretical" relation to things. Instead, it is a kind of coming to contact with them, an encounter in which each of the parties stretches toward the essence of the other, thereby finding also its own essence; thinking is not some cognitive operation, but rather a special kind of relation with the world, with things and with the way they unfold.

Heidegger suggests, accordingly, to think of thinking as craft, a *handi*craft. The hand is crucial here: it is very different from the grasping organs other animals have: "The hand does not only grasp and catch, or push and pull. The hand reaches and extends, receives and welcomes – and not just things: the hand extends itself, and receives its own welcome in the hands of others" (1976, p. 16). Thinking about thinking as a kind of handicraft, then, means the thinker extends and hands part of himself to the thing that is thought, and the latter stretches out to welcome the thinker, to receive thought. Thinking of something is granting it full attention, focusing on it and letting it be what it is, what it can be only when encountering someone who cares and thinks about it.

It comes as no surprise, then, that Heidegger's example for learning, through which he tries to explain how we must learn to think, is not taken from the academic or scientific context but from that of handicraft: the apprentice of a cabinetmaker. To learn how to build cabinets and similar objects out of wood theoretical knowledge is not enough, nor are practical skills. "If he is to become a true cabinetmaker", Heidegger says of the apprentice, "he makes himself answer and respond above all to the different kinds of wood and to the shapes slumbering within wood – to wood as it enters into man's dwelling with all the hidden riches of its nature" (1976, p. 14). Such learning requires not only exercise but also attention, focus, full directedness toward the essences addressing the apprentice at every moment (p. 4) – one needs to think hard when learning to build cabinets, when learning to think. Furthermore, one also needs a good *teacher*, and not every good cabinetmaker is good at teaching cabinetmaking. Heidegger claims that teaching is more difficult than learning, for "what teaching calls for is this: to let learn. The real teacher, in fact, lets nothing else be learned than – learning" (p. 15). Teaching, then, does not involve conveying theoretical knowledge, nor simple demonstration; it requires restraint, minimal guidance meant to let the student-apprentice learn by himself, pave his own path by feeling his way around. Hence all a teacher can do, all Heidegger can do for his listeners, his readers, even himself, is take them to the foothills of thought (p. 12); from there, they must make the leap by themselves, and leaping requires courage because it calls into question the student, the one who attempts to think, no less than that which is thought.

* * *

The above discussions of three key continental philosophers were not meant to exhaust their conceptions of thinking or their relevance to education, but merely to indicate that the continental philosophical tradition is preoccupied from the very beginning with a reexamination of thinking in a way that yields significant educational implications. Marx, Nietzsche and Heidegger are no exceptions among continental philosophers in challenging the Cartesian conception of thinking. Although thinking is not always at the center of the philosophical discussions of that tradition, many philosophers attend to it, examining its relations with other concepts such as consciousness, intentionality and rationality. I believe the reason for that is not only the influence of those three dominant voices; continental philosophy, as already mentioned, is often engaged with self-examination of the philosophical tradition, including the meaning and role it ascribes to thinking. Yet the continental conceptions of thinking are only rarely applied to the educational field – a lacuna this book aims at filling.

Again, just as much as it would be a mistake to ascribe to continental philosophy a sweeping critique of Descartes' conception of thinking, so it would be erroneous to draw a sharp distinction between the conceptions of thinking elaborated in the continental tradition and those of the analytic one. Apart from the vast variety of approaches within each tradition, some cross-tradition similarities can be discerned. Thus Williams – whose attempt to establish a kind of dialogue between Heidegger and Siegel was mentioned above – discusses the similarity between Heidegger's conception of thinking and that of British philosopher Gilbert Ryle (2016, pp. 58–88), and contemporary discussions in the phenomenology of thinking appeal to an analytic philosophy of mind attempting to learn and engage in dialogue (Breyer and Gutland 2015). While I have no intention of deepening the divide and arguing for the superiority of one tradition over the other, I also do not insist on establishing dialogues and looking for points of convergence. The importance of breaking traditional boundaries notwithstanding, such a task would give the book a polemic nature that might come at the expense of the attention given to each of the philosophers. The book is therefore anchored in the continental tradition, and except for an appeal to Dewey in the chapter on Adorno, remains within its confines.

1.5 About the Book

In this book, I explore connections between education and some of the conceptions of thinking developed within the continental philosophical tradition. In do not aim to exhaust the discussions of thinking in that tradition, or even to cover its most important trends – this would be practically impossible in light of the vast variety of schools, systems and worldviews within continental philosophy. The five philosophers I focus on – Adorno, Arendt, Deleuze, Derrida and Rancière – are not examined as representatives of some trends or schools in continental philosophy, but simply as interesting cases in their own right.

Yet these philosophers have been selected not only because of their central place in twentieth-century continental philosophy (and in Rancière's case, the 21st as well). Each of them develops an original conception of thinking that is by no means an obvious matter even within the continental tradition. While this tradition is characterized by a strong tendency for self-reflexivity, this tendency is often expressed in reflections on the role and nature of *philosophy*, leaving thinking itself unthought. Another reason for selecting these particular philosophers is the significant political dimension in each. To be sure, the existing field of education for thinking also has a political aspect: developing thinking skills is supposed to foster active, critical citizens able to engage thoughtfully in democratic politics. However, none of the philosophers in the field of education for thinking develops his own conceptions of politics; they rely on widespread conceptions of democracy and social justice, explaining how education for thinking can contribute to raising democratic citizens and to narrowing achievement gaps. The philosophers discussed below, on the other hand, develop their own unorthodox conceptions of politics and political activity, which challenge the liberal-democratic order in different ways. Their conceptions of thinking are inseparable from their political views: thinking itself is conceived by all in relation to politics and to questions of thoughtful political activity. For this reason, politics is a central axis in this book: each of its chapters generates a three-dimensional encounter between education, thinking and politics.

While all five philosophers discussed in the book are political philosophers (or at least "critical" in a politically relevant way), none is a philosopher of education. To be sure, each has written about educational issues – some more, like Adorno, Rancière, and to a certain extent Derrida, and some less, like Arendt and Deleuze – but these issues are not at the heart of their philosophical engagements. Just as most of the articles, books and academic courses dedicated to their work do not address education, almost all the articles, books and academic courses on educational theory in the twentieth century do not mention any of them (Rancière being somewhat of an exception). However, the five are no strangers to educational philosophy: there is vast secondary literature discussing the implications and relations of their ideas to the educational context, at times developing existing aspects, and at times creating new connections that do not exist in the original. But even this literature barely touches upon the conceptions of thinking these philosophers develop, leaving the implications of their views to education for thinking mainly in the dark. My aim in this book, accordingly, is not to introduce these philosophers to the educational discourse, but rather to focus on the unique intersection between education, thinking, and politics in their writings, and thereby contribute both to the field of philosophy of education and to the study of each of the philosophers individually.

Moreover, the orientation of the discussion is philosophical-theoretical, and emphasis is *not* on how to apply the conceptions of thinking to conventional educational practice. As these have not been developed with an eye to education, it is not always clear how the philosophical insights can be translated into curricular products. While I do try to elaborate on practical implications when these are relevant, it is important not to force the practical question on the discussion, allowing unique conceptions of education and politics to arise from the discussion alongside those of thinking. Every constellation of thinking-education-politics is singular, and its mode of practical applicability changes accordingly. This is also the reason why in the title, as well as many passages in the book, I renounced use of the term "education *for* thinking", which seems to assume an education that influences and shapes thinking, and used the conjunctive "education *and* thinking", which leave the nature of the relation open.

To recap, although the five philosophers are part of the continental tradition, they do not form a distinct school or trend within it. Fundamental differences exist between them, far exceeding the discussions of thinking, education and even politics: each philosopher opens up an entirely new philosophical world. Undoubtedly influenced by previous as well as contemporary philosophers, each asks his or her own questions and develops his or her own philosophical and conceptual worlds. Accordingly, each chapter focuses on one philosopher, allowing the full complexity of each philosophical world to come to light. While points of similarity and difference are marked along the discussions, I am careful not to force them, so as to let each philosopher develop his or her own unique voice without interruption. Accordingly, the comparative discussion is left almost entirely to the conclusion. Each chapter is therefore independent, and can be read on its own. The chapters are ordered more or less chronologically, but it should not bind the reader. Just like in the process of thinking (at least according to some of the conceptions discussed below), following a strict, pre-given order of progression might feel too restricting to some readers, while wandering around or focusing on certain parts rather than the bigger picture may yield surprising insights.

The next chapter deals with Adorno, bringing together two subjects on which he wrote extensively while leaving the connection between them underdeveloped: political education and the nature of thinking. While often stressing the need for education for independent, autonomous thinking in the spirit of Kantian enlightenment, Adorno's discussions of education rarely draw on the elaborate analyses of the nature of thinking that appear elsewhere in his writings. To allow a better understanding of the uniqueness and complexity of his conception of thinking and its relation to education, it is examined against another educational view that gives thinking prominent role: John Dewey's. Although Adorno and Dewey belong to distinct philosophical traditions, both insist not only on the importance of thinking in education but also on the centrality of *experience* in thinking. For Dewey, to think is to search for order and regularity in experience, and education for thinking, accordingly, must allow the student to experience the world on his own and attempt to discover the rules governing it. Adorno shares Dewey's view that thinking arises out of direct experience with the world, as well as that education should summon such experiences and not be limited to knowledge transfer. However, he strongly objects to the claim that thinking amounts to recognizing rules and regularities. For him, such "identity thinking", which applies the logic of economic exchangeability to the mental sphere by limiting itself to subsuming different things under the same category, is not at all worthy of its name. When the subject really thinks, argues Adorno, his experience is open to the uniqueness of the particular object, establishing with it relations that are not founded on identification and domination. Thinking, therefore, problematizes not only existing linguistic, scientific, and social categories, but also the very social logic that rests on categorization and identification. As such, it is political activity in its own right, resisting the sociopolitical order dominated by the exchange principle and instrumental rationality. Political education, accordingly, should not focus on active citizenship within the existing order but on encouraging thinking: directing the students to reflect upon objects as particulars, not representatives of some general category. Such thinking, it is finally argued, is best achieved through the writing of essays: an essay, for Adorno, is a written text that does not force some preexisting form on the object but rather gives itself over to its inner logic, articulating its unique place in the world. After Adorno's *Minima Moralia*, I call this education *Minima Pedagogica*, as it renounces traditional educational and political methods, opting instead for minor activities of thinking and writing, which are the only non-compromising actions possible in our late-capitalist world.

Unlike Adorno, Arendt hardly wrote on educational issues; in the very few essays she dedicated to the subject thinking was not mentioned at all. Although thinking is important for Arendt, who famously highlighted the devastating results of thoughtlessness, she only rarely engaged with the question of how to encourage people to think. The third chapter analyzes Arendt's conception of thinking and examines the possible ways education can foster thinking in students. At the heart of the chapter is a distinction between two different conceptions of thinking found in Arendt: the first involves temporary withdrawal from the world in order to engage in inner dialogue about the meaning of things, whereas the second follows the Kantian notion of "enlarged mentality", namely thinking about the world from various perspectives. Although the two are of opposing orientations – turning away from the world as opposed to trying to look at it from multiple points of view – this chapter argues that education must foster both. This is because while thinking about meanings is important *morally*, it can nevertheless be dangerous *politically*: turning away from the common world may make accepted norms appear in their true, immoral meaning, and prevent the thinker from taking active part in atrocities, but it also undermines the very commonality of the world, putting in danger the space in which political action can appear. Thinking in enlarged mentality, on the other hand, strengthens the connections between the thinker and other people with whom she shares the world, reinforcing political common sense and creating the conditions in which political action can appear. A clear example of thinking in the sense of inner dialogue about meanings, which also indicates Arendt's approach to education for thinking, is found in her discussion of Socrates: not only did he chose death over life devoid of the ability to think, when operating as gadfly, midwife and paralyzing electric ray he also encouraged his interlocutors to reject prejudices and start thinking for themselves. Moreover, the Greek philosopher's case shows how dangerous the "wind of thinking" can be to the polis, as some of his followers betrayed the city for reasons not unconnected, according to Arendt, to the withdrawal demanded by the activity of thinking. Education, therefore, must not settle for Socratic education but complement it with thinking in an enlarged mentality that fosters the students' ability to judge. This can be done, as argued at the end of the chapter, not only through conversations in which the participants are exposed to various perspectives of the world, but also by presenting examples of remarkable people using their power of judgment to make difficult decisions in crucial situations.

While for Arendt taking care of the common dimension of the world is a highly important political and educational task, Deleuze, discussed in the fourth chapter, presents a conception of thinking that makes sense by *rejecting* common sense. For him, thinking is much different from mere thought: the latter conforms to a dogmatic, commonsensical image according to which its natural activity is to recognize objects, whereas the former undermines ordinary structures of knowledge and action, transcending what is usually taken for granted in society. The Cartesian *cogito* is a clear example of the dogmatic, commonsensical image of thought, for even while presuming to have no unfounded presuppositions it still assumes that the meaning of thinking is unproblematic – that everybody knows what thinking is. Yet the dogmatism of common sense thought concerns not only *doxa*, the common opinion that is supposed to be self-evident; following Aristotle and Kant, Deleuze understands common sense also as the cooperation between the cognitive faculties – sensibility, imagination, memory, etc. – needed to recognize an object. Such thought, therefore, subsumes a plurality of faculties (and people) under a unifying model, thereby eradicating the differences between them. Unlike thought in which each faculty is limited so as to fit in with the others and produce a world common to different people, thinking for Deleuze is the independent activity of the faculties. Such activity cannot begin voluntarily, for the will does not cooperate with the other faculties; rather, it results from an encounter of sensibility with a problem that awakens it, forcing it to act in its own unique way and making the other faculties do the same. Such thinking is not aimed at recognizing the truth, but at making sense. Sense, for Deleuze, does not reside in language alone and has no meaning that can be shared; it is pure event at the encounter of language and world, when the interaction of the two generates a problem that has no simple solution in the peaceful world of thought and knowledge. After analyzing Deleuze's conceptions of thinking and sense, the chapter confronts the problem of how thinking can be taught and learned. Taking up Deleuze's discussion of learning to swim it is argued that this is in fact an example of education for thinking. The problem created when the body touches the water does not require a solution in the form of theoretical knowledge, harmonious cooperation of the senses with other faculties. Feeling the water and hearing the instructions of the teacher, sensibility is called to react on its own, to make sense of the problem in its own unique way while also passing it on to other faculties and other people, generating more thinking activities. This discussion is finally turns to Deleuze's reading of Marcel Proust's *In Search of Lost Time*: the journey through which the narrator becomes a "man of letters" is presented as an educational process of apprenticeship in which he encounters signs demanding interpretation, namely thinking and making sense of the world in a way that is not limited to the dogmatic image of though.

Derrida, the focus of the fifth chapter, also rejects the traditional view that the thinker is in full control over his thoughts and their meanings. The chapter argues that for Derrida, thinking, like language, should be understood not according to the structure of spoken language but rather that of the written one: the thinker is not entirely present in thought and its meaning is consequently essentially open and indeterminable. To substantiate this claim, the first part of the chapter examines the place of madness in thought as it arises from Derrida's debate with Foucault concerning Descartes' *cogito* and its relation to madness. In his *History of Madness* Foucault argues that Descartes raises the possibility that the thinking subject is mad only to immediately reject it, just like his contemporaries incarcerated people deemed insane. For the seventeenth-century philosopher – unlike the philosophers and poets of the Renaissance – thinking cannot be mad: when I think about my thinking, I realize I am not mad. In Derrida's interpretation, on the other hand, madness is integral to the *cogito* and the skeptical philosophical move that leads to it: whether I am mad or not, I think, therefore I am. Contra Foucault, Derrida argues that confinement of madness takes place not when the *modern* thinking subject is constituted, but rather each time the thinker enters into discourse, the space of common meanings. Every discourse necessarily excludes madness, without ever getting rid of it altogether – madness is inseparable from thought, making it possible for it to change and develop even beyond discursive limits. Hence, madness within thought also has educational significance: while education introduces the student into discourse, thereby deeming thoughts that do not fit the discursive presuppositions as mad, a good teacher – like Foucault might have been for Derrida – also leaves the student with enough madness to be able to think his own way and burst out of the discursive frame set by the teacher. This approach to education and thinking is examined through Derrida's discussions of two educational issues: teaching philosophy in schools and the role of the university. In both, he emphasizes the role of thinking vis-à-vis "the other of philosophy", which philosophy rejects as irrational or mad while being in fact inseparable from it, allowing it to change and develop. Education, then, should turn thinking toward itself, toward its own conditions of possibility; it should open thinking to people and voices that usually have no place in philosophy, that it seems mad to let into the class of philosophy. Thinking must look into the historical and material conditions making it possible, among them the state and the institution hosting it, as well as the various people – administrators, service providers and of course students – whose work is indispensable for philosophy although it seems mad to think of them as part of it.

The sixth chapter turns to Rancière, arguing that the notion of thinking is crucial for understanding his views of education and politics. A key term for Rancière is *intelligence*: the entire sociopolitical order, he argues, rests on the assumption that there are fundamental differences between the intellectual capacities of different people, and social divisions into roles and ranks are supposed to be in accordance with these natural capacities. This differential assumption is clearly at work in mainstream school education, which assumes that the student cannot learn by himself, using his own intelligence, but is rather in need of a teacher, whose intelligence is superior. Although Rancière does not use these terms, such education is a kind of education for thinking, which assumes that there is only one way to think and learn: the teacher's superior intelligence is a thinking skill, and the heart of all teaching is instruction in gradual, methodical thinking. Emancipatory education, on the other hand, which rests on the assumption of equality of intelligence, accepts the plurality of ways of thinking and recognizes the irreducible singularity of thought. To be emancipated one has to realize that his or her intelligence is not inferior (or superior) to that of anyone else, that he or she is already a thinking being, capable of thinking just like anybody else. This radical equality reveals the arbitrariness of the entire social order, but Rancière insists that the political effect of emancipatory education is limited, for intelligence, and consequently emancipation, belongs only to an individual and not to a collective. This chapter argues, however, that thinking, as well as education, plays a crucial role in Rancièrian politics. Politics, for him, operates through the formation of a collective political subject, who acts in the name of the equality of anyone with everyone, challenging the fundamental distinction between those capable and those incapable of thinking. Since the political subject involves a plurality of individuals, each of whom learns to think of oneself as part of the political subject and as equal to everyone else, the formation of political subjectivity necessarily involves emancipatory education for thinking. Such education teaches the individual, who is used to thinking according to the differential logic of the existing order, to think also in terms of equality: he is to hold the two heterogeneous thoughts together in his own unique way. This plurality of singular thoughts within the political subject, it is finally argued, makes it possible for politics to multiply, as one political subject gives birth to others who learn to think and demand equality in the name of other groups who are not supposed to be able to think.

The concluding chapter brings the five philosophers together to examine the differences and similarities between their views on thinking, education, and politics. The comparison indicates lack of common ground on which a comprehensive theory of continental education for thinking can be founded. The five approaches may be better seen as splitting paths passing through the same territory on the way to very different directions. Applying them to educational practice, therefore, requires choosing a path and paying careful attention to its uniqueness as well as the philosophical complexity giving it depth and meaning.

References

Alston, K. (1995). Begging the question: Is critical thinking biased? *Educational Theory, 45*(2), 225–233.

Bailin, S. (1995). Is critical thinking biased? Clarifications and implications. *Educational Theory, 45*(2), 191–197.

Bailin, S., & Buttersby, M. (2016). Fostering the virtues of inquiry. *Topoi, 35*(2), 367–374.

Bailin, S., & Siegel, H. (2003). Critical thinking. In N. Blake, P. Smeyers, R. Smith, & P. Standish (Eds.), *The Blackwell guide to the philosophy of education* (pp. 181–193). Hoboken: Blackwell.

Bailin, S., Case, R., Coombs, J. R., & Daniels, L. B. (1999). Conceptualizing critical thinking. *Journal of Curriculum Studies, 31*(3), 285–302.

Baron, J. B., & Steinberg, R. J. (1987). *Teaching thinking skills: Theory and practice*. New York: W. H. Freeman and Company.

Bonnett, M. (1994). *Children's thinking*. London: Cassell.

Breyer, T., & Gutland, C. (2015). Introduction. In T. Breyer & C. Gutland (Eds.), *Phenomenology of thinking* (pp. 1–24). New York: Routledge.

Burden, R. (2015). Do they really work? Evidence for the efficacy of thinking skills approaches in affecting learning outcomes: The need for a broader perspective. In R. Wegerif, L. Li, & J. C. Kaufman (Eds.), *The Routledge international handbook of research on teaching thinking* (pp. 291–304). New York: Routledge.

Butler, H. A. (2015). Assessing critical thinking in our students. In R. Wegerif, L. Li, & J. C. Kaufman (Eds.), *The Routledge international handbook of research on teaching thinking* (pp. 305–314). New York: Routledge.

Cole, M., & Scribner, S. (1978). Introduction. In L. S. Vygotsky, M. Cole, V. John-Steiner, S. Scribner, & E. Souberman (Eds.), *Mind in society: The development of higher psychological processes* (pp. 1–14). Cambridge, MA: Harvard University Press.

Cottingham, J. (1993). *A Descartes dictionary*. Hoboken: Blackwell.

Cuypers, S. E. (2004). Critical thinking, autonomy and practical reason. *Journal of Philosophy of Education, 38*(1), 75–90.

Descartes, R. (1985a [1628]). Rules for the direction of the mind. In *The philosophical writings of Descartes* (J. Cottingham, R. Stoothoff, & D. Murdoch, Trans.) (Vol. 1, pp. 9–78). Cambridge: Cambridge University Press.

Descartes, R. (1985b [1637]). Discourse on method. In *The philosophical writings of Descartes*. (J. Cottingham, R. Stoothoff, & D. Murdoch, Trans.) (Vol. 1, pp. 111–151). Cambridge: Cambridge University Press.

Descartes, R. (2008 [1641]). *Meditations on First Philosophy* (M. Moriarty, Trans.). Oxford: Oxford University Press.

Dewey, J. (1997 [1910]. How we think. Mineola/New York: Dover Publishing, Inc.

Dewey, J. (2004 [1916]). Democracy and education. New Delhi: Aakar Books.

Di Nicola, V. (2018). Slow thought: A manifesto. *Aeon*. Retrieved from https://aeon.co/essays/take-your-time-the-seven-pillars-of-a-slow-thought-manifesto

Engels, F. (1940 [1883]). The dialectics of nature. New York: International Publishers.

Ennis, R. (1987). A taxonomy of critical thinking dispositions and abilities. In J. B. Baron & R. J. Steinberg (Eds.), *Teaching thinking skills: Theory and practice* (pp. 9–26). New York: W. H. Freeman and Company.

Ennis, R. (1991). Critical thinking: A streamlined conception. *Teaching Philosophy, 14*(1), 5–24.

Fauconnier, G., & Turner, M. (2002). *The way we think: Conceptual blending and the mind's hidden complexities*. New York: Basic Books.

Feuerstein, R., et al. (1980). *Instrumental enrichment: An intervention program for cognitive modifiability*. Baltimore: University Park Press.

Fromm, E. (2004 [1961]). Marx's concept of man. New York: Continuum.

Gray, J. G. (1976). Introduction. In M. Heidegger (Ed.), *What is called thinking?* (J. Glenn Gray, Trans., vi–xvi). New York: Harper Perennial.

Gregory, M. R., & Loverty, M. J. (Eds.). (2017). *Community of Inquiry with Ann Margaret Sharp: Childhood, philosophy and education*. New York: Routledge.

Hamby, B. (2015). Willingness to inquire: The cardinal critical thinking virtue. In M. Davies & R. Barnett (Eds.), *The Palgrave handbook of critical thinking in higher education* (pp. 77–87). New York: Palgrave Macmillan.

Harpaz, Y. (1991). Introduction. In Y. Harpaz (Ed.), *Education for critical thinking* (pp. 11–19). Jerusalem: Magnes Press.

Harpaz, Y. (2015). Teaching thinking: An ideological perspective. In R. Wegerif, L. Li, & J. C. Kaufman (Eds.), *The Routledge international handbook of research on teaching thinking* (pp. 29–44). New York: Routledge.

Harpaz, Y., & Lefstein, A. (2000). Communities of thinking. *Educational Leadership, 58*(3), 54–57.

Heidegger, M. (1976 [1952]). *What is called thinking?* (J. Glenn Gray, Trans.). New York: Harper Perennial.

Heidegger, M. (2008 [1964]). The end of philosophy and the task of thinking (J. Stambaugh, Trans.). In ed. D. F. Krell (Ed.), Basic writings (pp. 427–449). New York: Harper Perennial.

Heidegger, M.. (2010 [1927]. *Being and Time* (J. Stambaugh, Trans.). Albany: SUNY Press.

Higginsm, S. (2015). A recent history of teaching thinking. In R. Wegerif, L. Li, & J. C. Kaufman (Eds.), *The Routledge international handbook of research on teaching thinking* (pp. 19–28). New York: Routledge.

Hitchcock, D. (2017). Critical thinking as an educational ideal. In *On reasoning and argument: Essays in informal logic and on critical thinking* (pp. 477–497). Dordrecht: Springer.

Hitchcock, D. (2018). Critical thinking. In *The Stanford Encyclopedia of Philosophy* (E. N. Zalta, Ed.). Retrieved from https://plato.stanford.edu/entries/critical-thinking/

John-Steiner, V., & Souberman, E. (1978). Afterword. In L. S. Vygotsky, M. Cole, V. John-Steiner, S. Scribner, & E. Souberman (Eds.), *Mind in society: The development of higher psychological processes* (pp. 121–134). Cambridge, MA: Harvard University Press.

Kant, I. (2000 [1781]). *Critique of Pure Reason* (P. Guyer, & A. W. Wood, Trans.). Cambridge: Cambridge University Press.

Kant, I. (2003 [1784]). An answer to the question: "What is enlightenment?". In H. S. Reiss (Ed.), *Political writings* (pp. 54–60). Cambridge: Cambridge University Press.

Kant, I. (2004 [1783]). *Prolegomena to any Future Metaphysics* (G. Hatfield, Trans. and Ed.). Cambridge: Cambridge University Press.

Knight, S., & Littleton, K. (2015). Thinking, interthinking, and technological tools. In R. Wegerif, L. Li, & J. C. Kaufman (Eds.), *The Routledge international handbook of research on teaching thinking* (pp. 467–178). New York: Routledge.

Kozulin, A. (2004). The socio-cultural psychology of Lev Vygotsky. In L. S. Vygotsky, M. Zellermayer, & A. Kozulin (Eds.), *Mind in society: The development of higher psychological processes* (pp. 13–36). Tel Aviv: Hakibbutz Hameuchad.

Lee, S. (2019). Thinking in nearness: Seven steps on the way to a Heideggerian approach to education. *Journal of Philosophy of Education, 53*(2), 229–247.

Lipman, M. (2003 [1991]). *Thinking in education.* Cambridge: Cambridge University Press.

Lipman, M., Sharp, A. M., & Oscanyan, F. S. (1980). *Philosophy in the classroom.* Philadelphia: Temple University Press.

Marx, K. (2000a [1845]). Theses on Feuerbach. In Selected writings, David McLellan, 171–174. Oxford: Oxford University Press.

Marx, K. (2000b [1846]). The German ideology. In Selected writings, David McLellan, 175–208. Oxford: Oxford University Press.

Marx, K. (2000c [1844]). Preface to *A Critique of Political Economy.* In D. McLellan (Ed.), *Selected writings* (pp. 424–428). Oxford: Oxford University Press.

McPeck, J. (1981). The meaning of critical thinking. In *Critical thinking and education* (pp. 1–21). New York: Martin Robertson.

Mill, J. S. (2003 [1859]). *On liberty.* New Haven: Yale University Press.

Nietzsche, F. (1989 [1887]). *The Genealogy of Morals, Ecce Homo* (W. Kaufmann, & R. J. Hollingdale, Trans.). New York: Vintage Books.

Nietzsche, F. (2002 [1886]). *Beyond good and evil* (J. Norman, Trans.). Cambridge: Cambridge University Press.

Passmore, J. (1980). Teaching to be critical. In *The philosophy of teaching* (pp. 166–182). London: Duckworth.

Perkins, D. N. (2014). *Future wise: Educating our children for a changing world*. San Francisco: Jossey-Bas.

Piaget, J. (2001 [1923]). *The Language and Thought of the Child* (Marjorie, & R. Gabain, Trans.). New York: Routledge.

Siegel, H. (1988). *Educating reason: Rationality, critical thinking, and education*. New York: Routledge.

Siegel, H. (2017a). *Education's epistemology: Rationality, diversity, and critical thinking*. Oxford: Oxford University Press.

Siegel, H. (2017b). Epistemology in excess? A response to Williams. *Journal of Philosophy of Education, 51*(1), 193–213.

Smith, K. (2015). *The Descartes dictionary*. London: Bloomsbury.

Swartz, R. J. (1987). Critical thinking, curriculum, and the problem of transfer. In D. N. Perkins, J. Lochhead, & J. C. Bishop (Eds.), *Thinking: The second international conference* (pp. 261–285). Hillsdale: Lawrence Erlbaum Publishers.

Taylor, C. (1995). *Philosophical arguments*. Cambridge, MA: Harvard University Press.

Thayer-Bacon, B. J. (1992). Is modern critical thinking theory sexist? *Inquiry: Critical Thinking Across the Disciplines, 10*(1), 3–7.

Turri, J., Alfano, M., & Greco, J. (2017). Virtue epistemology. In *The Stanford encyclopedia of philosophy* (E. N. Zalta, Ed.). Retrieved from https://plato.stanford.edu/archives/win2017/entries/epistemology-virtue/

Vygotsky, L. S. (1978). *Mind in society: The development of higher psychological processes* (M. Cole, V. John-Steiner, S. Scribner, & E. Souberman Cambridge, MA.: Harvard University Press.

Vygotsky, L. S. (2012 [1934]). *Thought and language* (A. Kozulin, Ed.). Cambridge, MA: The MIT Press.

Vygotsky, L. S., & Luria, A. R. (1994 [1930]). Tool and symbol in child development. In R. van den Veer, & Jaan Valsiner (Eds.), *The Vygotsky Reader* (pp. 99–174). Hoboken: Wiley-Blackwell.

Vygotsky, L. S., & Luria, A. R. (2013 [1930]). *Studies on the history of behavior: Ape, primitive, and child*, (Victor I Golod, & J. E. Knox, Ed. and Trans.). Hillsdale: Lawrence Erlbaum Publishers.

Wegerif, R. (2007). *Dialogic education and technology: Expanding the space of learning*. Berlin: Springer.

Wegerif, R. (2010). *Mind expanding: Teaching for thinking and creativity in primary education*. London: Open University Press.

Wegerif, R. (2013). *Dialogic: Education for the internet age*. New York: Routledge.

Wegerif, R., Li, L., & Kaufman, J. C. (Eds.). (2015a). *The Routledge international handbook of research on teaching thinking*. New York: Routledge.

Wegerif, R., Li, L., & Kaufman, J. C. (2015b). Introduction. In R. Wegerif, L. Li, & J. C. Kaufman (Eds.), *The Routledge international handbook of research on teaching thinking* (pp. 1–8). New York: Routledge.

Wheary, J., & Ennis, R. (1995). Gender bias in critical thinking: Continuing the dialogue. *Educational Theory, 45*(2), 213–224.

Williams, E. (2015). In excess of epistemology: Siegel, Taylor, Heidegger and the conditions of thought. *Journal of Philosophy of Education, 49*(1), 142–160.

Williams, E. (2016). *The ways we think: From the stairs of reason to the possibilities of thought*. Hoboken: Wiley-Blackwell.

Wiske, M. S. (Ed.). (1998). *Teaching for understanding: Linking research with practice*. Hoboken: Wiley.

Wittgenstein, L. (1973 [1953]). *Philosophical Investigations* (G. E. M. Anscombe, Trans.). London: Pearson.

Yuran, N. (2012). Revolution. In A. Handel et al. (Eds.), *The political lexicon of the social protest (2011–)* (pp. 167–169). Tel Aviv: Hakibbutz Hameuchad.

Zagzebski, L. T. (1996). *Virtues of the mind: An inquiry into the nature of virtue and the ethical foundations of knowledge*. Cambridge: Cambridge University Press.

Zellermayer, M. (2004). Zone of proximal development and its implications for the work of the teacher. In L. S. Vygotsky, M. Zellermayer, & A. Kozulin (Eds.), *Mind in society: The development of higher psychological processes* (pp. 163–203). Tel Aviv: Hakibbutz Hameuchad.

Žižek, S. (2002). *Welcome to the desert of the real: Five essays on September 11 and related dates*. New York: Verso.

Žižek, S. (2012). *Don't act, just think*. Retrieved from https://www.youtube.com/watch?v=IgR6uaVqWsQ

Chapter 2
Theodor W. Adorno: *Minima Pedagogica* – Education, Thinking and the Experience of the Non-Identical

2.1 Introduction

Education occupies no small place in Theodor W. Adorno's rich and varied oeuvre. He touched upon educational questions throughout his writings, with growing interest in the last 10 years of his life (French and Thomas 1999; Heins 2012). An engaged intellectual who took active part in West Germany's postwar public and cultural life, Adorno highlighted education as the most significant arena for confronting the country's dark past and shaping its future. For him, this educational-political task was not limited to denazifying and rebuilding the education system, but required also its reinvention in order to cultivate the democratic spirit that was so lacking in the first half of the century.

The key for education in Germany and elsewhere, Adorno held, could not be traditional socialization, the piling of knowledge or even acquaintance with high culture, but rather developing the students' ability for independent, critical thinking. In the spirit of Kantian enlightenment, he argued that to be mature and autonomous students had to learn to think critically, namely to think for themselves and to break free of all external authorities. Nevertheless, in his discussions of education, Adorno says little about the *nature* of thinking, and the secondary literature on his educational theory addresses this question only cursorily (Gur-Ze'ev 2010).

Important claims on the nature of thinking appear elsewhere in Adorno's work. From his early writings to his very last, Adorno is preoccupied with thinking: he criticizes prevalent ways of thinking, examines the relations of thought to rationality and emotions, and sketches the outlines of critical-dialectical thought. In *Negative Dialectics*, he writes that "if negative dialectics calls for the self-reflection of thinking, the tangible implication is that if thinking is to be true – if it is to be true today, in any case – it must also be a thinking against itself" (Adorno, 2003a, p. 365). This is a most radical view: true thinking should not only examine itself, be self-conscious of its own flaws. It is to turn against itself, against its own condition of possibility.

I. Snir, *Education and Thinking in Continental Philosophy*, Contemporary Philosophies and Theories in Education 17,
https://doi.org/10.1007/978-3-030-56526-8_2

Such thinking is clearly critical, but Adorno's understanding of critical thinking goes much further than the familiar claim that thought must be ready to doubt its own content, to take nothing for granted. As will be seen, he argues that thinking must apply its conceptual means to looking for the non-identical that escapes the conceptual attempt at unification and totalization, and thereby offer an alternative to the logic of domination in form no less than in content. This is an impossible mission, which is nevertheless the most urgent in contemporary reality, out of which the demand for education also arises.

Still, these reflections on the nature of thinking rarely touch upon educational questions, and the Adorno scholarship has yet to establish this link. Unlike studies that read Adorno's educational thought against the backdrop of the history of education and the German *Bildung* tradition in particular (Thompson 2006; Pongratz 2008), or with relation to art and aesthetics (Kertz-Welzel 2005; Papastephanou 2006), the present chapter brings together Adorno's ideas on education and thinking in an attempt to develop an original approach to education, thinking, and the political significance of education for thinking.

The remainder of the chapter proceeds as follows. I start with discussing Adorno's radio talks and lectures on education brought together in a book titled *Erziehung zur Mündigkeit* (1971), to outline his reasons for conceiving of education for autonomous thinking as a task of the outmost importance. Next, I turn to other texts in which Adorno engages with thinking, to allow for a richer understanding of the concept. Of particular importance is the distinction between "identity thinking", which amounts to nothing more than subsuming particulars under general categories, and genuine thinking, which rejects identification and is in fact a form of critical activity. The key for genuine thinking, according to Adorno, is experience, namely openness on the part of the subject to the object's particularity. To better understand the connections between education, thinking and experience in Adorno, Sect. 2.3 examines how they are linked together in the thought of another important political and educational philosopher – John Dewey. Although Adorno and Dewey belong to very different philosophical traditions, I show that the two philosophers in fact have much in common, as both not only put thinking at the center of education but also argue that intelligent thinking involves careful reflection on experience. In the following section. I highlight the differences between them, arguing that while for Dewey thinking of an object amounts in the last instance to discovering the laws applying to it, thereby being able to control and dominate it, for Adorno thinking requires experiencing the object as "non-identical", transcending all general categories. Education for thinking, therefore, is education for real experience, for opening oneself up for experiencing the object in its irreducible singularity. Finally, in Sect. 2.5 I show that the proper form of genuine thinking, which should be the heart of encouraging students to think autonomously, is not public discussion but rather the writing of essays. I conclude by terming this type of education that is focused on thinking as action *minima pedagogica*.

2.2 Education for Autonomous Thinking

Adorno opens his famous 1966 lecture "Education after Auschwitz" by saying that "The premier demand upon all education is that Auschwitz not happen again. Its priority before any other requirement is such that I believe I need not and should not justify it" (2005f, p. 191). For him, Auschwitz – as a metonymy to the atrocities committed during the Second World War – is not a past long gone or an accidental, unpredictable outburst of evil but a direct result of the sociopolitical conditions in Germany of the first half of the century, and its recurrence remains an open possibility because these conditions have not changed significantly after the war. "National Socialism lives on", he says in "The Meaning of Working through the Past" (2005c, p. 89), because "the objective conditions of society that engendered fascism continue to exist" (p. 98). Uncritical education that does not acknowledge these conditions and struggle to contain their implications betrays its most urgent task.

This educational task is tightly linked to the "new categorical imperative" Adorno formulates in *Negative Dialectics*: "Hitler has imposed a new categorical imperative upon humanity in the state of their unfreedom: to arrange their thinking and conduct, so that Auschwitz never repeats itself, so that nothing similar ever happen again" (2003a, p. 365). This imperative, categorically binding albeit anchored in concrete historical events, far exceeds the educational context, and concerns all aspects of postwar life (Snir 2010). Nevertheless, education plays key role in applying this imperative, in preventing a second Auschwitz: "Since the possibility of changing the objective – namely societal and political – conditions is extremely limited today, attempts to work against the repetition of Auschwitz are necessarily restricted to the subjective dimension" (2005f, p. 192). That is to say, the struggle against future atrocities should focus on education, influencing subjects in order to create "an intellectual, cultural and social climate in which a recurrence [of Auschwitz] would no longer be possible" (p. 194). As preventing a second Auschwitz is linked to the general intellectual, cultural and political conditions, education is for Adorno the last barricade not only against the recurrence of Nazism, but also against the deterioration of the whole of society to barbarism: "The pathos of the school today, its moral import, is that in the midst of the status quo it alone has the ability, if it is conscious of it, to work directly toward the debarbarization of humanity" (2005e, p. 190).

Although Adorno's conception of education is inseparable from the image of an "enlightened", knowledgeable person, he insists that "I do not at all refer to the idea of 'the formation of man' [*Menschenformung*], because no one has the right to form people from without. But I also do not refer to the idea of education as mere provision of knowledge" (1971b, p. 107, my translation). Rather, he anchors education in the idea of *Mündigkeit* – rendered in English as both maturity and responsibility – as presented by Kant, perhaps the brightest light of European enlightenment. In his seminal 1784 essay "An Answer to the Question: What is Enlightenment?" Kant writes that "Enlightenment is man's emergence from self-incurred immaturity [*Unmündigkeit*]" (2003, p. 4). Such immaturity, he explains, refers not only to actual age, but also to the lack of resolution to think without the guidance of others. The motto of enlightenment, for Kant, is therefore "Have courage to use your own understanding!" (p. 54). The crux of Kant's text is that one's maturity depends not only on personal psychological or intellectual qualities but also and primarily on the sociopolitical surrounding, which encourages or discourages autonomous thinking. Personal and social enlightenment are therefore mutually reinforcing: it is very difficult to be an enlightened person in a dark age, but enlightened people can create a social environment that promotes enlightenment in others and brings about significant social change. In Adorno's context, education is tasked with nurturing enlightened people who will in turn make society less barbarous: "The genuine power standing against the principle of Auschwitz is autonomy, if I might use the Kantian expression: the power of reflection, of self-determination, of not cooperating" (2005f, p. 195). Stressing the "subjective dimension" of the struggle against barbarism amounts therefore to education for critical thinking and critical thinking is first and foremost autonomous thinking.

To be sure, Adorno does not endorse the Kantian notion of autonomy as it is. As Iain Macdonald points out, Kantian autonomy posits "a purely formal sphere of rational interiority in which the self-legislating subject is bound by the moral law" (2011, p. 2). Adorno, following Hegel (1977, p. 386), views Kantian autonomy as an abandonment of the lived material experience that calls for action and in which action takes place. While Kant emphasized the need to develop an open public sphere in which opinions could be freely voiced (Macdonald 2011, p. 13), for Adorno freedom of thought is more than the ability to express it in public but primarily its content, namely the explicit critique of unfreedom it formulates.

Furthermore, Kant wrote that although his was not yet an "enlightened age", it was nevertheless "an age of enlightenment" in which obstacles to man's emergence from self-incurred immaturity were being gradually removed (2003, p. 58). Conversely, Adorno thinks that society in his own age – most significantly but not only in Germany – does *not* promote independent thinking but rather its opposite. The line connecting Germany of the 1930s and 40s to that of the 60s is authoritative, heteronomous thought-structures:

> National Socialism lives on today less in the doctrines that are still given credence – and it remains questionable whether its doctrines were ever believed – than in certain formal features of thought. These features include the eager adjustment to the reigning values of the moment; a two-tiered classification dividing the sheep from the goats; the lack of immediate, spontaneous relations to people, things, ideas; a compulsive conventionalism; and a faith in the established order no matter what the cost. Structures of thought and syndromes such as these are, strictly speaking, apolitical in their content, but their survival has political implications (2005b, p. 27).

Instead of combatting this state of affairs and fostering autonomous thinking, education clings to traditional principles that reproduce heteronomy rather than autonomy. In (2003b), Adorno uses the term *Halbbildung*, or semi-education, to designate the way culture and education, which are supposed to be free of socioeconomic pressures, are in fact determined by the existing conditions, reinforcing rather than challenging them (Thompson 2006, p. 75). German education stresses, for example, the idea of responsible civic commitment (*Bindung*), which Adorno describes as nothing but "dependence on rules, on norms that cannot be justified by the individual's own reason" (2005f, p. 195), namely a form of heteronomy. It also stresses the ideal of "being hard" (p. 197), which generates indifference and inability to empathize with the suffering of others – psychological conditions without which Auschwitz would not have been possible (p. 201).

Moreover, not only does contemporary education not challenge the prevailing patterns of thought, it is also directly influenced by the widespread anti-intellectual atmosphere that is suspicious of education and enlightenment (Adorno 2005b, p. 31), denouncing any attempt to think things through as an expression of weakness. This is reflected in the low appreciation of teachers, who enjoy far less prestige than university professors still do: while the latter are allegedly occupied with high-quality intellectual work, the teachers are believed to be weak individuals whose position allows them to exercise unfair disciplinary violence against those below them (2005e, p. 182).

Adorno's critique of this distorted image of the teaching vocation does not mean he does not aim his arrows also at the teachers themselves, or rather at the student teachers he meets while serving as an examiner in philosophy exams included in teacher training in Germany. Future teachers, he argues, have no real interest in the philosophical aspects of the subjects they are about to teach (2005b, pp. 31–2). Even they do not think autonomously. However, Adorno by no means blames present or future teachers for contemporary education's inability to foster independent thinking. Just like their students, they are influenced by the prevailing social conditions. "We really must start by recognizing the enormous difficulties blocking maturity in the very way our world is arranged", he says in a radio conversation with Helmut Becker. "As long as this remains the case, society will continue to mould people through a vast number of different structures and processes, in such a way that, living within this heteronomous framework, they swallow and accept everything, without its true nature even being available to their consciousnesses" (1999, pp. 29–30). As Becker points out earlier in that conversation, "a certain inherent immaturity" is already presupposed by the very fact that the German education system engages in tracking, for this amounts to telling the students that their abilities and potentials are given in advance and categorizing most of them as incapable of abstract thinking and theoretical studies (p. 22).

Yet despite the seeming vicious circle in which unenlightened society reinforces semi-education and vice versa, Adorno does not think the situation is hopeless and believes education for enlightened, autonomous thinking is possible even under contemporary conditions. Barbarous elements have indeed penetrated and contaminated the educational sphere, but for this very reason, Adorno believes education can contribute to the debarbarization of society:

> The meaning of debarbarization… must not be sought along the lines of being moderate, avoiding strong feelings, or even eliminating aggressions… I think that to combat and overcome barbarism an aspect of rage is necessary, one that if examined from a formal humanist perspective might also be condemned as barbarism. But since we are all trapped in the guilty context of the same system, no one is completely innocent of barbarous characteristics,

> and the whole idea is to harness these characteristics against the principle of barbarism instead of allowing them to lead to disaster (1971c, pp. 122–3, my translation).

Barbarous rage turns out to be as dialectic as enlightenment itself: just as it contains a destructive potential so it can turn against itself, against the very conditions generating it. This requires, of course, conscious systematic reflection on the social factors generating rage, frustration, and violence in the young.

Reflection, therefore, is at the heart of education for enlightenment, for *Mündigkeit* in the sense of autonomous thinking. The subject must look into himself to be aware of the values, norms and narratives he received from society, and become a conscious, critical thinker (Giroux 2004; Bicker 2018, p. 4). "One must come to know the mechanisms that render people capable of such deeds", Adorno writes regarding the crimes of Auschwitz, but also "reveal these mechanisms to them, and strive, by awakening a general awareness of those mechanisms, to prevent people from becoming so again… The only education that has any sense at all is an education toward critical self-reflection" (2005f, p. 193). The struggle against racist prejudices, accordingly, does not require presenting anti-racist arguments, but rather turning the racist students' attention to the mechanisms that generate racism in their minds (2005c, pp. 100–1). Enlightenment, in other words, is not about knowing things or holding some "correct" views – it is about asking the right questions, including putting question marks on oneself: "Simply posing such questions [about what made one become a collaborator] already contains a potential for enlightenment. For this disastrous state of conscious and unconscious thought includes the erroneous idea that one's own particular way of being – that one is just so and not otherwise – is nature, an unalterable given and not a historical evolution" (2005f, p. 200).

Education for autonomous thinking is thus inseparable from psychoanalytic examination of the personality, aimed at bringing to consciousness the impulses society directs toward violence, racism and indifference to the suffering of others. People must be "psychologically ready for self-determination" (2005f, p. 194) to be able to cope with the collapse of traditional authorities without succumbing to fascism. Accordingly, Adorno stresses the importance of education for enlightenment already in early childhood (2005f, p. 193), and argues that psychoanalytic training must be an inseparable part of training in the teaching vocation (2005e, p. 187). Furthermore, as collective unconscious in contemporary societies is shaped mainly by mass media – most notably television – the psychological process of bringing to consciousness ideological or racist prejudices must also include "guided watching" (1971a, p. 55) of culture industry products, in an attempt to recognize the ways they influence and distort people's understanding of the world by imposing simplistic "identity thinking".

Adorno is well aware, however, that rational thought does not lead directly to enlightenment, or rather, that it is dialectic like enlightenment itself – namely, harbors a destructive and not only progressive potential. He agrees with Becker, who says that "thinking and rationality themselves do not necessarily indicate lack of barbarism" (1971c, p. 125, my translation), for one may rely on rational considerations to design an atomic bomb or meticulously plan a genocide. In Adorno's own words, "thinking in itself can indeed serve… both blind domination and its opposite" (p. 125, my translation). Even education for critical thinking and independent problem solving, as Lucas Lundbye Cone rightly argues (2018, p. 1025), becomes semi-education the moment it is brought in as an efficient tool for succeeding in the business world. This is precisely why Adorno rejects Kant's formalistic conception of autonomous thinking and the liberal notion of free public sphere it entails, demanding that thinking be directed to "clear, humanistic ends, not abstract theoretical ideas" (1971c, p. 125, my translation). That is to say, thinking must not be limited to following rational procedures but rather be linked to matter, to experience.

Moreover, Adorno is also well aware that looking at concrete reality is not enough to protect thought against barbarism, for "rationality is essentially also an examination of reality, and always involves a dimension of adaptation" (1971b, p. 109, my translation). Education for critical self-consciousness and autonomous thinking, therefore, requires a thick conception of thought, namely, systematic account of the nature of thinking and its relation to human experience and political action. While Adorno's lectures and radio talks on education, directed to a general audience, remain relatively thin, more elaborate discussions of thinking appear elsewhere in his writings, and it is important to weave them into his educational position to gain better understanding of education for enlightened, independent thinking.

2.3 Thinking as Action

Adorno is concerned with the notion of thinking in many of his works, including the celebrated *Dialectic of Enlightenment* (2007), co-authored with Max Horkheimer. Thinking, as Adorno and Horkheimer argue in this seminal book, is never completely abstract, detached from the sociohistorical context. The primary illness they diagnose in the development of Western civilization, in enlightenment in the transhistorical sense, is domination (*Herrschaft*). Domination originates in the basic need for survival: humanity dominates nature to protect itself from the dangers it harbors. But domination is not limited to the sphere of economics and relations of production, but penetrates all aspects of psychic and social life. As already understood by Marx, "Consciousness can never be anything else than conscious existence, and the existence of men is their actual life-process" (2000, p. 180). Hence, consciousness is also shaped by relations of domination and it plays an active part in reproducing them. Unlike orthodox Marxism, however, Adorno does not think that the relation between domination and consciousness is limited to ideology in the simple sense of explicit and implicit beliefs (knowledge and prejudice, respectively). Following György Lukács (1972), he claims it influences the very forms and structures thinking assumes; the fetishistic nature of culture brings about the reification of the mind (Thompson 2006, p. 72).

The heart of the matter is the concept of reason. Originally a means of self-preservation (Adorno 2005h, p. 272), reason has been of crucial importance in protecting human beings against nature, but has become through the process of enlightenment an instrument through which the rational subject dominates not only the objective world but also other subjects, as well as oneself (Adorno and Horkheimer 2007). Instead of reflecting on the values and meanings of human existence – what Max Horkheimer (2004) called "objective reason" – reason reduces itself to finding efficient means to given ends; given, that is, by existing society. Aimed only at future benefits, such reason ignores the unique qualities of every object and is reduced to what Adorno calls "identification", namely recognition of what is similar in different things in order to subsume them under the same concept, while neglecting what is unique to each: "the concept does not exhaust the thing conceived" (2003a, p. 5), Adorno writes, "the name dialectics says no more, to begin with, than that objects do not go into their concepts without leaving a reminder, that they come to contradict the traditional norm of adequacy" (ibid.), namely, the conception of truth as correspondence between concept and object. Identity thinking, which is tightly connected to the social structure dominated by the principle of exchange that quantifies and equalizes all values, is therefore inherently blind to un-exchangeable particularity, conforming plurality and heterogeneity to unity and totality. Under identity thinking, the subject ignores the differences not only between objects, but also between oneself and other subjects: everything and everyone become identical.

For Adorno, however, identification is not true thinking at all. Unlike Descartes (2008), who took everything that occurs in the mind to be a kind of thought, for Adorno mental processes that accept reality as given and proceed only along rigorous, predictable logical procedures, are not fully worthy of the title "thinking": "Those alone think who do not passively accept the already given" (2005h, p. 264). Hence positive science, which rests on unconditional acceptance of data and applying logical procedures of truth preservation, in fact turns thinking into an empty ritual, a mere sequence of actions, exempting those engaged in it from the trouble of thinking (2005b, p. 33). Without thinking, all that remains is identification (Bicker 2018, p. 5), which is social no less than epistemological: he who does not think identifies with the existing order of things, blends in without asking questions: "When men are forbidden to think, thinking sanctions what simply exists… The culture of its environment has broken thought of the habit to ask what all this may be, and to what end" (2003a, p. 85). Furthermore, such thinking allows the reality of domination to persist uninterrupted by creating a façade of depth and wisdom, to which Adorno offers the most startling analogy: "If thought is not measured by the extremity that eludes the concept, it is from the outset in the nature of the musical accompaniment with which the SS liked to drown out the screams of its victims" (2003a, p. 365).

Replacing thought with empty procedures of identification and calculation results in the decoupling of theory and praxis, and consequently in renouncing theory, assuming praxis has no need of it. This is evident not only in capitalist, anti-intellectual mass culture, but also characterizes the few who still try to challenge it:

Adorno laments the fact that even among those who oppose capitalism whoever chooses to dwell on theory rather than devote oneself to practical activity is accused of being a "traitor to socialism" (2005h, p. 263). This impatient approach, which Adorno calls "actionism" or "pseudo-praxis", necessarily fails because it reproduces the very thing it is up against: "actionism acquiesces to the trend it intends or pretends to struggle against: the bourgeois instrumentalism that fetishizes means because its form of praxis cannot suffer reflection upon its ends" (p. 269). In refusing to devote time to true thinking about ends and reflecting on meanings, actionism yields to the logic of identity, namely to subjective, instrumental reason, and turns into a façade covering the oppressive, administered world; it deceives regarding the existence of free, autonomous agent who no longer exists (p. 270), instead of striving to generate this subject. This is not a hypothetical problem, but the reason so many mass movements in the twentieth century have turned into "the bloodiest reality" (p. 260) – unwilling to stop and think, they brought disasters no smaller than the ones they were fighting against. But precisely because it expresses the spirit of the time, actionism is so popular: "it is more comfortable to swim with the current, even when one declares oneself to be against the current" (p. 263). Going against the current requires effort, engaging in patient reflection, namely true thinking.

Yet although Adorno rejects thinking that takes place in an independent "inner realm" (2005a, p. 15) detached from social reality, being able to think against the current in a way that transcends the prevalent social logic is by no means eliminated by reality: "Whereas theory cannot be extracted from the entire societal process, it also maintains an independence within this process" (2005h, p. 277). Real, critical thinking, which recognizes objects in their non-identical particularity, is always an open possibility.

However, while identity thinking is not true thinking, the whole point of negative dialectics is that in contemporary conditions thinking cannot escape the need to conceptualize, namely to identify, unify and totalize: "the appearance of identity is inherent in thought itself, in its pure form. To think is to identify. Conceptual order is content to screen what thinking seeks to comprehend. The semblance and the truth entwine" (2003a, p. 5). To paraphrase one of Adorno's most famous aphorisms, there is no true thinking in the false one: identification is inherent in the nature of thought, and the non-identical which true thinking tries to comprehend necessarily eludes its grasp. This is what Adorno means when he writes, in the passage quoted above, that thinking "must also be a thinking against itself": it is to work against its own nature, seek for the non-identical using conceptual means designed to identify, look for heterogeneity with tools that always homogenize whatever they perceive. True thinking can therefore never fulfil its task. "Inevitable insufficiency" (2003a, p. 5) pushes it forward, unhappy and unsatisfied, and therefore also always negative and critical.

Hence, even as theoretical thinking is necessary for real praxis, this does not mean it has to answer the question, "What is to be done?" (2005h, p. 261). Unlike Kant, for Adorno enlightened thinking does not follow "practical reason". Theory must not be detached from praxis, but it must also not yield to practical considerations. Practicality, according to Adorno, lies in thought itself: "There is no thought, insofar as it is more than the organization of facts and a bit of technique, which does not have its practical telos. Every meditation upon freedom extends into the conception of its possible realization, so long as the meditation is not taken in hand by praxis and tailored to fit the results it enjoins" (2005h, p. 265). It is by distancing itself from praxis that theory becomes practical: "The theory that is not conceived as an instruction for its realization should have the most hope for realization" (p. 277). Genuine thinking is able to penetrate through reified consciousness, cut through the ideological veil covering social reality, and by touching reality pave the way to enlightenment in the form of sensitivity to the non-identical that eludes the concept: "If these ideologies are in fact false consciousness, then their dissolution, which diffuses widely in the medium of thought, inaugurates a certain movement toward political maturity, and that, in any case, is practical" (p. 278).

As mentioned, such thinking is first and foremost negative, as it fractures "the so-called train of thought that is unrefractedly expected from thinking" (2005d, p. 131), thus rejecting reality as it is and refusing to settle for preserving the "truth" of its appearance. As Macdonald (2011, p. 10) observed, autonomy rests with the process Hegel called "determinate negation", in which consciousness recognizes the contradictions in reality not as meaningless or aporetic but rather as forces pushing it forward, making it think of ways to resolve them. In this sense, true thinking is always also a form of challenging reality – a form of political resistance: "Thinking is a doing, theory a form of praxis; already the ideology of the purity of thinking deceives about this. Thinking has a double character: it is immanently determined and rigorous, and yet an inalienably real mode of behavior in the midst of reality" (2005h, p. 261). Adorno, in short, rejects the simplistic distinction between theory and praxis, between thought and action; thinking is for him not only a necessary condition for oppositional activity but also action in its own right: "Whoever thinks, offers resistance" (p. 263).

The ultimate expression of critical, oppositional thought is of course philosophy. Not institutional philosophy, the two dominant trends of which – American pragmatism and European ontology – notwithstanding their fundamental differences, share the positioning of metaphysics as an enemy and the view of thought itself as "a necessary evil" (2005a, pp. 8–9). Philosophy worthy of its name, which insists on actively thinking the non-identical, is "the force of resistance inherent in each individual's own thought, a force that opposes the narrow-minded acquisition of factual knowledge, even in the so-called philosophical specialties" (2005b, p. 22). The rejection of mainstream institutional philosophy also means, therefore, that resistant thinking is by no means the exclusive business of professional philosophers, and its proper abode is not necessarily academia. Recognizing no predetermined limits, philosophy may be practiced by the commonest people in the most ordinary places.

Can such thinking be practiced by children, however? And if so, can it find a place at school, the quintessential disciplinary site (Foucault 1995) identified by Marxist tradition as an ideological state apparatus where conformism is inculcated (Althusser 1971)? And can critical, autonomous thinking be at all taught? I suggest the answers that can be given to these questions through Adorno's thought are affirmative.

2.4 Dewey on Education, Thinking and Experience

We have seen that autonomous thinking objects to accepting the given and identifying with the collective. For Adorno, however, it is by no means introspective contemplation or what Hannah Arendt describes as temporary withdrawal from the world (1978, p. 47; see Chap. 3). Any attempt by the thinking subject to disengage from the object is not only impossible, but primarily an expression of bourgeois individualist ideology which rests on the assumption of an abstract, ahistorical subject. The real subject always exists in relation to the objective world, and reflective thought must "surrender itself to the subject matter" (Adorno 2005d, p. 129), and give precedence to the particular, non-identical object before it dialectically returns to the subject. As Macdonald (2011) explains, Adorno's concept of autonomous thinking differs from Kant's in that it involves live contact with things' "warmth". For this reason, "The key position of the subject in cognition is experience" (2005g, p. 254).

The relation between thinking and experience, particularly in the educational context, has been put forward by John Dewey, one of the founding fathers of the modern philosophy of education. Despite the belonging to very different philosophical traditions, Dewey's groundbreaking work on education and thinking shares many concerns with Adorno and is therefore a proper background for addressing Adorno's views. Despite being immersed in the American cultural and philosophical context, Dewey was highly influenced by Hegel's philosophy, and this influence is evident throughout his writings just as much as it is in Adorno's. As Paul Fairfield (2009, p. 18) points out, one of the main expressions of Hegelianism in Dewey's thought is the rejection of simple dichotomies in favor of more complex, "dialectical" views which synthesize differences rather than opting for one side over the other. This applies not only to the distinction he emphatically rejected between "progressive" and "conservative" education (Dewey 1997b), but also to that between Continental and Anglo-American philosophy. The proximity Fairfield recognizes between Dewey and European thinkers such as Husserl, Heidegger and Gadamer clearly also applies to the relation between Dewey and Adorno.

Like Adorno, Dewey objects to education as the piling of knowledge by an active teacher in the minds of passive students. Careful not to undervalue the importance of the curriculum, Dewey shifts the emphasis from knowledge transference to active, independent thinking and learning processes (1997a, p. 201). In *Democracy and Education* (2004), Dewey presents the importance of thinking to education as a reaction to Plato's paradox of learning. As Socrates explains in *Meno* (1997, p. 880), learning is impossible because if we know in advance what we are searching for, no learning can take place; and if we do not, we would not know that we have found it. According to Dewey, this paradox rests on the false assumption that there are only two possibilities – complete knowledge or complete ignorance – and that learning is an instantaneous transition from one to the other, while it in fact requires a process of thinking which is a hypothetical journey in an unknown land – "feeling one's way along provisionally" (2004, p. 161), as he puts it.

The lack of a paved way along which thought can advance means rejecting the Cartesian assumption of an a-priori method of right thinking one can apply to every subject matter. Thinking cannot be reduced to formal logic, and the activity of thinking is not identical to following deductive or inductive rules. It is an *art*, not an algorithmic procedure (Fairfield 2009, p. 6). Rather than a prescriptive discussion intended to guide thought, Dewey opts for a phenomenological investigation of the nature of thinking, aimed at describing how we actually think (Fairfield 2009, p. 101). In this sense, the key to understanding thinking is experiencing it, and the role of the philosopher or theoretician is to be attentive to experience, attempting to articulate what people do when they think.

Experience, however, not only tells us what thinking is – it is also integral to thinking itself. To find its way, claims Dewey, thought has to be attentive to its surroundings: "The material of thinking is not thoughts, but actions, facts, events, and the relations of things" (2004, p. 170). In his 1910 *How We Think*, he explains that "To think means, in any case, to bridge the gap in experience, to bind together facts or deeds otherwise isolated" (1997a, p. 80). That is to say, thinking is nothing but an intelligent investigation of experience, not very different from the everyday activity of trial and error – the gradual progression in understanding the world through tentative attempts of explaining it and careful examinations of the suggested explanations.

The best paradigm of intelligence-oriented experience is therefore the scientific experiment (1997a, p. 152). Scientific investigation starts with a phenomenon incompatible with what is already known, posing a hypothesis able to account for the oddity, and then examines the proposition to see whether it can be accepted pending future problems. Thinking arises from and ends in experience, for its outcome is the ability to better understand phenomena in the sense of recognizing causal connections and predicting future events. It is "that operation in which present facts suggest other facts (or truths) in such a way as to induce belief in the latter upon the ground or warrant of the former" (pp. 8–9).

The thinker here is no passive observer, and experience is not something that "happens" to her. Rather, she asks questions, makes suggestions, and looks for new experiences able to refute or confirm her ideas. Thinking, as Dewey makes clear in *Democracy and Education*, is connected to experience both as sensation and as experimentation; it involves recognizing the connection between the *active* element of experience (trying) and its *passive* element (undergoing), between what we do to things and what they do to us:

> Thinking… is the intentional endeavor to discover specific connections between something which we do and the consequences which result, so that the two become continuous. Their isolation, and consequently their purely arbitrary going together, is cancelled; a unified developing situation takes its place. The occurrence is now understood; it is explained; it is reasonable, as we say, that the thing should happen as it does (2004, p. 158).

In this way, thinking aims at finding new ways for coping with the problems encountered while experiencing the world. It results in the ability for future action in a world that has become more understandable. Like Adorno, then, Dewey rejects the dichotomy between theory and praxis: for him thinking is always a kind of action, just as unthoughtful realization of drives and instincts, characteristic of animals, is not action but mere behavior. Thinking and acting presuppose each other (Rømer 2015).

While Dewey emphasizes that everyone can think, he nevertheless insists that everyone can *improve* their thinking powers, and make investigative thinking a habit. The primary task of education, therefore, is developing thinking habits (1997a, p. 28). These "habits", to be sure, do not mean that thinking becomes some technical, automatic skill, but rather that active, independent thinking becomes an inseparable aspect of the student's interaction with the world. From this perspective the subject matter is not the most important thing – even science is significant not as a body of knowledge but rather as providing the paradigm of thinking as intelligent investigation of experience (Fairfield 2009, p. 108). Yet Dewey distances himself from those versions of "progressive education" that utterly reject the importance of subject matter arguing that education must put the student at the center and adjust itself to the individual needs of each. The center of gravity of Deweyan education is not the student herself but rather her *experience* (Fairfield 2009, p. 52) – nothing educates for thinking more than reasoned interaction with the world.

As thinking is inseparable from experience, clearly it is not an independent mental faculty that can be isolated and trained irrespective of specific fields of study (Dewey 1997a, p. 38, p. 45). In Dewey's words, thinking "no more exists apart from this arranging of subject matter than digestion occurs apart from the assimilating of food" (p. 188). This is why subject matter has a crucial role in education, although emphasis is put not on its direct acquisition but rather on learning it by way of active, independent investigation, that Dewey calls intelligent experiencing. Furthermore, the subject matter need not be academic in the traditional sense: "intelligent consecutive work in gardening, cooking, or weaving, or in elementary wood and iron, may be planned which will inevitably result in students not only amassing information of practical and scientific importance in botany, zoology, chemistry, physics, and other sciences, but (what is more significant) in their becoming versed in methods of experimental inquiry and proof" (1997a, p. 169). At the Laboratory School he founded in Chicago in 1894, Dewey arranged educational situations around subjects such as woodworking, domestic farming and cooking (Fairfield 2009, p. 58). In all these cases, the task of education is "to organize and relate these subjects so that they will become instruments for forming alert, persistent, and fruitful intellectual habits" (1997a, p. 168). Thus, one of the essential aspects of Dewey's educational view is that educational experiences in class must not be very different from everyday experiences – a continuation must exist between education and life (Fairfield 2009, p. 28).

Obviously, Deweyan education cannot amount to a one-way transfer of "thinking skills" from teacher to student, but must involve an encounter of the student with the world itself; an encounter in which she is encouraged to attend to connections between phenomena and look for creative ways of doing things with them, of using them to solve problems. As suggested by the title of Dewey's book, such education is democratic, but not only in the direct, civic-political sense of raising engaged political subjects, but rather as an overarching ethos. This ethos includes cooperative discussions and respect for different views among the students, as well as rejecting the traditional hierarchy of knowledge and replacing it with independent student activity, in which the teacher is merely a partner: "In such shared activity, the teacher is a learner, and the learner is, without knowing it, a teacher" (2004, p. 174). The teacher is far from superfluous in this process, as he has to create the conditions in which the student's surroundings appear to her as a challenging problem – not a trivial hindrance or unsurpassable obstacle, but a thought-provoking difficulty (2004, pp. 167–171; 1997b, pp. 51–60). The teachers' role, in other words, is "to protect the spirit of inquiry, to keep it from becoming blasé from overexcitement, wooden from routine, fossilized through dogmatic instruction, or dissipated by random exercise upon trivial things (1997a, p. 34). Thus, the teacher actively encourages the student to become a mature, independent thinker, and consequently an autonomous political subject.

2.5 Subject, Object, and Subject Matter

As we have seen, both Dewey and Adorno emphasize independent thinking and relate it to political subjectivity. Nevertheless, the differences between the two are no less significant, and even though the harsh criticism Adorno often directed at American pragmatism was not necessarily based on thorough acquaintance, it still reflects real differences. While it would be a mistake to reduce Dewey's views of experience and thinking to raw pragmatism which values everything only according to utility and instrumental reason (Garrison 1999; D'agnese 2017), from Adorno's point of view Dewey's approach leads to identity thinking and the logic of domination. Pinpointing the reasons for that will help us understand Adorno's position, especially the unique way he conceives of the relation between thinking experience in education and other contexts.

Dewey's version of pragmatism is far from vulgar utilitarianism, of the kind that looks only for the "cash value" of ideas and theories. He differentiates between "concrete thinking" focused on finding efficient means to given ends and "abstract thinking" which is "employed simply as a means to more thinking" (1997a, p. 138), and highlights the educational importance of the latter. He writes that education should take interest in "intellectual matters for their own sake, a delight of thinking for the sake of thinking" (p. 141). However, he is quick to clarify that "abstract thinking… represents *an* end, not *the* end. The power of sustained thinking on matters remote from direct use is an outgrowth of practical and immediate modes of thought, but not a substitute for them" (p. 142, emphasis in the original). The point, then, is to learn to enjoy thinking regardless of its practical outcomes; but even when delight is taken from the mere activity of thinking, the meaning of this activity is derived from the end to which it is directed. Pragmatic efficiency and applicability, then, reign over Dewey's conception of thinking. This is also Fairfield's conclusion, as he writes that for Dewey "Thought in general… crucially bears upon the pragmatic – 'how things work and how to do things' – not as a secondary matter but ultimately" (2009, p. 107). Thinking, in Dewey's words, "is the actual transition from the problematic to the secure" (quoted in Fairfield 2009, p. 109): it is inseparable from the ability to change the world, control and dominate it.

Furthermore, by adopting the model of thinking as experiential investigation, Dewey's pragmatism in fact succumbs to the principle of identity. From Adorno's perspective, as Deweyan thinking consists of understanding the lawful connections between objects, it must perceive each object as representative of a general category. It looks for similarities in an attempt to subsume them under conceptual categories, to be able to control them by formulating permanent connections. Hence, the experience presupposed by such thinking is also "identical", in Adorno's terms: even though Dewey (1997b) stresses the importance of the new and unexpected in experience, thinking strives to reduce perplexity, overcome inconsistency and make the unexpected predictable; this means that the aim of thinking is ultimately to assimilate the new in an "experiential continuum" (p. 33) where past experience is used to come to terms with the future and control it. Indeed, intelligent experience opens the way for more experiences that may be very different from the familiar ones, but when thinking confronts such experiences, its ultimate goal is to identify them, thereby forming a consistent worldview in which the future and present are in principle identical to the past. Even the experiencing subject, therefore, does not change significantly as a result of her experiences; she only "grows" as she accumulates experiences (p. 36), becoming equipped with more cognitive and conceptual means to deal with new experiences.

For Adorno, on the other hand, identical experience, in which everything new becomes more of the same, reduced to utility and use value, is no experience at all. When contact with things is limited to operation alone, he writes, the result is "the withering of experience" (2002, p. 40). This is no coincidental or personal problem but a socio-historical one, a result of the way capitalism commodifies everything (2005c, p. 91). Adorno writes that "the gravest problem today is that people have completely lost the ability to experience, and instead they insert between themselves and the object of experience the very stereotypical dimension one must object to" (1971b, p. 113, my translation). Replacing experience with identification, therefore, opens the way to antisemitism (2005c, pp. 101–2), which perceives Jews as essentially identical to each other and subsumes them all under pre-given categories of enemies or even subhuman parasites.

Real experience, on the other hand, involves encounter with the non-identical as such, with what transcends available concepts. Unlike Bicker's suggestion (2018, p. 3), experiencing the non-identical is not only about encountering unorthodox views and ideas. Non-identical experience is coming close to encountering the thing itself, in a way that is irreducible to any conceptual scheme: "the experiencing subject is confronted with a difference in itself, that is, the *nonidentical* that it cannot surmount" (Thompson 2006, p. 83, emphasis in the original). Macdonald (2011, p. 3) explains this disappearing experience through Adorno's discussion of intimacy, or "live contact with the warmth of things" (2002, p. 43), in contrast with the coldness and alienation of instrumental thinking. "The ideal of warmth as the counter-concept to the reduction of difference", he writes, "is developed along the lines of a utopian image of thingly intimacy: a relation in which thought reflects its object noncoercively, that is, by respecting and reflecting the object's difference" (Macdonald 2011, p. 6).

That is to say, to experience the non-identical, thinking must "turn against itself", namely be engaged with "the moment of the subject matter itself" (Adorno 2005d, pp. 130–1), in a way that allows it to appear non-identical – that does not attempt to capture and exhaust it with pre-given concepts, but rather lets the object act upon the subject (Thompson 2005, pp. 525–6). Thinking, therefore, plays a crucial role in enabling experience: it does so by giving itself to the object and opening itself to its unique singularity, not by searching for its lawful causal relations with other objects: "Thought acquires its depth from penetrating deeply into a matter, not from referring it back to something else" (Adorno 2000, p. 99). Hence, real experience cannot be accumulated: not only are past experiences inefficient means for dealing with new ones, they might even stand in their way, for thinking habits acquired through past experiences may blind one to the non-identical in the object and thereby thwart thinking. Non-identical experience *transcends* the familiar conceptual scheme, making it possible to understand Deweyan experience, despite its emphasis on change and renewal, as being trapped in a paradigm of immanence (Biesta 2017, p. 623): it tries to absorb the new while keeping the old as unaltered as possible. Encountering the non-identical, on the other hand, always involves an experience of the deceptiveness of existing reality, a call for radical change. Hence, Adorno argues that education for *Mündigkeit* must not only appeal to experience but also actually teach students how to experience their world afresh: "education for experience and education for independent thinking are one and the same" (1971b, p. 116, my translation).

To be sure, most subject-object encounters cannot but obey the logic of identity and domination. In everyday life, people must attain various goals, and the things around them are inevitably means to given ends. Contrary to Dewey's demand that whatever happens in class is to be a continuation of the outside world, for Adorno giving precedence to the object over the subject's needs requires a certain suspension of the everyday world and its practical demands; thinking requires its time and space. School is the ultimate site that can provide such time and space – it takes children away from family and society and offers them a place where the demands of the outside world are suspended, rendered inoperative (Masschelein and Simons 2013). Adorno's view of thinking and experience can therefore be understood as a call to turn schools from sites in which knowledge of the world is treated as possession and investment – what he called "semi-education" (*Halbbildung*) (2003b) – into ones in which the world is an object of thinking.

For school education to provoke thinking it must not place the student – and certainly not the teacher – in the center. Center stage must be given to the object of experience, to subject-matter over the subject-student and subject-teacher. The subject-matter on the table at school is there not only as an object of knowledge to be transferred from teacher to student, nor as an object of scientific investigation. It is there rather as a kind of subject in its own right: the object, so to speak, is invited to speak and act, while the subject (student) is required to listen and attend. The material to be studied needs not be "material" in the simple, physical sense, and the sensory aspect of experiencing it may be minimal. Despite Adorno's emphasis on experiencing aesthetic objects in which conceptual identification is never exhaustive (Thompson 2006, p. 77), not only artworks can be educational subject matter, and not only the aesthetic aspects of the object are important. Much like in Dewey, the nature of the object is inessential, since every subject-matter can provoke thinking, be it a philosophical text or historical document, mathematical formulae or physical phenomena, diesel engine or woodwork. Every lesson on every subject is an opportunity for critical, philosophical reflection (2005b, p. 21) – all that is needed is the time and space to take the subject matter as an object of thought rather than knowledge. The teacher, of course, cannot teach students to think the way he teaches knowledge, but he can certainly provide them with the *conditions* for thinking, primarily time and space.

Moreover, for Adorno thinking of the subject matter cannot abide peacefully with knowledge, as a complementary or parallel process. Critical thinking is reflection not on the knowledge of the object but on the object itself; it seeks the truth of the object, which contradicts accepted knowledge: "knowledge comes to us through a network of prejudices, opinions, innervations, self-corrections, presuppositions and exaggerations, in short through the dense, firmly-founded but by no means uniformly transparent medium of [accumulated] experience" (2002, p. 80). In the activity of thinking the subject who gives herself over to experience "rends the veil [knowledge] weaves about the object" (2005g, p. 254). Seeking the truth of the object is therefore an attempt – always only partly successful – to remove the cataract of social categories, to contact the object not through its possible uses, its place in the established historical narrative, or its value according to the mainstream culture industry.

This is why thinking that gives itself over to the object always also expands beyond the specific object and into the broader sociopolitical context. Although such thinking does not look for lawful connections between its object and others, it by no means treats the latter as isolated from its surroundings. It rather operates in a way Adorno calls "expansive concentration": "By gauging its subject matter, and it alone, thinking becomes aware of what within the matter extends beyond what was previously thought and thereby breaks open the fixed purview of the subject matter" (2005d, p. 131). As Macdonald puts it, such thinking is "the ability to reflect objectivity… in order to reveal the (dys)functional context of the status quo" (2011, pp. 10–11). That is to say, in the gap between how the object ordinarily appears and its truth that flickers through the activity of thinking, the alienation and distortion of the entire social reality is disclosed and brought to consciousness: every single object testifies that society views everything as interchangeable and does not allow it to appear as what it really is. Thus, every object of study is essentially a synecdoche: it can become subject matter through which the whole is revealed; to borrow a turn of phrase from Jacques Rancière (see Chap. 6), "everything is in everything" (1991, p. 19).

This is why, for Adorno, critical thinking is no mere theoretical work, but "a praxis that lives within the contradictions of the moment in order to articulate them in its very form" (Lewis 2006, p. 4). This praxis is of course essentially negative: it does not offer a positive alternative, and consists of the refusal to accept the object as it usually appears (Stojanov 2012, pp. 126–7). But even negativity is not simply given to thought, does not reveal itself as such to experience; the thinking subject must actively negate the object, thereby constituting it as a problem. Unlike Dewey, for whom the teacher is responsible for setting the stage in which the student experiences the problems and remains in control of the educational situation, here problematization is part of the thinking activity and is under the thinking student's full responsibility. This is, then, a much more radical form of democratic education: democratic relations of equality are founded on a relation of non-domination with the object, and are reflected in student-teacher relations, for the latter is responsible for creating the *negative* conditions for thinking, for providing the time and space it requires, but *not* for generating thought through artificial positive intervention. We can even say, in fact, that when the student thinks, it is not the teacher but rather the object that educates her: as the subject-student opens herself up to the subject-matter she cannot retain her identity after experiencing the non-identical. Her conceptual categories, the presuppositions guiding her everyday interaction with the world, are revealed to be insufficient and necessarily change through the act of thinking the non-identical (Thompson 2006, p. 83).

Moreover, it is only through genuine thinking that prioritizes the object that the student really becomes a subject. Whoever accepts preexisting knowledge takes the object to be an empirical given in an existing web of concepts, or limits oneself to logical procedures, is not exactly a subject; he is merely an abstract, general and illusory subject, hence somewhat of an object, a product of the social process of reification. The activity of thinking which seeks the truth of the object makes the thinker a real subject – a concrete person, anchored in her sociopolitical surrounding without being completely absorbed into it. Education for thinking, therefore, politicizes both object and subject, enabling them to temporarily suspend the logic of identification and domination. Not, to be sure, to reach a safe haven, but rather to develop a point of view from which the danger inherent in this logic – within living memory in Adorno's time but just as threatening in ours – is even more clear and present (Thompson 2005, 528).

2.6 The Essay as a Form of Thinking

As we have seen, thinking involves not only passive openness to material, but also active work with it. This activity is much different from that described by Dewey, which is aimed at dominating the object and is valued according to a practical test of results. For Adorno the activity of thinking takes place in language, or more precisely in the passage to language, in translating the object into the linguistic dimension: "Thinking begins in the labor upon the subject matter and its verbal formulation" (2005d, p. 133). This does not mean that there is pre-linguistic thought that needs to be given linguistic articulation, but rather that thought itself is a dynamic relation between concepts and objects, a spark resulting from the collision of these two incommensurable elements, the material and the linguistic.

However, encouraging the student to give the experience of the object linguistic form is not exactly an invitation to engage in dialogue or opine in a discussion. The linkage between thinking and open discussion is prevalent in Anglo-American scholarship on education for thinking (see Chap. 1), in which active participation in public deliberation is understood as necessary for giving form to thought, for elucidating and refining it (Lipman 2003). For Adorno, on the other hand, the discursive practice is completely subordinated to instrumental reason and the logic of domination, namely to the attempt to win the argument at any cost:

> [E]verywhere discussion is called for, certainly initially out of an anti-authoritarian impulse. But discussion, which by the way, like the public sphere, is an entirely bourgeois category, has been completely ruined by tactics… Discussion serves manipulation. Every argument, untroubled by the question of whether it is sound, is geared to a purpose… The opponent in a discussion becomes a functional component of the current plan:… If the opponent does not concede, then he will be disqualified and accused of lacking the qualities presupposed by the discussion (2005h, pp. 268–9).

Furthermore, the very presupposition of a possible "a-priori agreement between minds able to communicate with each other", namely the exchangeability of opinions, implies the unconditional surrender of each interlocutor to standards set by the collective, and is thus founded on "complete conformism" (Adorno 2002, p. 70).

Thinking, therefore, requires a special kind of interaction not only with the object but also with other subjects. Rather than being an attempt to directly influence and control the interlocutors, such interaction would be mediated by the object, as each student offers his or her perspective on the subject matter. Thus, each student would be exposed to the non-identical ways in which others use concepts, undermining the previous perception of the object and calling for a re-articulation of previous conceptions and dispositions.

Accordingly, for Adorno the most hospitable medium in which thinking may take place is not speech but writing. This is evident in his critique of student teachers, only "exceedingly few" of whom "have any idea of the difference between language as a means of communication and language as the precise expression of the matter under consideration; they believe that knowing how to speak is sufficient to know how to write, although it is true enough that whoever cannot write most often is also incapable of speaking" (2005b, pp. 28–9). The candidates' loss of connection to their own language, expressed primarily in their sloppy, style-less writing, is indicative of their inability to genuinely think. A complimentary case is Adorno's reluctance to publish his own lectures and radio talks (Kadelbach 1971, p. 7), as he believed that the spoken word does not allow space for sensitivity and linguistic precision, so needed for thorough thinking.

Writing here is not an external expression of a prior mental process or an auxiliary to such a process, but rather an inseparable aspect of thinking itself. The thinking student must become an active subject through writing on the object without dominating it, and without attempting to dominate others through it; she must write in a way that allows the object to remain subject-matter rather than a mute thing. Writing, therefore, must not impose a preexisting form on the object, a logical-conceptual scheme designed to analyze and exhaust it, formalize its relations with other things or use it as means to an end. It must be a form that always remains sensitive to content, to experience; a form that acknowledges the inherent impossibility of separating form and content. Adorno calls such form or writing style an "essay". Unlike the argumentative article or research report, the Adornian essay does not attempt to formulate a logical argument, or prove a point in a way that squeezes the rich material into an empty logical vessel: "In the essay, concepts do not build a continuum of operations, thought does not advance in a single direction, rather the aspects of the argument interweave as in a carpet. The fruitfulness of the thoughts depends on the density of this texture. Actually, the thinker does not think, but rather transforms himself into an arena of intellectual experience, without simplifying it" (2000, p. 101). The essay is a formless form, a flexible form that changes according to its content instead of imposing itself on it. It goes wherever the inner logic of its subject matter takes it, well aware of the inherent failure of every attempt at direct contact with the object, opting instead for a plurality of indirect routes, of groping in an unknown terrain. This way it preserves the active side of experience, that of trying, as well as its passive side, namely receptivity.

The essay welcomes any content. Unlike traditional philosophical texts which are preoccupied with big questions and abstract contents, it "revolts above all against the doctrine – deeply rooted since Plato – that the changing and ephemeral is unworthy of philosophy" (2000, p. 98). There is no hierarchy among the objects of thought, and if we assume in advance that certain objects are more important than others – that we can determine which are worthy of thinking and writing and which are not – we will be giving in to fixity and lack of self-reflection, prone "to neutralize the key phenomena of social injustice as mere exceptions" (2002, p. 125). Hence not only ordinary curricular subject matter, brought to the table by the teacher, can be food for thought; it can be anything the student encounters in her everyday life, no matter how seemingly trivial. The essay, moreover, welcomes any length. As it is carried away by its object, it may be quite lengthy in the attempt to break through the veil of given categories; but it is often very short: "It thinks in fragments just as reality is fragmented and gains its unity only by moving through the fissures, rather than by smoothing them over" (2000, p. 104).

The best example of such fragmentary writing is of course *Minima Moralia*, the collection of aphorisms completed by Adorno in 1947, in which he develops moral and sociopolitical critique of contemporary society through "micro-analyses" of various objects of experience, from the most mundane to the most refined products of high culture. As Roger Foster makes clear, such writing, which lingers with the particular to the point where social conditions are disclosed through it, which exaggerates to reveal the truth, is "not simply... a theory of resistance to wrong life, but rather… a performance of ethical resistance through its intrinsic aesthetic arrangement" (2011, p. 85). One does not have to be educated like Adorno to write an essay, however. No previous knowledge or experience are required, only willingness to study the objects, to be a student.

Note that Adorno explicitly posits the writing of essays against the kind of teaching usually practiced in school. He writes that "[t]he way in which the essay appropriates concepts is most easily comparable to the behavior of a man who is obliged, in a foreign country, to speak that country's language instead of patching it together from its elements, as he did in school" (2000, p. 101). Schoolteachers attempt to protect their students by teaching them the Cartesian wisdom that studying must proceed carefully from the most simple and elementary to the more complex, while the Adornian essay jumps right into the heart of the matter, ready to confront the object of experience in its full richness and complexity – to speak the language of the object rather than the one the subject already masters. In much the same way, Adorno invokes "the words of the schoolmaster" as blaming the essay for not being exhaustive, for failing to fully grasp the object and systematically present all its relevant aspects (p. 103).

Nevertheless, this does not mean the essay cannot find its place in school. Adorno's position may also be understood as a call for alternative teaching, very different from the one accepted today. I suggest that for him, the essay is the scholastic form par excellence – the one most fit for school, as it privileges neither the teacher's knowledge nor the subject-student's needs, but rather subject-matter itself. The teacher's role may therefore be characterized as one of inviting and helping the students write essays. It is no doubt impossible to teach how to write essays the same way more formal and structured writing styles can be taught, but the teacher may certainly lend the struggling student a hand. The authority of such a teacher need not contradict the freedom essayist writing and thinking is supposed to allow: as Adorno says to Becker in their talk on "education for maturity and responsibility [*Mündigkeit*]", "The way in which the individual – psychologically speaking – becomes an autonomous, and therefore mature, responsible person, is not simply to kick against every kind of authority… As a causal factor, the factor of authority is, in my opinion, the precondition for the whole process of maturation [*Mündigwerden*]" (1999, pp. 26–7).

Note that the essay is not an automatic, expressive or associative style of writing centered on the writer's inner world. Rejecting the absolute authority of logical formality does not amount to total freedom of all rationality: "the essay is not situated in simple opposition to discursive procedure. It is not unlogical; rather it obeys logical criteria in so far as the totality of its sentences must fit together coherently" (2000, p. 109). Although the essay enjoys aesthetic autonomy, it is distinct from art "through its conceptual character and its claim to truth free of aesthetic semblance" (p. 94). Its writing, therefore, needs to vacillate constantly between the rationale of pure logic and that of the object, and respect both without yielding to either. In writing an essay, even more than in other writing styles, the author must pay heed to the most precise nuances in describing the object (2002, p. 221), and make sure that in every paragraph "the central motif stands out clearly enough" (2002, p. 85). This requires "unlimited efforts" (2000, p. 105). The teacher, therefore, is often needed as an external support and even authority that can demand the effort, insist on the rewriting of drafts and facilitate thoughtful, attentive writing.

Adorno's criticism of common communicative and discursive practices, therefore, does not mean rejecting any form of interaction or collaboration in education. The central place given to writing in Adornian education for thinking – especially the writing of essays focused on objects rather than on the readers – may reinforce the false impression that such education is best achieved in isolation, in the intimacy of student and teacher, hence running against one of the essential features of school education, namely the plurality of students. I argue, however, that this is not the case – that plurality is essential to the Adornian essay and that school is its natural abode. Although communication with readers is not the ultimate aim of the essay form, as it is founded on dialogue with the object rather than other subjects, it need not be a kind of closet writing. Essays need to be read, and a certain form of interaction between writers and readers is certainly welcomed by the essay form. An essay written by one student may be read by others and compel them to react, think, and write. A school where essays are written thus becomes a special kind of community: not one of argumentation or discussion but one of writers and readers, a collective of thinkers. Communication in such a community is mediated and requires time and effort (Heins 2012, p. 78). It renounces in advance all attempts to persuade, to influence directly. It is what Adorno calls a "message in a bottle" (Hellings 2012), sent to the world without knowing in advance who would pick it up and what effects it may have. This is precisely why the essay is political – not in the "actionist" sense, which renounces thinking, but in the Adornian sense of recognizing that thought itself is always already critical and political.

This brings us to the final point. The reflection on essayist writing as a form of thought and of thinking as a form of political resistance reveals an interesting aspect of Adorno's relation to childhood. Various references to contemporary youth as infantile and stupid (2002, p. 22), as well as the adoption of the Kantian concept of *Mündigkeit*, create the impression that Adorno, like Kant, limits political subjectivity to grown-ups. However, the essay, to which "luck and play are essential" (2000, p. 93), is explicitly linked to childhood: "Instead of achieving something scientifically, or creating something artificially, the effort of the essay reflects a childlike freedom that catches fire, without scruple, on what others have already done" (p. 93). There is a childlike quality in the essay's essential freedom, in the rejection of accepted forms to avoid assimilation into existing society. Children, writes Adorno in *Minima Moralia*, are aware "of the contradiction between phenomenon and fungibility that the resigned adult no longer sees, and they shun it. Play is their defence" (2002, p. 228). The playful essay is therefore reluctant yet merry, lacking in positive vision yet critical, naïve yet political. The political subject who thinks and writes essays is childlike, and every child can be a political subject. After all, who knows better than do children to simply say no?

2.7 Conclusion: *Minima Pedagogica*

I have shown how in Adorno's view, education, and education for thinking in particular, can be an active form of political resistance. This does not mean that such education promises wonders. This is not exactly "educational activism", as Tyson E. Lewis suggests (2006), for according to Adorno activism implies simplistic separation of theory and praxis in which the latter is given precedence. Education for thinking that follows in Adorno's footsteps challenges many existing educational practices, but its political aspirations are rather modest. I suggest calling this education *minima pedagogica* – not in a sense that would imply that education is unimportant, of course, or in the sense of non-interventionist, "hands off" education, but in the sense Adorno gave his own writing in *Minima Moralia*: philosophical activity that refuses to be *magna moralia*, namely a unified, fully elaborated grand theory aimed at guiding the perplexed. This would be a minor, minimal pedagogy of liberation – it can offer the student nothing but better understanding of the reality of domination, in which lies only a glimmer of hope for something different, the exact nature of which cannot be known.

The problems attendant on this educational project are obvious. Education for thinking as discussed here is in clear conflict with other purposes Adorno ascribes to education, such as bequeathing high culture (French and Thomas 1999, p. 3), or the claim that students need to be "shown" how false and distorted cultural products are (p. 31). Moreover, Adorno's rejection of any action apart from thinking, his refusal of any concrete political action, even one which may bring temporary, partial relief from suffering, borders on practical resignation and acceptance of social reality for what it is. It seems, sometimes, that it would not be a bad idea to bring into Adorno's thinking something of the Deweyan pragmatic spirit – a desire to do something beyond thinking, reading and writing; to get out of the classroom, lecture hall or library, to expect results. In this chapter, however, I tried to suspend such criticisms, to surrender as much as possible to the object that is Adorno's writings, and let it be a subject matter that speaks through its and my own writing.

References

Adorno, T. W. (1971a [1963]). Fernsehen und Bildung. In G. Kadelbach (Ed.), *Erziehung zur Mündigkeit – Vorträge und Gespräche mit Hellmut Becker 1959 bis 1969* (pp. 50–69). Frankfurt: Suhrkamp.

Adorno, T. W. (1971b [1966]). Erziehung – Wozu? In G. Kadelbach (Ed.), *Erziehung zur Mündigkeit – Vorträge und Gespräche mit Hellmut Becker 1959 bis 1969* (pp. 105–119). Frankfurt: Suhrkamp.

Adorno, T. W. (1971c [1968]). Erzirhung zur Entbarbarisierung. In G. Kadelbach (Ed.), *Erziehung zur Mündigkeit – Vorträge und Gespräche mit Hellmut Becker 1959 bis 1969* (pp. 120–132). Frankfurt: Suhrkamp.

Adorno, Theodor W. (1999 [1969]). Education for maturity and responsibility. Trans. Robert French, Jem Thomas and Dorothee Weymann. History of the Human Sciences 12.3: 21–34.

Adorno, T. W. (2000 [1958]). The essay as form. Trans. Bob Hullot-Kentor and Frederic Will. In B. O'Connor (Ed.), *The Adorno reader* (pp. 91–111). Oxford: Blackwell.
Adorno, T. W. (2002 [1951]). *Minima Moralia* (E. F. N. Jephcott, Trans.). New York: Verso.
Adorno, T. W. (2003a [1966]). *Negative Dialectics* (E. B. Ashton, Trans.). New York: Continuum.
Adorno, T. W. (2003b [1959]). Theorie der Halbbildung. In: *Gesammelte Schriften*, Band 8 (pp. 93–121). Darmstadt: Wissenschaftliche Buchgesellschaft.
Adorno, T. W. (2005a [1962]). Why still philosophy. In *Critical models: Interventions and catchwords* (H. W. Pickford, Trans.) (pp. 5–18). New York: Columbia University Press.
Adorno, T. W. (2005b [1961]). Philosophy and teachers. In *Critical models: Interventions and catchwords* (H. W. Pickford, Trans.) (pp. 19–38). New York: Columbia University Press.
Adorno, T. W. (2005c [1959]). The meaning of working through the past. In *Critical models: Interventions and catchwords* (H. W. Pickford, Trans.) (pp. 89–103). New York: Columbia University Press.
Adorno, T. W. (2005d [1964]). Notes on philosophical thinking. In *Critical models: Interventions and catchwords* (H. W. Pickford, Trans.) (pp. 127–134). New York: Columbia University Press.
Adorno, T. W. (2005e [1965]). Taboos on the teaching vocation. In *Critical models: Interventions and catchwords* (H. W. Pickford, Trans.) (pp. 177–190. New York: Columbia University Press.
Adorno, T. W. (2005f [1966]). Education after Auschwitz. In *Critical models: Interventions and catchwords* (H. W. Pickford, Trans.) (pp. 191–204). New York: Columbia University Press.
Adorno, T. W. (2005g [n/a]). On subject and object. In *Critical models: Interventions and catchwords* (Henry. W. Pickford, Trans.) (pp. 254–258). New York: Columbia University Press.
Adorno, T. W. (2005h [n/a]). Marginalia to theory and praxis. In *Critical models: Interventions and catchwords* (H. W. Pickford, Trans.) (pp. 259–278). New York: Columbia University Press.
Adorno, T. W., & Horkheimer, M. (2007 [1944]). *Dialectic of enlightenment* (E. Jephcott, Trans.). Palo Alto: Stanford University Press.
Althusser, L. (1971). Ideology and ideological state apparatuses. Notes towards an investigation. In *Lenin and philosophy and other essays* (B. Brewster, Trans.) (pp. 127–186). New York: Monthly Review Press.
Arendt, H. (1978). *The life of the mind*. New York: Harcourt Brace & Company.
Bicker, J. (2018). Teacher-led codeswitching: Adorno, Race, Contradiction, and the Nature of Autonomy. *Ethics and Education, 13*(1), 73–85.
Biesta, G. (2017). P4C after Auschwitz: On immanence and transcendence in education. *Childhood and Philosophy, 13*(28), 617–628.
Cone, L. L. (2018). Towards a university of *Halbbildung*: How the neoliberal mode of higher education governance in Europe is half-educating students for a misleading future. *Educational Philosophy and Theory, 50*(11), 1020–1030.
D'agnese, V. (2017). The essential uncertainty of thinking: Education and subject in John Dewey. *Journal of Philosophy of Education, 51*(1), 73–88.
Descartes, R. (2008 [1641]). *Meditations on first philosophy with selections from the objections and replies* (M. Moriarty, Trans.). Oxford: Oxford University Press.
Dewey, J. (1997a [1910]). *How we think*. Mineola/New York: Dover Publishing.
Dewey, J. (1997b [1938]). *Education and experience*. New York: Thouchstone.
Dewey, J. (2004 [1916]). *Democracy and education*. New Delhi: Aakar Books.
Fairfield, P. (2009). *Education after Dewey*. New York: Continuum.
Foster, R. (2011). Lingering with the particular: *Minima Moralia*'s critical modernism. *Telos, 155*, 83–103.
Foucault, M. (1995 [1975]). *Discipline & punish: The birth of the prison* (Alan Sheridan, Trans.). New York: Vintage Books.
French, R., & Thomas, J. (1999). Maturity and education, citizenship and enlightenment: An introduction to Theodor Adorno and Helmut Becker, 'Education for Maturity and Responsibility'. *History of the Human Sciences, 12*(3), 1–19.
Garrison, J. (1999). Dewey's theory of practical reasoning. *Educational Philosophy and Theory, 13*(3), 291–312.

Giroux, H. (2004). Education after Abu Ghraib: Revisiting Adorno's politics of education. *Cultural Studies, 18*(6), 779–815.

Gur-Ze'ev, I. (2010). Adorno and Horkheimer: Diasporic philosophy. Negative theology, and counter-education. *Policy Futures in Education, 3*(4), 298–314.

Hegel, G. W. F. (1977 [1807]). *Phenomenology of spirit* (A. V. Miller, Trans.). Oxford: Oxford University Press.

Heins, V. (2012). Saying things that hurt: Adorno as educator. *Thesis Eleven, 110*(1), 68–82.

Hellings, J. (2012). Messages in a bottle and other things lost to the sea: The other side of critical theory or a reevaluation of Adorno's aesthetic theory. *Telos, 160*, 77–97.

Horkheimer, M. (2004 [1947]). *Eclipse of reason*. London: Continuum.

Kadelbach, G. (1971). Vorwort. In T. W. Adorno & G. Kadelbach (Eds.), *Erziehung zur Mündigkeit – Vorträge und Gespräche mit Hellmut Becker 1959 bis 1969* (pp. 7–9). Frankfurt: Suhrkamp.

Kant, I. (2003 [1784]). An answer to the question: "what is enlightenment?". In H. S. Reiss (Ed.), *Political writings* (pp. 54–60). Cambridge: Cambridge University Press.

Kertz-Welzel, A. (2005). The Pied Piper of Hamelin: Adorno on music education. *Research Studies in Music Education, 25*, 1–12.

Lewis, T. E. (2006). From aesthetics to pedagogy and back: Rethinking the works of Theodor Adorno. *InterActions: UCLA Journal of Education and Information Studies, 2*(1), 1–17.

Lipman, M.. (2003 [1991]). *Thinking in education*. Cambridge: Cambridge University Press.

Lukács, G. (1972 [1923]). *History and class consciousness: Studies in Marxist Dialectics* (R. Livingstone, Trans.). Cambridge, MA: The MIT Press.

Macdonald, I. (2011). Cold, cold, warm: Autonomy, intimacy and maturity in Adorno. *Philosophy and Social Criticism, 37*(6), 669–689.

Marx, Karl. (2000 [1846]). The German ideology. In *Selected writings*, ed. David McLellan, 175–208. Oxford: Oxford University Press.

Masschelein, J., & Simons, M. (2013). *In defence of the school. A public issue* (J. McMartin, Trans.). Leuven: E-ducation, Culture & Society Publishers.

Papastephanou, M. (2006). Aesthetics, education, the critical autonomous self, and the culture industry. *The Journal of Aesthetic Education, 40*(3), 75–91.

Plato. 1997. Meno. In J. M. Cooper (Ed.), *Plato: Complete works* (J. McMartin, Trans.) (pp. 870–897). Indianapolis: Hackett Publishing Company.

Pongratz, L. (2008). The liquidation of the subject: Reflections on subjectivity and education after Adorno. *Critique and Humanism Journal, 26*, 123–140.

Rancière, J. (1991). *Disagreement: Politics and philosophy* (J. Rose, Trans.). Minneapolis: University of Minnesota Press.

Rømer, T. A. (2015). Thought and action in education. *Educational Philosophy and Theory, 47*(3), 260–275.

Snir, I. (2010). The "new categorical imperative" and Adorno's Aporetic moral philosophy. *Continental Philosophy Review, 43*(3), 407–437.

Stojanov, K.. (2012). Education as social critique: On Theodor Adorno's philosophy of education. In P. Siljander, A. Kivelä, & A. Sutinen (Eds.), *Theories of* Bildung *and growth: Connections and controversies between continental educational thinking and American Pragmatism* (pp. 125–134). Rotterdam: Sense publishers.

Thompson, C. (2005). The non-transparency of the self and the ethical value of *Bildung*. *Journal of Philosophy of Education, 39*(3), 519–533.

Thompson, C. (2006). Adorno and the Borders of experience: The significance of the nonidentical for a 'Different' theory of *Bildung*. *Educational Theory, 56*(1), 69–87.

Chapter 3
Hannah Arendt: Thinking as Withdrawal and Regeneration of the World

3.1 Introduction

Hannah Arendt has given much thought to the activity of thinking. This may seem surprising, for in *The Human Condition* she describes her intellectual project as a challenge to the traditional hierarchy ranking *vita contemplativa*, namely contemplative life dedicated to thoughts and ideas, above *vita activa*, the active life of labor, work and action (1998, p. 17). Moreover, thinking has not been widely discussed even within this tradition of contemplation; indeed Arendt points out that even "professional thinkers", namely philosophers, rarely pay much attention to the experience of thinking (1978. P. 12). Thinking about thinking is therefore an aspect of her reevaluation of tradition: she thinks of thinking as an activity, part of *vita contemplativa*, which is nonetheless as active as *vita activa*.

Although the concept of thinking is already discussed in her works from the 1940s and 50s, Arendt writes that her special interest in the activity of thinking was aroused during her writing on Adolf Eichmann's trial in 1961, as part of her attempt to understand what made possible the horrible crimes for which he was responsible (1978, p. 3). In *Eichmann in Jerusalem: A Report on the Banality of Evil*, she writes that "his was obviously no case of moral let alone legal insanity" (2006a, p. 26). Eichmann was no sadistic pervert but rather "terribly and terrifyingly normal" (p. 276). Namely, not a man characterized by diabolical evil or extreme malevolence, but simply someone who did not think through what he was doing: "Eichmann was not Iago and not Macbeth, and nothing would have been farther from his mind than to determine with Richard III 'to prove a villain.' Except for an extraordinary diligence in looking out for his personal advancement, he had no motives at all… He merely, to put the matter colloquially, never realized what he was doing… [But] He was not stupid. It was sheer thoughtlessness – something by no means identical with stupidity – that predisposed him to become one of the greatest criminals of that period" (p. 287).

I. Snir, *Education and Thinking in Continental Philosophy*, Contemporary Philosophies and Theories in Education 17,
https://doi.org/10.1007/978-3-030-56526-8_3

This does not mean that Eichmann was just an "ordinary person" like you and me, that we are all Eichmanns, or that Eichmann can be relieved of responsibility for his actions because anyone would have done the same (Minnich 2017, p. 33). Arendt insists that his most prominent characteristic, which he by no means shares with everybody else although he is also not unique in it, was the inability to stop and think about his actions, to give himself a reflective account of the meaning of what he did.

Thinking, it turns out, is strongly related to morality, to the ability to tell right from wrong. If horrible crimes are not necessarily caused by evil intentions or vices such as hatred or jealousy but are rather made possible by mere thoughtlessness, than active engagement with thinking may prevent atrocities. Arendt was led, consequently, to fruitful discussions not only of the activity of thinking as such, but also of thinking's relations to historical and political circumstances. However, she does not say much about the ways education can encourage or stimulate thinking, and the two texts she dedicated to educational questions – "Reflections on Little Rock" (2003c) and "The Crisis in Education" (2006c) – never address the concept of thinking. Nevertheless, the possible connections between education and thinking raise growing interest in Arendtian scholarship (Duarte 2001; Novak 2009; O'Donnell 2012), and their relevance seems greater than ever as atrocities of the kind Arendt wrote about seem to be visited upon the Earth on a scale painfully reminiscent of her era.

In this chapter, I analyze Arendt's conception of thinking and examine how education can facilitate thinking activities. I argue that education for thinking in Arendt's approach is indeed possible and of great importance, but may also be hazardous to the thinker as well as her political community. Confronting this danger does not require less thinking (or education encouraging it), but rather engaging in two different but complementary kinds of thinking. That is to say, taking up the educational potential of Arendt's conception of thinking requires acknowledging the difference between two distinct kinds of thinking she discusses – a distinction which often escapes existing scholarship – and using the second as an antidote to the dangers of the first. The first kind of thinking is a mental activity demanding *withdrawal* from the world and from the company of other people in order to think about meanings, while the second follows Kant's notion of "enlarged mentality", attempting to view the world from the points of view of these very others.

Although Arendt relates the latter to the activity of judging and argues that the basic mental activities of thinking, willing and judging cannot be reduced to a common denominator (1978, p. 69), her discussion of judging indicates that it involves thinking through various perspectives, and there is no clear-cut distinction between the two. To be sure, Arendt nowhere presents a systematic typology of thought and at times even seems to neglect the differences between them, but both kinds that interest me are clearly present in her writings, and each is important to politics and morality in a different way, posing very different challenges to education.[1] To wit, while stopping to think about meanings is important morally but may be dangerous

[1] For a systematic discussion of the different conceptions of thinking and judging in Arendt, see Kateb 2010, pp. 34–8.

politically, thinking in the form of enlarged mentality involves the regeneration of political common sense.

The remainder of this chapter is organized as follows. I start by discussing Arendt's first concept of thinking, understood as a silent dialogue of me and myself, and then move to analyze its relations to the ability to tell right from wrong. Although thinking, for Arendt, cannot yield moral values or principles, the inner dialogue can nevertheless be a significant barrier against evildoing because it may involve reflection on the meanings of one's actions and a need to continue living with oneself as the doer. In the third section, I examine the possibility of education for thinking through Arendt's discussion of Socrates' self-description as gadfly, midwife and electric ray – this will show how a teacher can sting the student into thinking and help her deliver her thoughts by purging her of prejudices. Yet thinking, as the case of Socrates and some of his companions indicates, is also a dangerous activity. Next, I discuss Arendt's analysis of how withdrawal and alienation from the world brought about the destruction of political common sense in modernity. The fifth and last section is dedicated, accordingly, to discussing thinking in an enlarged mentality, examining how it may contribute to the regeneration of common sense, and looking into how such thinking can be taught through encouraging thoughtfulness and providing illuminating examples.

3.2 I Think Therefore I Am Not

Arendt thinks through conceptual distinctions and the starting point for her systematic reflection on thinking is the distinction between *thinking* and *knowledge*. The first to articulate this distinction was Kant – in his terms it is that between reason (*Vernunft*) and intellect (*Verstand*) – who also clearly saw that man has an inclination, often felt as a need, to think beyond given knowledge and even beyond all possible knowledge (1978, pp. 13–14). Kant was indeed wrong in arguing that the passion for thinking concerns only the great metaphysical questions of God, freedom and immortality – for everything, even the most mundane things, can be food for thought (p. 78). He nevertheless understood quite well that we have a capacity for thinking which is different from cognition, namely from the search for knowledge of the world. When we think, we put the question of existence aside, within brackets, and ask about meanings: thinking "does not ask what something is or whether it exists at all—its existence is always taken for granted—*but what it means for it to be*" (p. 57, emphasis in the original). To take a very Kantian example, thinking about God can never prove God's existence but may be full of meaning (p. 61). The fact that the sun revolves around the earth, to take another, may be positive knowledge, but in itself meaningless until we engage in thinking about the question of what the fact that our planet is not the center of the universe means to us. Truth, in other words, needs thinking to be humanized, to be made meaningful for human life (Minnich 2017, p. 64).

To be sure, thinking plays an important part in the intellect's search for true knowledge, but it does so only in the service of another enterprise, namely science (Arendt 1978, p. 61); in this case, it is a means to an external end, not an activity in its own right as it is when speculating about meanings (p. 64). Similarly, thinking in the proper sense differs also from other uses of our mental capacities, such as calculations, problem solving, or utilitarian speculations about efficient means to given ends. All those mental activities may involve thinking, but they harness it to their own ends and it comes to a halt when that end is reached. When thinking is independent of such external goals, on the other hand, the questions it poses can never have definite answers and no ultimate goal is ever reached. This is why thinking is also different from what we usually call reason, namely the rigorous following of logical inferences, deriving valid conclusions from given presuppositions. Reason, in this sense, strives for solid, sustainable proofs, while meanings, the fruits of pure thought, are by nature evasive, slippery, always open to doubt or reinterpretation. Arendt thus describes thinking as "swift" like the blink of an eye (1978, p. 44), so evasive that it is very difficult for the thinker to hold on to her thoughts before they are lost in the stream of consciousness.

Thinking's indifference to the existence of its objects has to do with the fact that the things it deals with are always absent – we think of mental representations, not objects present to the senses at the moment of thinking, although each representation stands for something sensed before being stored in memory and retrieved by imagination (Arendt 2003b, p. 165). Similarly, thinking does not produce anything tangible or visible, meant for presentation in the world of appearances: while the search for knowledge gives rise to an aggregate of truths that becomes part of the world, thinking leaves nothing behind (p. 163); it exists only in actualization, at the moment the thinker is engaged in the activity of thinking. To come back to yesterday's thoughts she would have to think them again. Thinking never accepts its outcomes as firm facts, and a second thought can always undo yesterday's conclusions or make previous insights seem trivial; thinking progresses like the veil of Penelope, undoing every morning what it had weaved the night before (p. 166) – it has an inherent drive for self-destruction.

Unlike knowledge, which is always both about the world and part of it, Arendt argues that when one thinks, it is as if one moves outside the world of appearances. Thinking, Arendt argues, involves a withdrawal from the world of experience to engage in dialogue with oneself rather than with the others with whom the thinker shares the world. In the activity of thinking, "I am both the one who asks and the one who answers" (1978, p. 185); it is a "silent dialogue of me with myself", in Plato's formulation from the "Theaetetus", which Arendt repeatedly quotes (1978, p. 185, 2003a, p. 92).[2]

As thinking abstracts and generalizes, it constantly drifts away from the world and from the particular objects appearing in it. What is meaningful for thought, what thought contemplates when reflecting on meanings, is what we may call

[2] In Levett and Burnyeat's translation, "A talk which the soul has with itself" (Plato 1997b, p. 210).

"essences", and essences do not exist in the world of particulars; the thinking ego who silently speaks with herself, therefore, is "homeless", having no proper place in the world (Arendt 1978, p. 199). The "I think", whose ultimate expression is the Cartesian *cogito* is characterized therefore as self-sufficient and world-less: "while, for whatever reason, a man indulges in sheer thinking, and no matter on what subject, he lives completely in the singular, that is, in complete solitude, as though not men but Man inhabited the earth" (p. 47). Thinking is a solitary activity, but the thinker is by no means lonely as she is keeping herself company, speaking silently with a friend more intimate than anyone in the outside world can ever be. It is no surprise, therefore, that thinking is often associated with walking: as portrayed for example in Leslie Stephen's "In Praise of Walking" (2014) and Walter Benjamin's discussion of Baudelaire as a *flâneur* (2006), is a solitary activity just like thinking, and offers a unique opportunity to leave the everyday world behind and engage in active inner dialogue.

No modern philosopher has understood the solitary nature of thinking better than did Descartes. The experience of thinking by himself, however, led him to lose all sense of reality and doubt the truth of the world of appearances, rather than grasp the temporary nature of the withdrawal from the world required by thinking. Moreover, Descartes was wrong to conclude from man's inability to think about his own non-existence – a result of the fact that in thinking one is engaged in a conversation with oneself – that man always thinks by the mere fact of existing as a thinking being. Following Heidegger, Arendt holds that genuine thinking is different from the ordinary mental processes that take place in our minds when we go around the everyday world, and to start thinking we must, in a sense, cease to exist. As Paul Valéry put it, "at times I think, and at times I am" (1978, p. 79); I think therefore I am not.

For this reason, the chief characteristic of thinking, according to Arendt, is that it interrupts all ordinary activities: "[T]he moment we start thinking on no matter what issue we stop everything else, and this everything else… interrupts the thinking process; it is as though we moved into a different world" (2003b, p. 165). Similarly, thinking is "out of order" – it demands to "stop-and-think" (1978, p. 78), disengage with any other activity. The search for meaning seems therefore to be unnatural, opposed to the human condition of living among other people in a world of appearances, and no wonder it has been compared with sleeping and even death (p. 79). This is so, however, only in the eyes of the external beholder. We by no means fall into thinking the same way we fall asleep or die – we must actively leave the everyday world to start thinking, and thinking itself is a very difficult, laborious activity. No wonder it is so rare (Berkowitz 2010b, p. 238); indeed, people can live their whole lives without ever engaging in serious thinking. Eichmann, to recall, was not an unusual man, only a man in unusual circumstances.

The relations between thinking and the world are therefore complex. On the one hand, only the world of appearances can provide food for thought; it surprises, perplexes, and fills us with wonder, thereby demanding we think and make sense of it. Eichmann's inability to think, Arendt writes, protected him against reality, that is, "against the claim on our thinking attention that all events and facts make by virtue of their existence" (1978, p. 4). On the other hand, the thinker is forced to return to reality "when the outside world intrudes upon the thinker and cuts short the thinking process" (p. 185). Thinking is *about* the world and *of* the world, but not *in* it; it feeds off the world while moving away from it, until the world pulls the thinker back to the mundane.

3.3 To Let a Murderer in

How, then, is thinking relevant to morality, to the practical distinction between good and evil? Arendt's answer is that if it is – and she is careful to use the conditional here, stressing that this issue is in itself a matter of thinking rather than knowledge – then the relation between the two is by no means simple or direct. Just as thinking does not produce knowledge, it also does not produce moral values or principles: "we cannot expect any moral propositions or commandments, no final code of conduct from the thinking activity, least of all a new and now allegedly final definition of what is good and what is evil" (2003b, p. 167). Thinking is essentially impractical, "good for nothing" (1978, p. 88), and even Kant, who was the first to articulate the distinction between thinking and knowledge, was wrong to expect thinking, in the form of practical reason, to yield moral imperatives. For Arendt, arguing that the results of thinking and philosophical examination can be directly applied to the actual world leads too easily to the belief in the superiority of the knowledgeable few over the lay masses, and consequently to the right of philosophers to rule over ordinary citizens – a belief she deems not only anti-democratic, but also utterly anti-political.

While philosophers from Plato to Kant appealed to rational thinking as a source for moral values and imperatives, the widespread view throughout history was that the validity of moral norms and standards was "supposed to be self-evident to every sane person either as part of divine or of natural law" (Arendt 2003a, p. 50). This belief collapsed overnight, of course, with the rise of totalitarian regimes in Nazi Germany and the Soviet Union. Then, Arendt writes, "it was as though morality suddenly stood revealed in the original meaning of the word, as a set of *mores,* customs and manners, which could be exchanged for another set with hardly more trouble than it would take to change the table manners of an individual or a people" (p. 50). For her, the unbearable ease in which one moral system can be replaced with another clearly shows that morality cannot be reduced to mere conventions. But even in the second half of the twentieth century and the beginning of the twenty-first, when "no one in his right mind can any longer claim that moral conduct is a matter of course" (p. 61), most people give very little thought to moral questions, and keep drawing their conceptions of right and wrong from their social surrounding.

To be sure, thoughtlessness, which is by no means rare, is very often not a problem at all in the moral context, as long as society follows the habitual way of life that kept it together for generations. The significance of thinking to politics and morality, according to Arendt, "comes out only in those rare moments in history" when "things fall apart" (2003b, p. 188), and traditional conventions that seemed to be safe and stable are replaced in surprising ease with others which allow for things that have been inconceivable up until now. In such moments – of which Nazism and Stalinism are the paradigmatic but by no means only examples – the ability to take a step back from the world, to stop and think, becomes of the highest importance.

Thinking becomes of critical importance in such moments precisely because it demands taking a distance from the everyday world and willingness to ask questions that are not normally asked. The thinking person raises herself to a position from which she can suspend all direct demands of reality, disregard the ways she is expected to behave and ignore the views she is expected to hold, in order think afresh on the meanings of what happens, of what other people are doing and of what she is asked to do. It is precisely this step away from reality that allows the thinker to reconnect to it again, freed from the prejudices of the time, and able to see things as they really are (Minnich 2017, p. 35). Acts and events that tend to be swallowed by the ordinary, banal flow of things may then appear to the thinker as crimes or even atrocities – as ones in which he or she will never participate.

Arendt further examines the complex relations between thinking and moral judgment through a discussion of two counterintuitive claims in Plato's *Gorgias* (1978, p. 181, 2003b, p. 181): "It is better to suffer wrong than to do wrong"; and "It would be better for me that my lyre or a chorus I directed should be out of tune and loud with discord, and that multitudes of men should disagree with me rather than that I, *being one,* should be out of harmony with myself and contradict *me*" (Plato 1997c, p. 813, p. 827).[3] According to Arendt, these two claims stem directly from the experience of thinking, namely from the dialogue between me and myself: when I appear to others I am necessarily one, otherwise it would have been impossible to recognize me. When I withdraw from the world to engage in thinking, however, I am split; thinking is quite literally reflecting – speaking with myself as if to my reflection in the mirror. Although I do not appear to myself the way I do to others, I always keep myself company, an experience we call consciousness: "So long as I am conscious, that is, conscious of myself, I am identical with myself only for others to whom I appear as one and the same. For myself, articulating this being conscious-of-myself, I am inevitably *two-in-one*" (2003b, p. 184, emphasis in the original). Consciousness is not identical with thinking, but it is its precondition – thinking's inner dialogue actualizes the split in consciousness.

These two in one, different yet same, are "out of harmony" not when they disagree on theoretical issues – in a sense, disagreement is necessary for actualizing the difference in consciousness, namely for starting the inner dialogue which is thinking – but when they contradict each other in such a way that does not allow them to remain partners or friends. This happens when they (together and each on one's own) are responsible for crimes: "It is better for you to suffer than to do wrong

[3] In "Some Questions of Moral Philosophy", Arendt discusses two other related claims that appear in "Gorgias": that "It is better for the doer to be punished than to go unpunished", and that "The tyrant who can do with impunity whatever he pleases is an unhappy man" (2003a, p. 82).

because you can remain the friend of the sufferer; who would want to be the friend of and have to live together with a murderer? Not even a murderer" (2003b, p. 185). If I do wrong, in other words, "I am condemned to live together with a wrongdoer in an unbearable intimacy" (2003a, p. 90).

This doppelgänger inherent to human consciousness is what we may call conscience. It is not the voice of a God or a Socratic demon telling us what to do but that of the inner dialogue, of thinking, helping us determine the moral meaning of our actions and at the same time demanding that we do not let in an evildoer. Note that in this interpretation, my conscience can never tell me what I *ought* to do, only what I *ought not* to: thinking does not produce moral knowledge or values, but only tells me what is unthinkable and does not allow me to cooperate with unbearable wrongs. Put differently, morality for Arendt depends on being unable to "do certain things, because having done them I shall no longer be able to live with myself" (2003a, p. 97). She writes that "He who does not know the intercourse between me and myself… will not mind contradicting himself, and this means he will never be either able or willing to give account of what he says or does; nor will he mind committing any crime, since he can be sure that it will be forgotten the next moment" (2003b, p. 187).

The role of self-consciousness as a necessary link between thinking and morality means that unlike the mainstream of post-Socratic philosophical tradition, according to which the criterion for telling right from wrong is absolute (2003a, p. 75), Arendt concedes that for her it is subjective in two senses. First, what I can bear to have done without losing my internal harmony might change from one individual to another, or depend on historical and political circumstances. Second, moral judgments turn on the question of with whom I wish to be, namely on something resembling concrete human interaction, not on abstract standards and rules that allow for Platonic objectivity (2003a, pp. 124–5). Nevertheless, Arendt's understanding of moral judgments is very different from what usually goes by the name of relativism – it means rather that morality deals with singular acts and historical situations, and that the ultimate responsibility for determining whether they are permissible rests with nothing but the thinking individual, who reflects on things among herself.

This subjectivism is at the heart of Arendt's critique of Heidegger's conception of thinking, according to which "I become a self qua self first and most properly insofar as I think" (quoted in Berkowitz 2017, p. 28). For Arendt, it is through thinking that I constitute myself as a *person*, as having "what we commonly call personality" (2003a, p. 95; Shuster 2018) – unlike Heidegger, she emphasizes not only the thinker's authentic human existence, but also the moral aspects of human subjectivity. Whoever renounces thinking, whoever prefers not to think too hard, renounces his or her status as person and retains only their raw humanity, which is not fully human.

We are now in a position to see why, at moments when social norms collapse, non-thinking becomes so dangerous: going about everyday life without the stop-and-think, "shields people against the dangers of examination, [and] teaches them to hold fast to whatever the prescribed rules of conduct may be at a given time in a given society" (2003b, p. 178). As Elizabeth Minnich puts it, at times like these our minds can be "intensely active, but they are also *occupied*. We are precisely not thinking around, about, outside the rules of the game. We are just trying to win by the rules of the occupation" (2017, p. 174). To be sure, knowledgeable or highly intelligent people are not immune to such collusion with evil reality. Accordingly, Shai Lavi explains that rationality is not the solution to totalitarianism: "thoughtlessness is not a revolt against reason and should not be confused with irrationality. To the contrary, it is the ability to act rationally without thinking" (2010, p. 232). When people begin weighing the pros and cons of collaborating with evil regimes, the game is already lost: as Roger Berkowitz writes, "all too often the arguments in favor of genocide, torture, and terror are made in the voice of reason", and "ordinary men can reason themselves into justifying what ought to be unthinkable" (Berkowitz 2010a, b, p. 5, p. 240).

The only source of light in dark times, therefore, is judgment that does not succumb to calculations of greater or lesser evil, namely one stemming directly from the activity of thinking, from the "internal conviction that rules out any cooperation from the outset' (Lavi 2010, p. 233). Berkowitz further writes that "Thinking—the habit of erecting obstacles to oversimplifications, compromises, and conventions—is an important part of Arendt's answer to Lenin's famous question: What is to be done?" (2010a, b, p. 239). It "demands that we continually recommit ourselves to the loss of a knowable and hospitable world and instead commit ourselves to the struggle of thinking and acting in a world without banisters. Only if we think and reconcile ourselves to the reality of our reconcilable world can we hope to resist the ever-present possibility of totalitarianism" (Berkowitz 2017, p. 27). In Arendt's words, "when everybody is swept away unthinkingly by what everybody else does and believes in, those who think are drawn out of hiding because their refusal to join is conspicuous and thereby becomes a kind of action" (2003b, p. 188).

3.4 The Gadfly, the Midwife and the Electric Ray

Like Kant, it is clear to Arendt that the connection between thinking and morality, however indirect, implies that every person, no matter how educated, is capable of thinking (2003b, p. 164) – otherwise philosophers, the "professional thinkers" would have been in a better position to make moral judgments than ordinary people would – a conclusion she deems unacceptable. The view that man is essentially a thinking being and that all men and women are equally capable of thought is for Arendt not an abstract philosophical assumption, let alone an empirical observation, but rather an implication of one of the objects of thinking, namely morality. However, we have seen that nobody thinks all the time, and many do not think about what is important or when it is important to think; thinking is not something we are born knowing how to do (Novak 2009, p. 87).

Yet thinking, as well as refraining from it, is a skill acquirable by training. Writing about people who cooperated with unthinkable atrocities, Minnich brings the testimony of a survivor of the genocide in Rwanda who describes how the killers trained themselves in dissociation from reality in a way that gradually allowed them to stop thinking about their victims as human beings, and in fact, stop thinking about what they were doing at all (2017, p. 42). "Thinking", she concludes,

> is not unlike running: we are born capable of it, most of us; some of us continue to delight in it and to practice despite all those parental efforts to calm us down and make us behave; most of us pretty much lose the capacity and the delight except, now and then, when startled into action… Ask us to think, ask us to run, when we are entirely unaccustomed and have internalized the feeling that it is more than a bit unseemly, that people will stare at you and worry if you suddenly burst into action… (2017, p. 113).

Arendt is faced, therefore, with the critical question: Can we encourage people to think? Is it possible to ignite in others this inner dialogue that no other can witness? Arendt does not ask this question in strict educational terms, nor does she raise it in either of her two articles on education. Her question is a more general one – "What makes us think?" (1978, p. 129) – acknowledging that throughout most of the history of philosophy questions about the origins of thinking were answered mainly by appealing to the relations between man and the world surrounding him rather than to interactions between people.

A significant exception to this rule is found in Socrates – the thinker who did not leave anything written behind, the teacher who did not take money nor was affiliated with any institution, the citizen among citizens who was out of order in the city and was destroyed by the wind he himself has given rise to (Arendt 2003b, p. 169). Arendt turns to Socrates to think about the meaning and possibility of thought-provoking interactions. Socrates, as is well known, did not teach anything – he had no positive knowledge to convey to his listeners. The most conspicuous characteristic of his dialogues, in which he questioned people about concepts with which they were supposed to be familiar, was their aporetic nature, namely the fact they never ended with a concrete answer, with a definition of the concept in question. Nevertheless, Socrates did believe, according to his "Apology", that his conversations helped improve the city and make it a better place (1997a, p. 28). Arendt analyzes the way Socrates conceived of the role he assumed vis-à-vis his interlocutors by discussing three similes he uses to describe himself: the gadfly, the midwife, and the electric ray.[4]

Socrates describes himself in the "Apology" as a *gadfly* who stings his fellow citizens (1997a, p. 28). He does this not just to hurt or annoy them, but also to wake them up. Socrates says that his conversations encourage his interlocutors to cultivate virtue, but for Arendt the full answer to the question, "What does the sting arouse them to?" is "to thinking and examination, an activity without which life, in his view, was not only not worth much but was not fully alive" (1978, p. 172). The slumbers, therefore, are not dogmatic thoughts like in Kant's famous self-description (2004, p. 10), but no thinking at all; and being awake simply means thinking actively, which is an inseparable aspect of leading a human life.

[4] The last of these was ascribed to Socrates by his interlocutor in the "Meno" (1997d, p. 879), but he acknowledged the description. The "electric ray" is, in fact, a torpedo fish, as is clear in the English translation of "Meno".

The image of the paralyzing *electric ray* (or torpedo fish) suits Socrates, as he makes clear, only if this ray paralyzes others by being itself paralyzed (1997d, p. 879), not due to some superior knowledge it holds. Paralysis is an adequate metaphor for describing thinking because it involves perplexity, delay, inability to go with the flow. Socrates says he makes others as perplexed as he is, and according to Arendt, this is the only way thinking can be taught. She points out that the image of the electric ray seems to contradict that of the gadfly – the former stops motion while the latter brings it about – but this is so only due to the unique nature of thinking, which appears still and silent from the outside while being experienced as living activity from within (1978, p. 173).

As *midwife*, Socrates takes the role of delivering the thoughts of others and judging whether they are healthy or stillborn (Plato 1997b, p. 167). Socrates assumes here the role of the old midwife who delivers other women's babies while being unable to bear children of her own. The problem, this time, is that all the "offspring" of Socrates' interlocutors appear upon examination to be false definitions, either self-contradictory or contradicting other views their parents hold. The value of Socratic midwifery, according to Arendt, lay in that "he purged people of their 'opinions', that is, of those unexamined pre-judgements that would prevent them from thinking" (1978, p. 173), because they made them think they knew what they in fact did not. In other words, Socrates led his interlocutors to the conclusions deriving from views they uncritically accepted as true, and showed them what they had to get rid of in order to engage freely in the activity of thinking.

Arendt does not develop her discussion of Socrates into a wider one on education for thinking, but several educational conclusions can be drawn from this discussion. Unlike Socrates, and even more so Plato, Arendt does not think that thought-provoking conversations can improve the polis, or that the value of thoughtful education can be used to argue for the rule of the philosophical few over the ignorant many. She claims that thinking, which produces no values or valid moral principles, is practically good for nothing – political power included – except of course for the sheer sensation of being alive one feels while engaged in thinking. It is only in rare moments of crisis and anomia that thinking becomes of great value, and education for thinking then becomes highly urgent and almost impossible: nothing is more important than making people avoid collaborating with atrocities, and nothing is more dangerous than turning thinking from invisible to visible when crime is the norm. Hence, education for thinking – the antidote to the evil of banality (Minnich 2017, p. 216) – must be provided even when times are not so dark and thinking has no tangible value for the individual student or society. The educational challenge, therefore, is institutionalizing education for thinking in schools despite thinking's obvious uselessness.

The role of the Socratic teacher is to sting, perplex and purge, and the means he has at his disposal is dialogue, in which the questions asked concern what seems most evident, in an attempt to shed new light on it, thereby provoking thinking. Such educational dialogue prepares the ground for thinking in the silent company of oneself, as the thinker models the inner dialogue after the one she has with the other, who may well be a teacher: "the guiding experience in these matters is, of course, friendship and not selfhood; I first talk with others before I talk with myself… and then discover that I conduct a dialogue not only with others but with myself as well" (1978, p. 189).

It is not insignificant that Arendt refers to the interlocutor, the teacher who provokes thinking, as a friend. For the educational dialogue to resemble the inner dialogue of the two-in-one, the teacher needs to be what Aristotle called "another-self", a friend with whom one can converse as reliably and peacefully as with oneself (1978, p. 189). Arendt's point is not that the teacher and the student should have similar abilities, preferences or backgrounds, but rather that they can trust each other: questioning one's deepest beliefs and presuppositions may be quite a shocking experience, and only mutual trust and sensitivity among friends can prevent the dialogue from harming the student. Indeed, in "The Crisis in Education", Arendt insists on the unbridgeable gap between the "newcomers" and the teacher who represents the old generation and draws her authority from taking responsibility for the world (p. 189). This does not mean, however, that teacher and student cannot be close, loving not only the world but also each other.

Since no previous knowledge is needed to be a teacher who engages students in thinking, apparently anyone can assume this role. The fact that Socratic teachers are so uncommon suggests, however, that one thing is necessary after all: previous experiences with the activity of thinking and the pleasure it involves. This does not mean that the teacher must be a "professional thinker", a philosopher of the Platonic or Kantian mold, but she does need to enter the conversation with the intention of thinking together with the student, not conveying knowledge. The relative ease with which Socrates contradicts his interlocutors can be ascribed, from this perspective, not to some unusual wit or wisdom, but simply to the fact that he has already thought through the questions other people answer by thoughtlessly quoting general opinion. To ignite thinking, in other words, one has to be himself a thinker (and since to be a thinker one has first to experience thinking with a friend, the teacher needs a teacher of her own).

Furthermore, the conversation in which thinking is provoked can take place practically everywhere, as the Socratic dialogues are located in all kinds of places. Arendt's discussion of Socrates clearly shows, however, that for her, the dialogue between the two friends can never replace the silent inner dialogue of me and myself. Thinking requires, to reiterate, withdrawal from the public world, and this movement has not only a metaphorical but also a spatial sense. The activity of thinking, that is, involves a kind of reduction, abridgment: just as the Socratic conversation has to be a dialogue rather than a multilogue (although many may witness the dialogue), so must the dialogue continue in the consciousness of each participant after the conversation is over. As Berkowitz observes, Arendt's insistence on the importance of the public realm must not lead us to overlook "her equally strong insistence upon a vibrant and secure private realm where active thinking is possible, secure from the unthinking habits, common opinions, and constraints of the social" (2010b, p. 239). Thus, even though one can immerse in thinking practically everywhere, thinking is best done in solitude and encouraging others to think regularly may include, therefore, arranging for a quiet place to which one can withdraw – a room of one's own, to borrow a phrase from a perhaps not so different context.

In this vein, Eduardo Duarte points out that education that encourages students to engage in dialogue with themselves has been cast aside by the prevailing contemporary version of education for thinking: cooperative education in communities of learning. Such educational models rest on Lev Vygotsky's claim that thinking develops only after and following communication with others, to argue that thinking is always a socially mediated process and therefore learning with others will lead to better results (Duarte 2001, p. 205). Although Arendt agrees with Vygotsky's claim that thinking as inner dialogue develops only after the experience of thoughtful dialogue with another, Duarte (2001) argues that the existing educational models, which demand of the students to constantly speak and be in the company of their fellows, do not leave much room for inner dialogue, thereby creating the conditions of non-thinking and bringing about "the eclipse of thinking" (p. 202). To counter that "positive *inter*dependence", Duarte offers, following the Arendtian conception of thinking, a pedagogy aimed at what he calls "positive *in*dependence", one that creates "experiences that privilege a student's desire and capacity to work independently and, more importantly, reflectively" (Duarte 2001, p. 216). Such pedagogy may still rely on philosophical texts to generate active thinking, but its ultimate goal is to make students withdraw from their everyday affairs, including the ordinary curriculum, and make inner dialogue part of their lives by developing "a habit of listening to an exhortation that interrupts the business of everyday life" (p. 217).

Yet we must not overlook the fact that Socratic dialogues are by no means merely preparations for future thinking; they are thinking events in their own right, in which both teacher and student actively think, reflecting on their preconceptions while talking to each other. This is true of dialogues in the Athenian agora as much as of dialogues in the modern-day school or university. Aislinn O'Donnell (2012) argues that even an academic seminar or lecture, in which the teacher stands in front of many students, can become a thinking event, for it "occupies a peculiar terrain between the sheer experience of thinking, that most private of activities which involves… an experience of the dialogue with self as two-in-one, and the exposure of oneself in the public domain" (p. 270). This is made possible, first and foremost, when the teacher does not transmit knowledge but rather thinks while teaching, encouraging the listeners to do the same. This is how Arendt described her own teachers Karl Jaspers and Martin Heidegger. Having heard Heidegger as a young student, she later wrote that with him thinking was brought back to life, that he made thinking his abode and that he was a teacher who made it possible to think (Arendt 2018; Minnich 2003, p. 103). In O'Donnell's words, "witnessing the experience of thinking by a master of thinking, like Heidegger, who performs thinking itself, allows thinking to be made manifest in speech" (2012, p. 270). There is, however, a big difference between Heidegger on the one hand, and Jaspers and Socrates on the other: Heidegger shows not just how thinking can be inspiring and inspired, but also that thinking does not make one immune to evildoing.

3.5 The Dangerous Wind of Thinking

Arendt's rejection of the claim that thinking improves the thinker and contributes to the polis goes even further than pointing to its uselessness, for she argues that thinking can in fact cause harm – if not to the thinker herself than by her to others. Here, too, Socrates points the way. He likens thinking to the wind, which is in itself evasive and invisible, discernable only through the manifestations of what it does to other things (Arendt 1978, p. 174); and this wind can at any moment turn into a storm, destroying not only its previous manifestations but also whatever and whoever happens to be in its way.

It is no accident, according to Arendt, that in the circle around Socrates there were men such as Alcibiades and Critias, who turned against and became a real threat to the polis. The direct cause of these men's actions was the sting of the gadfly, the unique Socratic way of teaching thinking: "not content with being taught how to think without being taught a doctrine, they changed the non-results of the Socratic thinking examination into negative results: If we cannot define what piety is, let us be impious" (Arendt 1978, pp. 175–6). Arendt makes clear that this conclusion is the complete opposite of Socrates' teaching, but this is part of the danger inherent to thinking: it blows all original intentions away.

This is why every thought can become dangerous, regardless of the nature of the thinker and the object of thought: "there are no dangerous thoughts; thinking itself is dangerous" (1978, p. 176). Put differently, although a reversal of all values is a possibility inherent to thinking, the danger to which Arendt refers does not lie in this reversal itself. As long as thinking turns values around repeatedly in order to examine their meanings, reversal is as futile as every thinking is. The danger stems rather from "the desire to find results that would make further thinking unnecessary" (p. 176). That is to say, thinkers may confuse the manifestations of the wind with concrete structures, forget that thinking is real only as long as it actively undermines its own conclusions, and be mesmerized by the novelty and radicalness of its manifestations regardless of their uselessness. The thinker may feel he can float in the air without having to think further, thereby defying thinking's own movement and bringing about non-thinking.

This proximity of thinking and its absence is evident in the two figures that are most associated with Nazi crimes in Arendt's life and work: Heidegger and Eichmann, the ultimate thinker and the ultimate non-thinker, who both collaborated in different ways with the evil regime. The danger, as we can see, is not limited to those unaccustomed to thinking, and even the most thorough and intelligent thinkers might lose touch with reality and be swallowed by a criminal storm.

Importantly, the destructive potential of thinking does not stem only from its unique characteristics – the inner dialogue and search for meanings – but also from its turning away from the world, a condition it shares with other mental activities and intellectual enterprises, most notably science. Understanding the challenge education for thinking faces requires therefore a fuller account of this very condition. I will provide such an account through a discussion of Arendt's concept of common sense. Although common sense is for her an essential aspect of a common world, she rejects the traditional conceptualizations, which sees it as a-priori natural light (Descartes 2008, p. 30) or a characteristic of every human society (Geertz 1993). She argues, rather, that common sense is a fragile construct, an achievement in need of constant maintenance, and that it has indeed been eroded and even lost due to modernity's turning away from the world.[5] The discussion of common sense will also allow us, in the next section, to outline a second way to educate for thinking, one focusing more on judgment and the cultivation of common sense than on an inner dialogue.

Arendt understands common sense (or *sensus communis*) as "a kind of sixth sense needed to keep my five senses together and guarantee that it is the same object that I see, touch, taste, smell, and hear… This same sense… fits the sensations of my strictly private five senses – so private that sensations in their mere sensational quality and intensity are incommunicable – into a common world shared with others. The subjectivity of the it-seems-to-me is remedied by the fact that the same object also appears to others though its mode of appearance may be different" (1978, p. 50). That is to say, common sense creates a coherent picture of the world out of the plurality of sense perceptions, and at the same time lets this world appear as common to a plurality of perceivers: "common sense presupposes a common world into which we all fit, where we can live together because we possess one sense which controls and adjusts all strictly particular sense data to those of all others" (1994, p. 318). Although Arendt calls it a "sense", common sense is very different from the five "private senses" in that it is not a natural capacity but rather acquired through experience of a common world; it is located first and foremost in the public domain before it is internalized. Through common sense, we are able to understand the world as common, and coordinate our life together.

Hence, any withdrawal from the world of appearances is necessarily withdrawal from common sense. This is why thinking often leads to nonsensical conclusions – in fact, the very question of meaning is meaningless to common sense (Arendt 1978, p. 57) – and the life of the "professional thinker" who dedicates her life to thinking in solitude cannot but seem odd to an ordinary man of common sense. From the perspective of common sense, the philosophical way of life is a rejection of life on earth, not unlike death: thinking looks like dying while being alive (p. 80). It is no surprise, therefore, that Plato tells in "Theaetetus" that the first philosopher, Thales, made a girl laugh when he fell into a well while walking and thinking (1997b, pp. 164–5). Nevertheless, although Plato seemed to believe that this story captured a permanent hostility on the part of the masses towards the few who dedicate their lives to thinking – the same hostility that led to the trial and execution of Socrates – Arendt thinks that "laughter rather than hostility is the natural reaction of the many to the philosopher's preoccupation and the apparent uselessness of his concerns. This laughter is innocent and quite different from the ridicule frequently turned on an opponent in serious disputes" (1978, p. 82).

[5] For a fuller discussion of Arendt's conception of common sense, see Snir 2015.

Moreover, Arendt insists that withdrawal from the world rarely leads to complete separation from it, and that the gap between thinking and common sense reasoning is hardly unbridgeable: "the reason that strangeness and absent-mindedness are not more dangerous, that all 'thinkers', professional and laymen alike, survive so easily the loss of the feeling of realness, is just that the thinking ego asserts itself only temporarily: every thinker no matter how eminent remains 'a man like you and me' (Plato), an appearance among appearances equipped with common sense and knowing enough common sense reasoning to survive" (1978, p. 53). The thinking ego "will disappear as though it were mere mirage when the real world asserts itself again" (p. 75). Withdrawal from the world is possible only temporarily, and even then, the thinker does not lose all eye contact with the common appearances – the world is the starting point of all thinking, providing it with the concepts, words and images with which it operates (p. 24), and it is also the safe harbor to which the thinker ultimately returns.

Despite this commitment of every individual thinker to common sense, however, Arendt argues that in the long run, turning away from the world results in loss of common sense, leading to an erosion of its power to bring together a plurality of sense perceptions and individuals. This is exactly what happened in modernity, due to the unprecedented achievements of science and the philosophical trends that followed them. To be sure, Arendt writes that like philosophy, science too stems from common sense: it is originally "an enormously refined prolongation of common-sense reasoning in which sense illusions are constantly dissipated just as errors in science are corrected" (1978, p. 54). Moreover, no matter how far scientific theories "leave common-sense experience and common-sense reasoning behind, they must finally come back to some form of it or lose all sense of realness in the object of their investigation" (p. 56). Yet modern science has altogether disengaged with the world of appearances and started a process that undermined common sense itself.

According to Arendt, the decisive event in the development of modern science, and of the modern age more generally, is the invention of the telescope, or more precisely the use Galileo made of the telescope when he turned it up to the sky. This allowed him to develop a new science which "considers the nature of the earth from the viewpoint of the universe" (1998, p. 248), freeing humanity from its dependency on sense perceptions and leading it to formulate laws of nature in mathematical language, valid beyond any possible human experience. Despite remaining tied to the world, it succeeded in thinking in universal terms and developing a worldview unrestrained by the human conditions on Earth, leading to the great achievements of modern science. This, however, also alienated humanity from the world: compared to the familiar, everyday world in which common sense makes it possible for us to feel at home, the world science studies – and teaches – appears strange indeed: the reality we are told is the only true one is not a haven we feel we can inhabit peacefully. In Arendt's words, "earth alienation became and has remained the hallmark of modern science" (1998, p. 264).[6]

---

[6] Alienation caused by modern scientific worldview is accompanied by two other historical events that stand, according to Arendt, on the threshold of the modern age and determine its nature: the "discovery" of America and the reformation (1998, p. 248).

When thinking contemplates the meaning of modern science, it cannot escape the conclusion that truth does not "lend itself" to the human senses, and therefore "only interference with appearance, doing away with appearances, can hold out a hope for true knowledge" (Arendt 1998, p. 274). The philosophical response to this radical challenge to appearing phenomena is of course Cartesian doubt, which is the philosophical version of the scientific distrust of the senses: "The outstanding characteristic of Cartesian doubt is its universality, that nothing, no thought and no experience, can escape it… Its universality spreads from the testimony of the senses to the testimony of reason to the testimony of faith because this doubt resides ultimately in the loss of self-evidence, and all thought had always started from what is evident in and by itself—evident not only for the thinker but for everybody" (p. 275). Unable to trust sense perceptions, modern philosophy – still looking for certainty – turned since Descartes to introspection, which is "not the reflection of man's mind on the state of his soul or body but the sheer cognitive concern of consciousness with its own content" (p. 280). That is to say, rather than deriving validity from the only source that can lend objectivity to sense perceptions – the fact that they are anchored in common sense, namely common to different people – the introspective path of modern philosophy takes it farther away from the world and deepens its alienation from it. To quote Arendt again, "World alienation, and not self-alienation as Marx thought, has been the hallmark of the modern age" (p. 254).

The important point is that this alienation did not remain the exclusive purview of professional thinkers and scientists, but gradually influenced the larger public and became a wide phenomenon, leading to what Arendt calls "loss of common sense":

> common sense, which once had been the one by which all other senses, with their intimately private sensations, were fitted into the common world, just as vision fitted man into the visible world, now became an inner faculty without any world relationship. This sense now was called common merely because it happened to be common to all. What men now have in common is not the world but the structure of their minds, and this they cannot have in common, strictly speaking; their faculty of reasoning can only happen to be the same in everybody (1998, p. 283).

In other words, science and philosophy, which owe their existence and development to common sense, have turned against it and brought about its demise.

This is the most radical aspect of Arendt's conception of common sense: she holds that common sense does not exist automatically in every society. It arises out of living together in a *common world*. Not every place inhabited by a human group is such a world – a world in the full sense of the word. In Arendt's terms, such a world is one that enables every person to find his or her unique place, and at the same time maintain close connection to others who share the world with them. It is a common arena upon which different people look from different perspectives, like a table which at the same time connects and divides those sitting around it (1998, p. 52). Such a world provides speech and action with a kind of stage, a "space of appearance" in which words and deeds can appear to others and become meaningful. World alienation and the loss of common sense have left behind them a society whose members "either live in desperate lonely separation or are pressed together into a mass" (2006b, pp. 89–90), undermining the very conditions for political action.

This is how the gradual loss of common sense in modernity is intimately connected to the rise of totalitarian regimes – the ultimate assault on the ability to speak and act in public. In the closing pages of the *Origins of Totalitarianism*, she states this explicitly:

> Totalitarian domination as a form of government is new in that… [i]t bases itself on loneliness, on the experience of not belonging to the world at all, which is among the most radical and desperate experiences of man…. loneliness is at the same time contrary to the basic requirements of the human condition *and* one of the fundamental experiences of every human life. Even the experience of the materially and sensually given world depends upon my being in contact with other men, upon our *common* sense… without which each of us would be enclosed in his own particularity of sense data which in themselves are unreliable and treacherous (1973, pp. 475–6, emphasis in the original).

The modern condition in which common sense is lost eradicates the platform from which thinking departs and to which it always must return, thereby creating a culture of thoughtlessness, in which active thinking is even rarer than it usually is. Eichmann's inability to think, we may recall, was not unique and was not the result of some perverted personality, but a radicalization of his zeitgeist.

There is, however, another kind of reasoning which totalitarianism does encourage as a substitute for common sense, namely ideology:

> [T]he peculiar and ingenious replacement of common sense with stringent logicality, which is characteristic of totalitarian thinking, is particularly noteworthy. Logicality is not identical with ideological reasoning, but indicates the totalitarian transformation of the respective ideologies. If it was the peculiarity of the ideologies themselves to treat a scientific hypothesis, like "the survival of the fittest" in biology or "the survival of the most progressive class" in history, as an "idea" which could be applied to the whole course of events, then it is the peculiarity of their totalitarian transformation to pervert the "idea" into a premise in the logical sense, that is, into some self-evident statement from which everything else can be deduced in stringent logical consistency… The chief political distinction between common sense and logic is that common sense presupposes a common world into which we all fit… whereas logic and all self-evidence from which logical reasoning proceeds can claim a reliability altogether independent of the world and the existence of other people… In other words, wherever common sense, the political sense par excellence, fails us in our need for understanding, we are all too likely to accept logicality as its substitute, because the capacity for logical reasoning itself is also common to us all (1994, pp. 317–8).

Unlike common sense, which is anchored in the world and is constantly being validated by other people, the logic of ideo*logy* is empty, out of touch with the world. *Ideo*logy develops its core idea in sheer logical consistency, following it blindly even if it leads to the destruction of the world. This is the only way totalitarian regimes succeed in "resolutely and cynically emptying the world of the only thing that makes sense to the utilitarian expectations of common sense" (1973, p. 457), namely that the others with which we share the world are not superfluous.

Ideology, like any rigorous application of formal logic, is very different from genuine thinking, which searches for meanings by way of a "silent dialogue of me with myself". But there is a clear connection, however indirect, between turning away from the world in order to think and the loss of common sense, followed by the rise of totalitarian regimes and their ideologies. Thinking may stop the thinker from collaborating with atrocities, but at the very same time, it supports the conditions that make atrocities possible.

Arendt was fully aware of this problem, which was manifested in Heidegger's disgraceful collaboration with the Nazi regime. As Lavi observes, she understood Heidegger's moral failure as the failure of philosophical thinking as such, a failure philosophy was unable to solve from within, with the mere power of thought (Lavi 2010, p. 229). This did not mean, however, that Arendt claimed we had better stop thinking. I suggest that Arendt's growing interest in the power of judgment in the 1970s (Berkowitz 2017, p. 29) can be understood as articulating another kind of thinking, one that need not replace the inner dialogue but rather complement it. Judging, for Arendt, is tightly connected to what she calls, following Kant, "enlarged mentality" – a kind of thinking that involves turning towards rather than away from the world and the others who inhabit it. Education for thinking, therefore, must work in two different directions: encouraging the students to both think and judge, take a step back from the world to converse with themselves and take a step back from themselves to examine other perspectives on the world. In the following section, I discuss the nature of Arendtian judgment, and examine what it means to educate for judgment.

3.6 Judging and Thinking in an Enlarged Mentality

Arendt's understanding of judgment, much like her distinction between thinking and knowing, follows Kant's footsteps. She accepts Kant's observation, in his *Critique of the Power of Judgment* (2002), that unlike thinking which deals with the most abstract and general things, judgment deals with particulars; it subsumes the particular under its appropriate general rule or category (1973, p. 69, 2003a, p. 137). Judgment plays a role in all three domains of Kantian critical philosophy: cognition, morality and aesthetics. It is the arbiter in questions of true and false (this particular is a tulip), right and wrong (I ought not to pick that tulip), as well as beautiful and ugly (this tulip is beautiful). The problem is that there are no rules for the subsumption – no rule can tell me which rule to apply – and sometimes, as in questions of aesthetic taste, the rule does not even exist a priori but must be seen as contained in the particular itself (I do not have a concept of beauty applicable to all tulips – I see beauty in this particular tulip) (2003a, p. 138).

Since there is no solid, rational foundation for judgment, the only ground from which it can spring is common sense, defined by Kant as "the idea of a *communal* sense, i.e., a faculty for judging that in its reflection takes account (*a priori*) of everyone else's way of representing in thought, in order *as it were* to hold its judgment up to human reason as a whole and thereby avoid the illusion which, from subjective private conditions that could easily be held to be objective, would have a detrimental influence on the judgment" (Kant 2002, pp. 173–4, emphasis in the original). Common sense, that is, allows judgment to achieve (or approximate) its most important feature, namely impartiality – it neutralizes subjective bias by submitting judgment to the objectivity of the common, of the community. As Kant further explains, "this happens by one holding his judgment up not so much to the actual as to the merely possible judgments of others, and putting himself into the position of everyone else, merely by abstracting from the limitations that contingently attach to our own judging" (p. 174). In other words, impartial judgment requires what Kant calls "enlarged mentality" or "a broad-minded way of thinking" (p. 174), in which the individual examines other people's perspectives in order to mitigate the inherent limitedness of one's own point of view.

Kant makes clear that considering different perspectives does not necessarily mean actually asking for other people's views whenever we judge – judging does not involve opinion polling, and the "merely possible judgments" of others may suffice. This is made possible as the faculties of thinking and imagination come to judgment's aid by making what is absent present to the mind as if to an "inner sense" (Arendt 1989, p. 65), enabling us to imagine and represent absent perspectives in our minds. In Arendt's words, like thinking, judging "still goes on in isolation, but by the force of imagination it makes the others present and thus moves in a space that is potentially public " (p. 43).

Yet although judgment's impartiality requires stepping back from one's actual, subjective conditions, this withdrawal is very different from the one in which thinking in the strict sense is involved. While thinking puts the world between brackets to engage in an inner activity, judging involves abandoning the role of an actor and assuming that of a viewer who reflects and forms opinions on the actions she sees. Judgment "does not leave the world of appearances but retires from active involvement in it to a privileged position in order to contemplate the whole" (Arendt 1978, p. 94). Moreover, unlike the philosopher who leaves his fellow men behind, the judger is not altogether independent of others' views (p. 94). Even though every instance of judgment can be a priori, with the others present only as mental representations, actual involvement with real people is a necessary precondition for judgment – one needs to be acquainted with other perspectives to be able to represent them to one's inner sense when called upon to judge. Without speaking and listening to other people, I will not be able to reflect on their perspectives: "The more people's standpoints I have present in my mind while I am pondering a given issue, and the better I can imagine how I would feel and think if I were in their place, the stronger will be my capacity for representative thinking and the more valid my final conclusions, my opinion" (Arendt 2006d, p. 237; see O'Donnell 2012, p. 271). Other people's opinions made present to the mind through imagination are not imaginary: they are concrete perspectives of actual people in the world. Hence, when we judge, we do so not as members of the human species or as rational animals, but as members of actual human communities who need each other's company to form our opinions (Arendt 1989, p. 27). It is only when we judge that some validity is lost to the Socratic "It is better to be at odds with the whole world than, being one, to be at odds with myself" – which, as we have seen, is a key for the experience of thinking (2003a, p. 142).

For this reason, commonality, namely interaction not with imaginary but with real people, is not only a necessary precondition for judging; the opposite is also true: as judging requires being acquainted with other people's views, it also plays an active part in *creating* commonality, bringing people together and strengthening the relations between them. The same goes for common sense, which is both the *ground* from which judgment grows and the *fruit* of judging and interacting: "the commonality among men produces a common sense. The validity of common sense grows out of the intercourse with people – just as we say that thought grows out of the intercourse with myself" (Arendt 2003a, p. 141). That is to say, while thinking harms common sense and erodes the very commonality of the world, judging works the opposite way, reinforcing common sense and making the world common.

Judging, therefore, is self-reinforcing: when we judge, we create the conditions from which our future judgments can arise. Much like thinking, the ability to judge impartially, although common to all humanity, requires training and improvement. As Arendt says in her lectures on Kant, "To think with an enlarged mentality means that one trains one's imagination to go visiting" (1989, p. 43). Yet although Arendt is aware of the need to train the imagination and hone the ability to judge impartially, she nowhere develops this idea into a discussion of *education* for judgment. She accepts Kant's saying that judgment is "a peculiar talent which can be practiced but cannot be taught" (1978, p. 215). As Stacy Smith points out, this should be understood in light of Arendt's claim in "The Crisis in Education" that education and politics must be separated (Smith 2001, p. 68): since judging is for Arendt a form of involvement in politics, she seems to believe it has no place in school or other educational institutions.

We do not have to accept Arendt's verdict on the matter. In fact, Smith suggests, following Seyla Benhabib, to think *with* Arendt *against* Arendt (2001, p. 75). Taking up Arendt's suggestion to train for the skill of judgment, while ignoring her reservation from education for judgment, we can see that her writings open two possible ways for education to foster students' ability to judge impartially: encouraging thoughtful conversations with others, and giving examples.

First, speaking and listening to others is neither natural nor easy: many people – children included – tend to be self-centered, shut themselves off to views other than their own, or are simply not engaged in any kind of contact with people who look at the world from significantly different perspectives. Education can undoubtedly contribute to remedying this problem by bringing together students from various social backgrounds, and introducing them to learning materials through which different perspectives can be unfolded. Most importantly, it can open their eyes to the fact that the world is revealed to us through interpretations, and that acquainting ourselves with stories through which others make sense of this world can make it much richer in meanings (Mackler 2010, p. 527).

As O'Donnell argues, this shows a way to a kind of thinking that is very different from the silent, inner dialogue of me with myself: thinking together with others, "in-concert" as Arendt is fond of saying: "thinking-in-concert is perhaps less close to the *dia-logos* – the speaking and thinking of two – than to the *con-vertere* and *con-versare* of conversation in which we turn towards one another to listen, to speak, to contest, embodying passionately our thinking" (O'Donnell 2012, p. 273). The point of such conversations is not to convince or reach consensus, but simply to "think aloud" and make up our minds in response to the multiple different views to which we have been exposed. This is how we train for enlarged mentality and learn to judge impartially.

The second route to education for judgment is opened in the closing pages of "Some Questions of Moral Philosophy", where Arendt returns to the fundamental problem of judgment: the lack of a solid criterion for deciding difficult questions of right and wrong. Taking her queue once again from Kant, she writes that "there is indeed something to which common sense, when it rises to the level of judging, can and does hold us to, and this is the example" (2003a, p. 143). To use an example, she explains, is "to single out, *eximere*, some particular instance which now *becomes* valid for other particular instances" (p. 144, emphasis in the original). A good example is a particular whose characteristics are so telling that it can function like a kind of general rule or standard in light of which it is possible to evaluate other particulars. Clearly, one has to be familiar with the particular instance for it to function as an example, but acquaintance with it sheds light on the question at hand, setting the standard other particulars will have to aim at to be subsumed under the concept it exemplifies. Examples of good examples are easy to find in the history of moral and political thought. Arendt mentions Achilles, who exemplifies courage, and Solon who exemplifies wisdom. Hence, examples are "the guideposts of all moral thought" (p. 144) – when we judge we represent in our mind some incident or person that have become examples, and compare to the issue at hand in order to evaluate it.

Arendt is somewhat aware of the educational implications of this insight: she quotes Thomas Jefferson saying that reading *Macbeth* or *King Lear* can leave a much stronger impression on a child than "the dry volumes of ethics and divinity", and adds in parenthesis that "This is what every ethics teacher should say but no other teacher" (2003a, p. 145). This comment can be understood in light of Arendt's "Crisis in Education" (2006c): examples cannot be enough in most educational fields, since they require the application of pre-given rules and/or non-judgmental encounter with the world. In the case of ethics and morality, however, where the important thing is not to know theories or facts but rather learning to judge and evaluate, good examples are indispensable – only they can provide students with the "guideposts" needed to make their own minds in the rocky terrain of moral problems.

The two paths, conversations and examples, are not so distant. Both provide opportunities for stepping back from oneself. Importantly, both are also deeply involved with the world and with the people inhabiting it – the one through bringing up multiple perspectives on it, and the other through focusing on paradigmatic cases that are by nature part of the common tradition and culture that keep the world together. Namely, unlike thinking that withdraws from common sense and even puts it in danger, education for judging – or for thinking in enlarged mentality – contributes to maintaining the commonality of the world, thereby strengthening common sense itself. Common sense, as we have seen, does not automatically exist in any society, and fostering judgment through conversations about the world and examples from it actually maintains common sense or even reconstructs it after having been lost in modernity.

3.7 Conclusion

The role of judgment in maintaining common sense, I suggest, ties the educational approach developed here to Arendt's conceptions of thinking and judging, to what she does say about education in "Crisis in Education". One of the central claims in that paper is that taking responsibility for the world is the prime prerequisite of educators: "Anyone who refuses to assume joint responsibility for the world should not have children and must not be allowed to take part in educating them" (2006c, p. 189). This responsibility, for Arendt, means siding with other adults in protecting the world against the newcomers who tend to reject things just because they are old. But reconstructing common sense and maintaining the common nature of the world may also be understood as assuming responsibility for it. A world that is not common is no world at all, argues Arendt, and educating children to think in an enlarged mentality and see the world as common protects it from destruction and is the most responsible thing to do.

To be sure, renouncing education for thinking as a silent dialogue of me and myself – even though it might work against common sense – would be an utterly *ir*responsible thing. The importance of protecting and regenerating common sense must not obscure the importance of reflecting on meanings, since such reflection may be the last barrier against collaborating with atrocities. In the educational context, fostering judgment must not come at the expense of providing students with the space and opportunity needed for conducting silent, inner dialogues – thinking about examples, thinking-in-concert and thinking in the solitude of me and myself are three complementary ways of thinking, and education must encourage and facilitate them all.

References

Arendt, H. (1973 [1951]). *The origins of totalitarianism*. New York: Harcourt Brace & Company.

Arendt, H. (1978). *The life of the mind*. New York: Harcourt Brace & Company.

Arendt, H. (1989 [1982]). *Lectures on Kant's political philosophy*. Chicago: University of Chicago Press.

Arendt, H. (1994 [1954]). Understanding and politics. In *Essays in understanding: 1930–1954* (pp. 307–327). New York: Schocken Books.

Arendt, H. (1998 [1958]). *The human condition*. Chicago: University of Chicago Press.

Arendt, H. (2003a [1965]). Some questions of moral philosophy. In J. Kohn (Ed.), *Responsibility and judgment* (pp. 49–146). New York: Schocken Books.

Arendt, H. (2003b [1971]). Thinking and moral considerations. In J. Kohn (Ed.), *Responsibility and judgment* (pp. 159–189). New York: Schocken Books.

Arendt, H. (2003c [1959]). Reflections on Little Rock. In J. Kohn (Ed.), *Responsibility and judgment* (pp. 193–213). New York: Schocken Books.

Arendt, H. (2006a [1964]). *Eichmann in Jerusalem, a report on the banality of evil*. London: Penguin Classics.

Arendt, H. (2006b [1961]). The concept of history: Ancient and modern. In *Between past and future: Eight exercises in political thought* (pp. 41–90). London: Penguin Classics.

Arendt, H. (2006c [1958]). The crisis in education. In *Between past and future: Eight exercises in political thought* (pp. 170–193). London: Penguin Classics.

Arendt, H. (2006d [1968]). Truth and politics. In *Between Past and Future: Eight Exercises in Political Thought, ed* (pp. 223–259). London: Penguin Classics.

Arendt, H. (2018 [1969]). Heidegger at eighty. In J. Kohn (Ed.), *Thinking without a banister: Essays in understanding 1953–1975* (pp. 419–431). Schocken Books: New York.

Benjamin, Walter. 2006 [1938]. The writer of modern life: Essays on Charles Baudelaire. Trans. Howard Eiland, Edmund Jephcott, Rodney Livingston, and Harry Zohn. Cambridge, MA: Belknap Press.

Berkowitz, R. (2010a). Introduction: Thinking in dark times. In R. Berkowitz (Ed.), *Thinking in dark times: Hannah Arendt on ethics and politics* (pp. 3–14). New York: Fordham University Press.

Berkowitz, R. (2010b). Solitude and the activity of thinking. In R. Berkowitz (Ed.), *Thinking in dark times: Hannah Arendt on ethics and politic* (pp. 237–245). New York: Fordham University Press.

Berkowitz, R. (2017). Reconciling oneself to the impossibility of reconciliation: Judgment and worldliness in Hannah Arendt's politics. In R. Berkowitz, & I. Storey (Eds.), *Artifacts of Thinking: Reading Hannah Arendt's* Denktagbuch (pp. 9–36). New York: Fordham University Press.

Descartes, R. (2008 [1641]). *Meditations on first philosophy* (M. Moriarty, Trans.). Oxford: Oxford University Press.

Duarte, E. (2001). The eclipse of thinking: An Arendtian critique of cooperative learning. In M. Gordon (Ed.), *Hannah Arendt and education: Renewing our common world* (pp. 201–224). Boulder: Westview Press.

Geertz, C. (1993). Common sense as a cultural system. In *Local knowledge: Further essays in interpretive anthropology* (pp. 73–93). London: Fontana Press.

Kant, I. (2002 [1790]). *Critique of the power of judgment* (P. Guyer, & E. Matthews, Trans.). Cambridge: Cambridge University Press.

Kant, I. (2004 [1783]). *Prolegomena to any future metaphysics* (G. Hatfield, Trans. and Ed.). Cambridge: Cambridge University Press.

Kateb, G. (2010). Fiction as poison. In R. Berkowitz (Ed.), *Thinking in dark times: Hannah Arendt on ethics and politics* (pp. 29–41). New York: Fordham University Press.

Lavi, S. (2010). Crimes of action, crimes of thought: Arendt on reconciliation, forgiveness and judgment. In R. Berkowitz (Ed.), *Thinking in dark times: Hannah Arendt on ethics and politics* (pp. 229–234). New York: Fordham University Press.

Mackler, S. (2010). And worldlessness, Alas, is always a kind of Barbarism: Hannah Arendt and the challenge of educating in worldless times. *Teachers College Record, 112*(2), 509–532.

Minnich, E. (2003). Arendt, Heidegger, Eichmann: Thinking in and for the world. *Soundings: An Interdisciplinary Journal, 86*(1–2), 103–117.

Minnich, E. (2017). *The evil of banality: On the life and death importance of thinking*. Lanham: Rowman & Littlefield Publishers.

Novak, B. (2009). The audacity of thought: Seeing thinking as the moral virtue pivotal to the re-founding of democracy on a moral basis. *Philosophical Studies in Education, 40*, 83–93.

O'Donnell, A. (2012). Thinking-in-concert. *Ethics and Education, 7*(3), 261–275.

Plato. (1997a). Apology. Trans. G. M. A. Grube. In J. M. Cooper (Ed.), *Complete works* (pp. 17–36). Indianapolis: Hackett Publishing Company.

Plato. (1997b). Theaetetus. Trans. J.M. Levett & M. Burnyeat. In J. M. Cooper (Ed.), *Complete works* (pp. 157–234). Indianapolis: Hackett Publishing Company.

Plato. (1997c). Gorgias. Trans. D. J. Zeyl. In J. M. Cooper (Ed.), *Complete works* (pp. 791–869). Indianapolis: Hackett Publishing Company.

Plato. (1997d). Meno. Trans. G. M. A. Grube. In J. M. Cooper (Ed.), *Complete works* (pp. 870–897). Indianapolis: Hackett Publishing Company.

Shuster, M. (2018). Hannah Arendt on the evil of not being a person. *Philosophy Compass, 13*(7), 1–13.

Smith, S. (2001). Education for judgment: An Arendtian oxymoron? In M. Gordon (Ed.), *Hannah Arendt and education: Renewing our common world* (pp. 67–92). Boulder: Westview Press.

Snir, I. (2015). Bringing plurality together. *The Southern Journal of Philosophy, 53*(3), 362–384.

Stephen, L. (2014 [1902]). In praise of walking. In *Studies of a biographer* (Vol. 3, pp. 254–285). Cambridge: Cambridge University Press.

Chapter 4
Gilles Deleuze: Thinking as Making Sense Against Common Sense

4.1 Introduction

For Gilles Deleuze, philosophy is all about thinking differently, in an unorthodox, non-commonsensical way. Thinking is one of the key concepts he repeatedly discusses throughout his work, attempting to conceive of alternatives to what he views as the traditional, "dogmatic" image of thought. Genuine thinking, according to Deleuze, is one that *makes sense* – yet sense must not be understood in a commonsensical way, but rather as an effect transcending and contradicting ordinary common sense. Deleuzian education for thinking therefore makes sense only by opposing commonsensical views, including those pertaining to the very notions of education and thinking.

It is generally thought that eliciting or cultivating common sense – whether considered a sociohistorical construct or ascribed to human nature – is a key role of education. In doing so, the community fosters shared values and meanings, and renders them self-evident for its members (see Chap. 3 above; Gadamer 2004; Kumashiro 2004; Gasparatou 2017). Thus, adherents of common sense tend to refer to it as fundamental to all thought, and claim that criticizing any aspect thereof must rely on others (Rescher 2005; Peirce, 2011, pp. 290–301). Deleuze disagrees: he believes that common sense is radically challenged by education for thinking, that thinking requires breaking free of common sense and of the image of thought that it produces. Thus, he argues, educating for common sense actually frustrates thinking, and only education focused on *making* sense can trigger thinking that transcends the self-evident and produce effects that are truly political.

Despite the fact Deleuze has barely concerned himself with educational questions (Morss 2000, p. 195; Bogue 2004, p. 327), his philosophy is increasingly attracting the attention of education scholars (Reynolds and Webber 2004; Semetsky and Masny 2013; Masny and Cole 2015). Indeed, several recent studies examine the

I. Snir, *Education and Thinking in Continental Philosophy*, Contemporary Philosophies and Theories in Education 17,
https://doi.org/10.1007/978-3-030-56526-8_4

relation between thinking and education in his works (Semetsky 2003, 2004; Kohan 2011; Munday 2012; Wallin, 2014). Nevertheless, the available literature tends to ignore the Deleuzian *sense* – a concept developed mainly in *Logic of Sense* (1990) and *Difference and Repetition* (1995). Also largely disregarded is the strong relation between sense and thinking. Consequently, that relation, as well as the relation between thinking and the different cognitive faculties in Deleuze's radical political philosophy is yet to be explored in the educational context. In the following, I try to put some sense into the Deleuzian brand of educating for thinking, thereby shedding new light on its counter-commonsensical, radical-political potential (see also Snir 2018). I show how making sense can serve as an educational encounter able to undermine hierarchies and to generate thinking independently of the knowledge available to the thinkers and of their sociopolitical status.

I start with an analysis of the Deleuzian concepts of common sense and good sense, which form the basis of the dogmatic image of thought. I then move on to discuss his concept of sense, and demonstrate that Deleuzian sense can never be common, for it resides not in ordinary, communicable linguistic propositions but rather in the surface in-between language and world, arising from a problematic encounter with the world rather than lying in the safety of the solutions. In the fourth section, I address the commonsensical relation between the human faculties to develop Deleuze's notion of thinking as an involuntary, unregulated exercise of the faculties and present his example of learning to swim as a case of education for thinking. Finally, in the fifth sect. I turn to Deleuze's discussion of Marcel Proust's *In Search of Lost Time* to elaborate on how thinking is generated by involuntary encounters with signs, and analyze the Proustian search as another example of education for thinking, in which the narrator both learns and makes others think.

4.2 Common Sense and the Image of Thought

The third chapter of Deleuze's *Difference and Repetition*, which he describes as "the most necessary and the most concrete" (1995, p. xvii) in the entire book, is titled "The Dogmatic Image of Thought", and presents eight postulates which "imprison" thought within a given model.[1] One of these is common sense: the very same concept that for Arendt marked the precondition for political thought and action is for Deleuze an essential aspect of the dogmatism suffocating traditional thinking and philosophy.

Deleuze argues that philosophical thinking is dogmatic from the very start, from the very premises of philosophizing. The roots of this dogmatism lie not only in the historical cradle of philosophy in classical Greece, but more importantly, in

[1] Deleuze discusses the dogmatic image of thought already in his 1962 book on Nietzsche, and in the introduction to its English translation he writes that "without doubt this is the most important point of Nietzsche's philosophy: the radical transformation of the image of thought that we create for ourselves" (2006, p. xii).

wherever a philosopher chooses to start thinking. Philosophers often try to eliminate any explicit presuppositions that Deleuze refers to as "objective" – such as the scholastic presumptions regarding rationality and animality that Descartes (1996) rejects in the second *Meditation*, where he is careful not to define man as a rational animal (pp. 17–18). Nevertheless, they just as often accept implicit or "subjective" ones, such as the presuppositions related to the meaning of being or the nature of thought, to use Descartes' example again. Not articulated explicitly or systematically, the latter are easy to accept as they are "contained in opinions rather than concepts: it is presumed that everyone knows, independently of concepts, what is meant by self, thinking, and being" (Deleuze 1995, p. 129).

Philosophers thus try not to presuppose any thought as true or any concrete content as real, but to examine it carefully. When, however, they accept the "form", assuming to know the meaning of being and thinking, they thereupon already accept some material "element". This element, argues Deleuze, "consists only of the supposition that thought is the natural exercise of a faculty, of the presupposition that there is a natural capacity for thought endowed with a talent for truth or an affinity with the true, under the double aspect of a *good will on the part of the thinker* and an *upright nature on the part of thought*" (1995, p. 131, emphasis in original). Thus, he continues, "It is because everybody naturally thinks that everybody is supposed to know implicitly what it means to think" (ibid.). In other words, philosophers presuppose the purpose and manner of operation of thinking as given. They presuppose that thought always progresses linearly towards knowledge and truth. In fact, moreover, these presumptions are far from neutral descriptions of the actual form thought naturally takes – rather, they are substantive. Above all, dogmatism lies in thinking about thinking, in characterizing thought as both the activity and its object. Thought operates dogmatically when it accepts a pre-given image of itself. The *cogito* is much more than a mere example for that dogmatism, but "is the common sense become philosophical" (p. 133), because it represents the most important and at the same time, most dogmatic philosophical presupposition: that everyone knows what thinking means, that everyone thinks the same way, and does so for the same purpose.

Philosophy's adherence to common sense, to what everyone knows, Deleuze concedes, expresses a reticence from dogmatism, a desire not to start from scholastic, arbitrary, and dogmatic presuppositions. "When philosophy rests its beginning upon such implicit or subjective presuppositions, it can claim innocence, since it has kept nothing back... It then opposes the 'idiot' to the pedant… the individual man endowed only with his natural capacity for thought to the man perverted by the generalities of his time. The philosopher takes the side of the idiot as though of a man without presuppositions" (1995, p. 130). Therefore, relying on the self-evident is inspired by an egalitarian, anti-hierarchical approach that is meant to bridge the gap between scholar and layperson by rejecting the scholastic premises accessible only to the former. According to Deleuze, however, common sense is actually *doxa,* or common opinion, obviously also abounding with untested, implicit theoretical and practical assumptions whose self-evidence only makes them more dogmatic: an *ortho-doxa*.

Accordingly, it is doubly dogmatic to educate for common sense. Doing so not only accepts certain assumptions as true uncritically, but it presumes to train students for critical thinking, while only legitimizing a thought pattern imbued by these very assumptions. According to common sense philosophy, students are able to reach the right conclusions by themselves, but only if they think "properly", and thereby succumb to the intellectual and political order grounded in the presuppositions (Gregoriou 2004).

When thinking follows the dogmatic image, it misses that which is central to *Difference and Repetition*, and possibly to the entire Deleuzian philosophy: the new, the radically different, described by Deleuze as "a concept of difference", which is not merely "conceptual difference" (1995, p. xv) – a difference that cannot be reduced to that between pre-given concepts or objects, for it ontologically precedes the differing things. The dogmatic image of thought erases differences, or rather prevents them from being formed, because it harbors presuppositions regarding the pre-given nature of the various life forces, thereby setting limits to acceptable thoughts, experiences and actions. The task of proper philosophy, therefore, is to be a genuine beginning in thought: "those who do not renew the image of thought are not philosophers but functionaries", as Deleuze and Guattari write in *What is Philosophy?* (1996, p. 51).

Philosophy makes new beginnings, argues Deleuze, by offering new concepts with which to think (Deleuze and Guattari 1996, p. 2), and his concept of common sense, while relying on previous conceptualizations, is unique and original. It integrates common sense as *doxa* with other conceptions, particularly Aristotle and Kant's. For the former, common sense (*koine aisthēsis*) combines the data of the five external senses, enabling us to know when properties without any common measure belong to the same object (Aristotle 1957, p. 103). Similarly, Deleuze argues that common sense operates by integrating data and recognizing objects – as does thought itself, assuming it abides by to the dogmatic pattern. Unlike Aristotle, however, he does not define common sense with reference to the five senses. Rather, he argues, following Kant (2002, §21) – whose common sense (*sensus communis*) refers to a relation between different cognitive faculties, those of imagination and understanding – that all faculties need to collaborate to recognize an object:

> Recognition may be defined by the harmonious exercise of all the faculties upon a supposed same object: the same object may be seen, touched, remembered, imagined or conceived.... No doubt each faculty – perception, memory, imagination, understanding... – has its own particular given and its own style, its peculiar ways of acting upon the given. An object is recognised, however, when one faculty locates it as identical to that of another, or rather when all the faculties together relate their given and relate themselves to a form of identity in the object (1995, p. 133).

In other words, according to the dogmatic pattern, the natural activity of thought is to facilitate the faculties' harmonious collaboration (*concordia facultatum*) in order to recognize objects and know what each of them really is. Therefore, thought "is not a faculty like the others but the unity of all the other faculties which are only modes of the supposed subject, and which it aligns with the form of the Same in the model of recognition" (p. 134).

Recognition, Deleuze further explains, necessarily involves representation, namely the placing of one thing instead of another. The representative takes the place of the represented, which thereby become exchangeable: recognizing an object such as a table means representing the particular individual by a general concept, which identifies the object as table by ignoring its unique characteristics and focusing on what it has in common with all other tables.[2] Much like Adorno, Deleuze argues that representation blurs the differences between the various represented: "the world of representation is characterized by its inability to conceive of difference in itself" (1995, p. 138). It understands each new thing by comparing it to what is already known and familiar, necessarily overlooking the pure, singular difference between the new and what has already been experienced and classified into the existing order.[3] Dogmatic commonsensical thinking, therefore, with the concept of representation at its center, is representative in a double sense: it seeks to represent the world in the subject's consciousness and at the same time to turn each subject into a representative of all others, assuming that everybody thinks essentially the same way: "*everybody knows, no one can deny*, is the form of representation and the discourse of the representative" (1995, p. 130, emphasis in the original).[4]

As a complementary to common sense (*sens commun*), Deleuze offers "good sense" (*bon sens*) – "the norm of distribution from the point of view of the empirical selves and the objects qualified as this or that kind of thing (which is why it is considered to be universally distributed)" (1995, pp. 133–4). Namely, while *common* sense governs the collaboration of cognitive faculties, the ability to identify and classify objects, *good* sense is in charge of placing particular objects in particular categories, for our ability to identify similar objects as members of the same categories. *Common* sense is responsible for the "capacity to account for the identity of things (*what is this?*)", whereas *good* sense is "a principle for the distribution of any possible object (*any possible object can take its place in a classification of objects according to predicates*)" (Williams 2008, p. 133; emphasis in the original; see also Williams 2004, p. 118). *Bon sens* enables different people to share the same *sens commun* and thus ground their thinking in the same presuppositions.

---

[2] In *The Logic of Sense*, Deleuze offers a different concept of representation, to which this claim does not apply: one taken from Stoic philosophy, where each representation also includes something non-representable (1990, p. 145).

[3] In his books on film, Deleuze attempts to develop an alternative to the model of representation through non-psychological metaphysics borrowed from Bergson (Deleuze 1986, 1989).

[4] The attack on representative thinking is evident also in Deleuze's reading of Nietzsche. Nietzsche's critique of philosophers such as Hobbes and Hegel, Deleuze writes, relies on that "The notion of representation poisons philosophy: it is the direct product of the slave and of the relations between slaves, it constitutes the worst, most mediocre and most base interpretation of power… When we make power an object of representation we necessarily make it dependent upon the factor according to which a thing is represented or not, recognised or not. Now, only values which are already current, only accepted values, give criteria of recognition in this way" (2006, pp. 75–6). Representation here is a placeholder replacing the direct, affirmative presence of power as difference with something enabling various consciousnesses to identify different things as being the same, and the conditions of representation –those making it possible to identify one thing as representing another – are the accepted commonsensical values.

In *The Logic of Sense*, Deleuze returns to the distinction between common sense and good sense to develop it in a way that accounts for the fact that *sens* in French means not only sensation and meaning but also direction. Good sense, Deleuze writes, provides the commonsensical world of subjects and objects with clear direction, for when it forms identities out of the plurality of faculties and sense data it establishes temporal order, linear movement from the past through the present to the future:

> Good sense is said of one direction only: it is the unique sense and expresses the demand of an order according to which it is necessary to choose one direction and hold onto it. This direction is easily determined as that which goes from the most differentiated to the least differentiated, from things to the primordial fire. The arrow of time gets its orientation from this direction, since the most differentiated necessarily appear as past, insofar as it defines the origin of an individual system, whereas the least differentiated appears as future and end (1990, p. 75).

The thermodynamic movement from the more to the least differentiated characterizes the temporal direction formed by good sense, because it is a movement "from the singular to the regular, and from the remarkable to the ordinary" (p. 76), namely one that conceals differences and distinctions, deepening the hold of the commonsensical principle of identity. Hence, the directionality of time, its linearity, makes the future predictable and foreseeable in principle; the paradoxical claim that the end toward which time progresses is "primordial fire" indicates how problematic Deleuze finds the imposition of one determined direction on time.

The direction introduced by good sense is not merely temporal but also spatial: "such a distribution, implied by good sense, is defined precisely as a fixed or sedentary distribution... Good sense is altogether combustive and digestive. It is agricultural, inseparable from the agrarian problem, the establishment of enclosures..." (1990, p. 76). That is to say, good sense is what enables the division and limitation of space, the erecting of fences and setting of borders, and the ensuing order is not only fertile and productive but also one allowing limitations, uses that are in fact abuses. The combination of good sense and common sense is responsible, therefore, for what Deleuze and Guattari call "territorialization" of time and space, namely the organization of identities and meanings in a controllable manner (1987, pp. 174–5). Each *doxa* produced by common sense and good sense is a complex bundle of perceptions, sensations and meanings, determining what may appear in time and space, thereby setting the course along which dogmatic, linear thought is allowed to proceed.

The presuppositions that the *doxa* accepts without criticism thus reflect relations between the faculties that are dictated by thought, which in turn, abides by both common sense and good sense. Together, they form an identifiable, unified *object* out of the multiplicity of sensory data and of faculties, an identifiable, unified *subject* that all ordered faculties belong to, and so also an integrated *community* all of whose subjects recognize the same objects. Commonsensical thought is thus not only a general framework where education can take place, but has an inherent educational dimension in that it generates and shapes subjects. More than a system of presuppositions, it is in fact an active force that operates within and among individuals and that determines what can be thought and perceived, what is considered meaningful and valuable – what is right and what is wrong. In every act of communication and identification, this force educates, laying the groundwork for "reasonable" experience and for action, and binding thought and life together to a predetermined order. This means that any attempt to tie education to common sense results in practice, and perhaps deliberately so, in a continuous effort to neutralize unorthodox thoughts (Deleuze and Guattari 1996, p, 70; see also Cole 2017).

To be sure, Deleuze concedes that common sense is valid in the banal, quotidian contexts in which we recognize objects. It is necessary for acting and communicating in the day-to-day world (Williams 2008, p. 30), and therefore, educating according to its presuppositions is unavoidable to a given extent. The problem, he argues, lies in the *imperialism* of common sense, in how it comes to dominate thought and action and cast them in conformist patterns: "On the one hand... acts of recognition exist and occupy a large part of our daily life: this is a table, this is an apple, this the piece of wax, Good morning Theaetetus. But who can believe that the destiny of thought is at stake in these acts, and that when we recognise, we are thinking?" (1995, p. 135).[5] Recognition takes place *in thought*, but does not involve *thinking*; it is rather "Incapable of giving birth in thought to the act of thinking" (p. 139), as it allows nothing that is radically different and new to happen. Daily experiences cast in ordinary language are simply incapable of exhausting the fields of thought and experience (Bogue 2004, p. 340; Hwu 2004, p. 183). Thus, even when subjects try to be critical, commonsensical thought reproduces the political order and the meanings that it assigns to both objects and subjects: "thought 'rediscovers' the State, rediscovers 'the Church' and rediscovers all the current values that it subtly presented in the pure form of an eternally blessed unspecified eternal object" (Deleuze 1995, p. 136). Dogmatic thought, in other words, is reduced to recognition also in the political domain: "how derisory are the voluntary struggles for recognition", Deleuze writes, "Struggles occur only on the basis of a common-sense and established values, for the attainment of current values (honours, wealth and power)" (p. 136).[6] Such struggles (re)produce rather than renew.

Therefore, in order to genuinely educate for thinking, what is needed is "the power of a new politics which would overturn the image of thought" (p. 137). The point of departure for this new, genuine education – and for that matter, any new philosophy – would necessarily be to reject *sens commun* as such, which could not be achieved by creating yet another common sense. A radical break is required with both common and good sense, with *doxa* and with the harmony of the faculties. However, what might be the nature of thought or philosophy unfettered by common sense? How will such thinking make sense? In what sense can it be educational?

---

[5] Deleuze points to Plato's *Theaetetus* (1997a) as one of the earliest expressions of commonsensical thought.

[6] This point echoes also in *A Thousand Plateaus*, in which Deleuze and Guattari write that "Ever since philosophy assigned itself the role of ground [on which thought stands] it has been giving the established powers its blessing, and tracing its doctrine of faculties onto the organs of State power. Common sense, the unity of all the faculties at the center constituted by the Cogito, is the State consensus raised to the absolute" (1987, p. 376).

4.3 On Sense and Common Sense

According to the dogmatic image of thought, all subjects sense and make sense of things the same way. Hence, sense is always at least potentially common: the sense of all that makes sense is common. However, Deleuze believes this view is informed by a misguided concept of sense, and therefore develops a new one to counter the traditional assumption that sense is always either common- or non-sense, opening the door for a new conception of education for thinking.

Deleuze contends that the philosophy of common sense defines sense as the condition of truth: a proposition must make sense in order to be true (1995, p. 153). A false proposition, however, also makes sense. Therefore, sense is broader than what it conditions, namely truth or falsehood. It lies in what the proposition expresses, and the latter is true when the dimension of expression is consistent with that of designation, or "denotation", as Deleuze calls it in *Logic of Sense* – with the object to which the proposition is applied. For example, when the person designated by "this is Theaetetus" is in fact Theaetetus. The sense expressed is derived from the dimension of manifestation, namely "the relation of the proposition to the person who speaks and expresses himself" *or* from that of signification, defined as the relation of the proposition to other propositions and concepts from which it is derived (1990, pp. 13–14).

From the vantage point of language as system (*langue*), sense is determined by signification and from that of the actual use of language (*parole*), sense is determined by manifestation. Both signification and manifestation, which supposedly endow the expression with sense and enable designation, depend in fact on the latter's ability to correspond with the expression – for signification or manifestation that are not either true or false make no sense in commonsensical understanding. This "circle", as Deleuze calls it (1990, p. 17), means that sense is limited to the dichotomy between truth and falsity, and is opposed only to non-sense or absurdity, namely to what has no sense at all and can be neither true nor false.[7]

This conceptualization of sense is perfectly dovetailed with the dogmatic image of thought and with the common sense, which is one of its postulates – the matching of expression and designation is none other than successful recognition, a harmonized operation of all faculties. This implies that thought operates properly when it recognizes objects successfully, whereas unsuccessful thought is basically misrecognition. The horizon open for thought is therefore constrained by the simplistic duality of correct and incorrect recognition, making error "the sole 'negative' of thought" (1995, p. 148). This means that deviation from the dichotomous, dogmatic image of thought is not erroneous: we err, rather, when our faculties do not cooperate properly, as when confusing something we see with something else we retrieve

[7] Deleuze does not ascribe this theory of sense to a specific philosopher. Williams (2004, pp. 127–29) argues that critiques of this view have been formulated in "traditional" analytic philosophy already before Deleuze, who therefore attacks a kind of a strawman. Be that as it may, Deleuze's critique is helpful in understanding his own concept of sense.

from memory. Even when errant, however, thought abides by common sense – only the specific harmony of the faculties, good sense, has been temporarily disrupted: "It is as though error were a kind of failure of good sense within the form of a common sense which remains integral and intact" (p. 149).

Throughout the history of thought, writes Deleuze, philosophers have been aware that thought simply cannot be reduced to true or false recognition. Accordingly, they have used other concepts to refer to different modes of failure in thought, including "stupidity", "inner illusion", "superstition", "alienation", and "madness" (1995, p. 150). However, the dogmatic image rejects all these as thought activities, assuming that any thought that cannot be reduced to a true or false proposition is senseless, and thus not exactly thought. The dogma attributes these failures to causes external to thought, rather than to internal failures that are indicative of the nature of thought. Conversely, Deleuze insists that "Cowardice, cruelty, baseness and stupidity are not simply corporeal capacities or traits of character or society; they are structures of thought as such" (p. 151). He does not commend these structures, but argues that rejecting them requires considering them, and realizing that they are indicative of the multifaceted nature of thought and its multiple modes of operation (Deleuze 2006, p. 98). The problem facing Deleuze is thus a Kantian inquiry into conditions of possibility: the transcendental question "how is stupidity (not error) possible?" (1995, p. 151). To answer it, he offers a new take on sense that does not reduce it to signification and strives to go beyond the narrow recognition/misrecognition binary.

Accordingly, rather than reduce sense dogmatically to one of the familiar dimensions of a given proposition, Deleuze considers it an independent dimension that is distinct from signification and manifestation. While the relation of sense to truth is merely external in the dogmatic image – given that sense is neutral with relation to truth and a proposition has the same sense whether true or false – Deleuze suggests that sense and truth are internally related: "Truth and falsity do not concern a simple designation, rendered possible by a sense which remains indifferent to it. The relation between a proposition and what it designates must be established within sense itself: the nature of ideal sense is to point beyond itself towards the object designated" (1995, p. 154). Namely, sense does not belong exclusively to language, oblivious to its relation to objects; it also does not lie in the silent objects themselves, which are necessarily meaningless without language – it is not about them. Sense "subsists in language, but it happens to things" (1990, p. 24). It is a "pure event" or "effect" on the surface in which objects and language interact; it is both what is said and what happens, what would not have transpired in the same way without having been said.

Sense not only makes truth possible, but actually *becomes* true. A "pure event" cannot be recognized or described truthfully, for language is instrumental in bringing it about (Deleuze 2006, p. 69). Truth is more than just correspondence between linguistic sense and a reality that lies beyond language, but is created in sense, in the event that occurs in but not only in language: "Sense is the genesis or the production of the true, and truth is only the empirical result of sense" (1995, p. 154). Thus, unlike the dogmatic image according to which both true and false can make sense,

sense for Deleuze makes truth (and not falsity). Sense that creates truth, true sense, marks an event where language encounters things, where things make something out of language and language makes something out of things – where they interact to make sense.

As demonstrated by several Deleuze scholars (e.g. Lecercle 2002, p. 99; Roy 2005, p. 102), sense is not simply meaning – it is not enough for someone to mean something for their words to make sense: sense "is closer to significance rather than meaning, that is to the way in which meaning matters or makes things matter" (Williams 2008, p. 3). Inna Semetsky explains that events make sense "not if we understand them theoretically but when we experience in practice the very difference that makes each singular event significant" (2013, p. 216, see also 2007, p. 34). Therefore, sense expresses all that is important in the world and makes a difference in it (Bolaños 2006, p. 575). There is no sense if things remain unchanged, if language and the world remain indifferent to each other. Contrary to the commonsensical belief that identifies sense with meaning and that meanings can be shared, for Deleuze, to reiterate, not every linguistic utterance that is meaningful also makes sense. In fact, he argues, most of what we say does not make sense; utterances such as "Good morning Theaetetus", "This is a table", are commonsensical, but make very little sense. They are perfectly understandable, but when uttered thoughtlessly in daily speech, hardly anything happens: words and objects pass each other by without leaving a trace.

Furthermore, not all sense is necessarily understandable or meaningful in the commonsensical way. A nonsense word such as Lewis Carroll's Snark can make sense, although it breaks the chain in which each word designates or expresses something different from itself because it expresses what it denotes and denotes what it expresses. It says nothing, "but at the same time it says the sense of what it says: it says its own sense" (1990, p. 67). Nonsense disrupts ordinary linguistic relations and is effective in that it indicates an immediate self-presence, that of an "important kind of sense that can only operate through nonsense" (Williams 2008, p. 68). Therefore, sense is not the opposite of nonsense; rather, it posits "between sense and nonsense an original type of intrinsic relation, a mode of co-presence" (1990, p. 68). This means that all words and expressions, not only Carrollean portmanteaus, have to function simultaneously, "momentarily and paradoxically" as sense and nonsense (Roy 2005, p. 104).

Yet even ordinary linguistic structures are not utterly devoid of sense. As there is no sense without language, so there is no language without sense. Not all linguistic components express sense – sense is an event, and therefore it is not marked by a noun or described by an adjective, but rather "enveloped in a *verb*" (1990, p. 182, emphasis in the original), even if it is not expressed explicitly. When we speak of a green tree, sense does not reside in "the tree" or "is green", nor in a proposition like "the tree is green"; it rather stems from "the tree greens", from "to green" (*verdioe*), and from the intensity of interrelations between this verb and others (e.g. "blow" or "fall") (1990, p. 21). Most of the time, as in this example, the interaction between the verbs is minute – they hardly operate on each other powerfully enough to make unusual, significant effects.

Now, what is the nature of a sense-rich linguistic expression whose encounter with reality is a true event? The answer provided by Deleuze lies in the question, or rather in its form (1995, p. 121). This does not imply that all questions necessarily make much sense, but it does imply that some call for thinking and thus generate meaningful effects. An utterance makes sense, claims Deleuze, when it asks something of the world, creating a problem within it. The activity of thinking is therefore means the generation of true, meaningful problems, whereas stupidity has nothing to do with error and all to do with the formulation of false problems to begin with, trivial problems without any real interest (Deleuze 1995, p. 159, 1998, p. 15).

We commonly think of problems and questions from the perspective of solutions and answers. Thus, we assume that a problem properly formulated can find, by definition, a solution within the existing intellectual order, and that a good question has a knowable answer. A question with no foreseeable answer is nonsensical; questions make sense as much as they take part in common sense. This kind of questioning or interrogation, Deleuze writes, "always takes place within the framework of a community: to interrogate implies not only a common sense but a good-sense, a distribution of knowledge and of the given with respect to empirical consciousnesses in accordance with their situations, their points of view, their positions and their skills, in such a way that a given consciousness is supposed to know already what the other does not" (1995, p. 157).

This presupposition is at the core of common sense education, as it assumes that teachers possess knowledge, and that their role is more than just to pass it along but rather to pose the right questions leading students to the right answers; the answer is implicit in the question, endowing it with sense. This conceptualization of education is thus essentially hierarchical, with the teachers being the only ones posing questions and making sense, empowered by the fact that they know all the answers in advance:

> According to this infantile prejudice, the master sets a problem, our task is to solve it, and the result is accredited true or false by a powerful authority. It is also a social prejudice with the visible interest of maintaining us in an infantile state, which calls upon us to solve problems that come from elsewhere… As if we would not remain slaves so long as we do not control the problems themselves, so long as we do not possess a right to the problems, to a participation in and management of the problems (1995, p. 158).

To be able to produce questions and problems that make sense, Deleuze argues, we must "rid ourselves of an illusion which belongs to the dogmatic image of thought: problems and questions must no longer be traced from the corresponding propositions which serve, or can serve, as responses" (p. 157). In other words, rather than assuming that a problem makes sense by virtue of its solution, for Deleuze sense lies in the *problem itself*. A problem that makes sense does not consist in the search for a solution, and does not disappear once one has been found. It has an existence of its own, which is not "the being of the negative", namely the lack of a solution, but rather "the being of the problematic", which Deleuze also dubs "(non-)being" or "?-being" (1990, p. 123). The problem is never converted into an item of knowledge, a part of the comprehensive set of common accessible knowledge: "Even if the problem is concealed by its solution, it subsists nonetheless in the Idea which relates it to its conditions and organizes the genesis of the solutions" (1990, p. 54; see also p. 123). That is to say, even when a solution offers itself, sense does not reside in it; at most, it resides in the encounter between the solution and the question in relation to which it appears, becomes interpreted, and receives meaning.

Therefore, the problem cannot be solved by any datum or knowledge item, for it generates more questions that in turn call for new and different solutions all the time. A problem that makes sense does not have a simple solution in common or good sense, as it problematizes both, challenging self-evident beliefs and hierarchies, or *doxa*. Thinking that begins with such problems proceeds in constant motion that teachers can never stop by providing solutions. It is problematic for them just as it is for their students, for experts no less than for laypersons, and hence for the hegemonic hierarchies designed to reproduce the power relations between these parties.

Deleuzian education for thinking, therefore, involves posing problems that make sense, asking questions to which the teacher does not know the answers. But where do these problems come from, if not from the teacher's knowledge? How can a teacher formulate questions that make sense without knowing the answers? And what exactly is communicated and learned when such questions and problems are posed?

4.4 The Unregulated Exercise of All Faculties

How is sense related to education and thinking? To better understand that relation, let us return to the collaboration of the faculties, and introduce the Deleuzian discussion of the deregulation of their commonsensical order. Since thinking conforming to *doxa* involves such cognitive collaboration, genuine thinking requires that commonsensical interrelations be disintegrated. In Kant, Deleuze finds the paradigmatic example of the commonsensical order of the faculties as well as the possibility of disrupting that order. Each of the three chapters of his 1963 book *Kant's Critical Philosophy* focuses on the relations between understanding, reason, and imagination in one of the three Kantian Critiques. Deleuze claims that each Critique focuses on one of "reason's interests" and on the faculty fulfilling it – understanding in the case of the speculative interest (first Critique), reason in the case of the practical interest (second), and imagination in that of the aesthetic one (third). The point is that no faculty can satisfy the relevant interest on its own, and is in need of the cooperation of the others. The entire Kantian system rests therefore on the doctrine of the faculties: "In each Critique understanding, reason and imagination enter into various relationships under the chairmanship of one of the faculties. There are thus systematic variations in the relationship between the faculties, depending on which interest of reason we consider… In this way the doctrine of the faculties forms the real network which constitutes the transcendental method" (Deleuze 2008a, pp. 8–9). Each time the three faculties cooperate to fulfill one of reason's interests they form a common sense.

Deleuze explains that the Kantian system needs the commonsensical cooperation of the faculties precisely because Kant is aware that each human faculty has its own unique character, incommensurable with the others: "One of the most original points of Kantianism", Deleuze writes, "is the idea of a *difference in nature between our faculties*" (2008a, p. 19, emphasis in the original). The principle of common sense limits and regulates the activity each faculty through that of others – the faculties cooperate by restraining each other. Kant's genius, however, lies in that he conceives also of the possibility of non-commonsensical operation of the faculties. This happens in the experience of the sublime: unlike natural beauty, which "carries with it a purposiveness in its form, by which the object seems as it were pre-determined for our power of judgment", Kant writes that "if something arouses in us, merely in apprehension and without any reasoning on our part, a feeling of the sublime, then it may indeed appear, in its form, contrapurposive for our power of judgment, incommensurate with our power of exhibition, and as it were violent to our imagination, and yet we judge it all the more sublime for that" (2002, §23). That is to say, while the beautiful produces a feeling of harmony between subject and object resulting from a free, harmonious exercise of the cognitive faculties, the sublime involves an unbridgeable gap between the subject and what she experiences, resulting from a counterproductive disharmony between the faculties. Rather than working together in a common sense, they operate violently against each other, pushing each other to "reach the maximum" of their individual operation (2002, §26).

As Deleuze puts it in his book on Kant, "it is as if the imagination were confronted with its own limit, forced to strain to its utmost, experiencing a violence which stretches it to the extremity of its power" and hence "the sublime thus confronts us with a direct subjective relationship between imagination and reason. But this relation is primarily a dissention rather than an accord, a contradiction experienced between the demands of reason and the power of the imagination" (2008a, pp. 42–3). In *Difference and Repetition*, Deleuze returns to the Kantian sublime, writing that the "paradoxical" activity of the faculties, opposed to their activity in a common sense, "can appear only in the form of a *discordant harmony,* since each communicates to the other only the violence which confronts it with its own difference and its divergence from the others. Kant was the first to provide the example of such a discordant harmony, the relation between imagination and thought which occurs in the case of the sublime" (Deleuze 1995, p. 146). The sublime, Deleuze explains, allows for a free, unregulated relation between the faculties, as

> it brings the various faculties into play in such a way that they struggle against one another, the one pushing the other towards its maximum or limit, the other reacting by pushing the first towards an inspiration which it would not have had alone. Each pushes the other to the limit, but each makes the one go beyond the limit of the other… It is a tempest in the depths of a chasm opened up in the subject. The faculties confront one another, each stretched to its own limit, and find their accord in a fundamental discord: a discordant accord is the great discovery of the *Critique of Judgement,* the final Kantian reversal (2008a, p. xi).

In the Kantian sublime, therefore, the faculties are not forced into a common sense and the way is open to new kinds of experience and thinking.

The sublime, however, is not the only case that calls for genuine, non-commonsensical thinking. Deleuze finds awareness of the distinction between perceptions that call for thinking and those that do not also in the *Republic*, where Plato writes:

[Socrates:] I'll point out, then, if you can grasp it, that some sense perceptions *don't* summon the understanding to look into them, because the judgment of sense perception is itself adequate, while others encourage it in every way to look into them, because sense perception seems to produce no sound result.
[Glaucon:] You're obviously referring to things appearing in the distance and to *trompe l'oeil* paintings.
[Socrates:] You're not quite getting my meaning.
[Glaucon:] Then what do you mean?
[Socrates:] The ones that don't summon the understanding are all those that don't go off into opposite perceptions at the same time. But the ones that do go off in that way I call *summoners*—whenever sense perception doesn't declare one thing any more than its opposite, no matter whether the object striking the senses is near at hand or far away. (Plato 1997b, p. 1140),

Unlike things such as a finger that is enough to see in order to recognize, Socrates further explains, sensations such as "bigness" or "thickness" are always sensed together with their opposite, for what is big or thick in relation to one thing is small or thin in relation to another; we never perceive bigness without also perceiving smallness, thickness without thinness, etc. The soul, therefore, "is puzzled as to what the sense means" and will "summon calculation and understanding" (Plato 1997b, p. 1140–1) to begin a process of thinking that will eventually distinguish between the visible and the intelligible. This is also how Deleuze describes the changes the protagonist undergoes in *Alice's Adventures in Wonderland* (Carol 1984): when she grows, she becomes larger than she was before; but so long as she continues growing she also becomes smaller than she will be the following moment. Hence, "it pertains to the essence of becoming to move and to pull in both directions at once: Alice does not grow without shrinking, and vice versa" (Deleuze 1990, p. 1). As a result, Alice loses her identity, her name, her being part of an order of stable, recognizable states of affairs (p. 3).

That is to say, Deleuze interprets the things that do not summon the understanding as objects of recognition that do not generate thinking because in recognizing them thought follows the dogmatic image: "thought and all its faculties may be fully employed therein, thought may busy itself thereby, but such employment and such activity have nothing to do with thinking. Thought is thereby filled with no more than an image of itself, one in which it recognises itself the more it recognises things: this is a finger, this is a table, Good morning Theaetetus" (1995, p. 138). Encountering unity of opposites, on the other hand, can provoke thinking precisely because it is impossible to classify and recognize; the problem such encounter poses to the senses cannot be solved by cooperating with other faculties, and forces interaction of a totally different kind:

> Something in the world forces us to think. This something is an object not of recognition but of a fundamental *encounter*… its primary characteristic is that it can only be sensed. In this sense it is opposed to recognition… It is therefore... imperceptible precisely from the point of view of recognition – in other words, from the point of view of an empirical exercise of the senses in which sensibility grasps only that which also could be grasped by other faculties, and is related within the context of a common sense to an object which also must be apprehended by other faculties. (pp. 139-140; emphasis in the original)

In this bewildering encounter, the sensible faculty cannot respond ordinarily, and for this very reason, it operates independently and uniquely, "transcending" in Deleuze's terms, the commonsensical empirical model of recognition. To be sure, this transcendent operation does not involve ascending towards some abstract Idea or essence existing above or beyond the world. Rather, this is transgression from ordinary common sense to what is most immanent to each faculty: "Transcendent in no way means that the faculty addresses itself to objects outside the world but, on the contrary, that it grasps that in the world which concerns it exclusively and brings it into the world" (p. 143), namely what is unique to it, distinguishing it from the other faculties.

The object of encounter, therefore, need not be sublime. It can be practically anything: "What is encountered may be Socrates, a temple or a demon" (p. 139), Deleuze writes, if only its effect on sensation is not translated into the language of recognition, known to the other faculties. The encounter awakening thinking is experienced as a shocking, startling, limitless happening, one Deleuze calls "mad becoming" or "becoming mad" due to its distance from ordinary, commonsensical thought. Such thinking is by no means natural or frequent, but it is also not limited to specific times and places, and educated, knowledgeable people have no privileged access to it.

Moreover, in the encounter that triggers thinking, the thinker is necessarily involuntary and passive, for the faculty of the will does not collaborate with sensibility – something external imposes itself violently on the senses. It is "an original violence inflicted upon thought; the claws of a strangeness or an enmity which alone would awaken thought from its natural stupor or eternal possibility: there is only involuntary thought, aroused but constrained within thought, and all the more absolutely necessary for being born, illegitimately, of fortuitousness in the world. Thought is primarily trespass and violence, the enemy, and nothing presupposes philosophy: everything begins with misosophy" (Deleuze 1995, p. 139).

According to Jonathan Dronsfield, "Thinking becomes no longer a natural capacity we all possess but an activity some of us are forced into doing by that which we do not recognize but sense; moreover sense in a way which differentiates the faculty of sensibility from all other faculties, indeed brings it into discord with them whilst at the same time confronting them with their own limits" (2012, p. 405). Thus, although the transcendent operation of sensibility is not sharable with or translatable into the language of other faculties, it does not remain within the bounds of sensitivity alone. The senses' encounter with the outside awakens other faculties, and in the absence of communicable and recognizable content, the violent shock caused by the encounter passes through the faculties, igniting in each – from sensibility to memory, imagination, and thought – an independent activity that is unrestrained by the others:

> Each faculty is unhinged, but what are the hinges if not the form of a common sense which causes all the faculties to function and converge? Each... has broken the form of common sense which kept it within the empirical element of *doxa*… Rather than all the faculties converging and contributing to a common project of recognising an object, we see divergent projects in which... each faculty is in the presence of that which is its 'own'. Discord of the faculties, chain of force and fuse along which each confronts its limit, receiving from (or communicating to) the other only a violence which brings it face to face with its own element, as though with its disappearance or its perfection (1995, p. 141).

A distinctly disharmonic relationship thus obtains between the faculties, as they do not collaborate in a common sense. The violence that generates this connection is not aimed at mutual limitation or annihilation. Rather, the cognitive faculties are liberated by the involuntary shock, enabling each one of them to operate "transcendentally": to sense that which is only sensible, to remember that which is only memorable, and to imagine that which is only imaginable (p. 145).

This does not mean that each faculty has a predetermined, "natural" mode of operation – there are infinite ways to sense that which is only sensible, to imagine that which is only imaginable, etc. Similarly, the faculties Deleuze writes about are by no means the only ones, and countless unique others may be discovered. Further inquiries may add "other faculties which would find their place in a complete doctrine – vitality, the transcendent object of which would include monstrosity; and sociability, the transcendent object of which would include anarchy – and even… faculties yet to be discovered, whose existence is not yet suspected" (1995, p. 143). This is an infinite variety of experiences that have one thing in common – they all transcend the commonsensical order of things, the familiar way we all understand and make sense of our world – thanks to which they are capable of giving rise to thinking not limited to common sense and to what everybody think.

As opposed to dogmatic *thought* involving commonsensical collaboration of the cognitive faculties, *thinking* is thus an independent activity of the faculties, which follows upon one's experience of something in the world as a problem, or as a sign that is not a recognizable object, but rather that requires unique interpretation (Bogue 2004). Thinking is differentiating, not only between events and objects in the world, but primarily between the faculties. It is not processing of existing data, nor reflection on pre-given concepts, but rather creative activity which brings something new into existence; an activity conditioned by passivity, by receptivity to the problem (Kohan 2011, p. 347).

In Deleuze's terms, the problem that passes through the faculties and awakens thinking in each in turn is called "Idea":

> There is, therefore, something which is communicated from one faculty to another, but it is metamorphosed and does not form a common sense. We could just as well say that there are Ideas which traverse all the faculties, but are the objects of none in particular. Perhaps… it will be necessary to reserve the name of Ideas not for pure *cogitanda* [objects of cognition] but rather for those instances which go from sensibility to thought and from thought to sensibility, capable of engendering in each case... the limit- or transcendent-object of each faculty (1995, p. 146).

The Idea of the problem is the violent element moving from one faculty to the other following the shocking encounter with the sign, touching each without residing in any. It does not fit into the order of common sense, and its sense is primarily the principle of communication itself, the "para-sense" generating the problem. This is not the communication of sense, through which sense is made common; what is communicated is problematics itself, the shocking restlessness that is expressed every time differently.

To reiterate, Ideas "run throughout all the faculties and awaken them each in turn" (1995, p. 164), driving each to the limit. They are thus provocative of thought, but are definitely not pure mental entities that can be reflected upon rationally. Like their Platonic counterparts, Deleuzian Ideas must arise from an encounter of the senses with the world while themselves transcending the sensible. And like Kantian ideas, they are the generators of thinking, but are unable to be objects of knowledge..

This conceptualization of thinking and communication of Ideas allows Deleuze to outline a unique understanding of education for thinking, which does not rest on dogmatic commonsensical assumptions. To differentiate the picture he draws from the more traditional understandings of education for thinking, he avoids even the term "education", using the word "apprenticeship" – used also by Heidegger to link learning to think with the handicraft of the cabinetmaker's apprentice (see Chap. 1) – to describe the revelatory process through which an Idea awakens thinking:

> The exploration of Ideas and the elevation of each faculty to its transcendent exercise amounts to the same thing. These are two aspects of an essential apprenticeship [*apprentissage*] or process of *learning* [*apprendre*]... an apprentice is someone who constitutes and occupies practical or speculative problems as such. Learning is the appropriate name for the subjective acts carried out when one is confronted with the objectivity of a problem (Idea), whereas knowledge designates only the generality of concepts or the calm possession of a rule enabling solutions (1995, p. 164).

Deleuze uses a famous example to illustrate this process: swimming at sea (1995, pp. 22–3, 165). Far from being a matter of abstract theoretical knowledge the student will obviously never acquire the skill by listening to a swimming teacher describe or demonstrate certain movements and practicing them on land. The untrained swimmer's first encounter with seawater imposes a novel problem, a shock for the senses involving a previously unexperienced mixture of wetness, coldness, and loss of control. At that moment of encounter, the world becomes unable to provide familiar representations and the situation is felt to be radically different from everything else. "For this athlete who finds herself in a novel situation, there is literally no solid foundation under her feet, and the world that she has to face loses its reassuring power of familiar representations" (Semetsky 2013, p. 223; see also Semetsky 2003, p. 19; Wallin 2011, p. 298). The collaboration of the faculties will not do for dealing with this problem. This is not a question of recalling previous knowledge, understanding the exact conditions at sea, or applying creative imagination. The swimmer's senses must address the problem independently by responding to and acting in tandem with the waves. The sea itself acts on the trainee, makes sense to her. The learning process is not knowledge acquisition, therefore, but rather discovering the sea as an Idea. As a challenge demanding confrontation, the sensed

Idea can influence other faculties: it can flood the imagination, fish memories from the deep, or even produce fresh insights – but each faculty remains independent of the others and does not act with them to reach a solution able to "drown" the problem. Such transcendent activity of the faculties is clearly thinking in the Deleuzian sense; learning to swim, therefore, is an example of education for thinking.

Even though such apprenticeship is not limited to formal educational contexts, such contexts are not necessarily counterproductive to thinking (Semetsky 2013, p. 223). Deleuze's attack on the orthodox, omniscient teacher, argues Ronald Bogue (2013, p. 22), does not minimize the latter's role, even in ordinary educational settings. "Giving courses has been a major part of my life… It's like a research laboratory; you give courses on what you are investigating, not on what you know" (Deleuze 1995, p. 139; see also Semetsky 2007, p. xxiv). Bogue (2013, pp. 25–6) confirms that Deleuze's teaching was perfectly consistent with the apprenticeship concept described above: he did not use the standard lecture format to deliver information, but as an encounter engaging all participants in active thinking. More than the teaching of given information, such a lecture is a performance of thinking in action, in that what is learned is not necessarily what is taught. The students may respond to the teacher's prompts in countless ways, often bearing little connection to the "subject". Even boredom can be beneficial, if it makes students drift into thinking. The problem or violent constraint is not only the content of the lecture but also the need to stay afloat, so to speak, while the teacher's voice resonates in the lecture hall. In that, an academic lecture is not all too different from a swimming lesson. There, too, thinking is generated by the violent encounter between the student's senses and a problem – here, the teacher's inescapable voice – which awakens memory, imagination, and other faculties into transcendent, original activity.

Obviously, not every lecture is evocative, and it is certainly not easy to make students think. The point is, rather, that nothing in this world is problematic "in itself", though every specific thing may be experienced as such. Common sense calls upon us to translate everything encountered by the senses into the language of recognition understandable to the other faculties – to understand and assimilate it to the prevailing order. The teachers' role is thus to counteract common sense by facilitating openness to problems by inspiring students to live the world as a question rather than be obsessed with recognizing and knowing (Colebrook 2008, p. 42; Wallin 2011, p. 295). To make sense, the teacher must be effective and make a difference by awakening the students out of their dogmatic slumber. The Deleuzian teacher's voice is part of the encounter awakening thinking in the student qua apprentice. It does not transfer meanings but generates meaningful encounters – it makes sense, it makes the world make sense, and when teaching makes sense, students start thinking. To make sense, the teacher cannot just throw the students into the proverbial cold water, but must find the right words and gestures to problematize their experience of the world and make them react forcefully by thinking. This does not mean, mind you, that the teacher can plan thinking or learning processes in advance, as they are never the necessary outcomes of previous causes: "We never know in advance how someone will learn: by means of what loves someone becomes good at Latin, what encounters make them a philosopher, or in what dictionaries they learn to think" (1995, p. 165). The teacher can try to make the world appear as a sign to be deciphered, but nothing guarantees that the student would comply and become an apprentice, and that experience would actually make sense.

In any case, the important point is that the problems that make sense are *for* the student but *in* the world – the world that common sense represents as a unified whole that is shared by all. Education that makes sense thus not only rejects the imperative to assimilate the students and knowledge into the commonsensical order, but also problematizes common sense itself. In the Deleuzian sense, such education is therefore always political in that it overturns the dogmatic image of thought, challenging the stable meanings and identities that form the very basis of the social order. It is not its content that makes Deleuzian education political, but rather the problematization event. Accordingly, a swimming lesson may be more political than a "political education" class. From seawater to philosophy, everything can be read disruptively and thereby deterritorialize the ordinary discipline, in both senses, and shake the student out of her comfort zone by making her think differently. As Diana Masny reminds us, the question "is no longer what a text means but rather how it works and what it produces" (2013, p. 76). The political aspect of such education rejects the politics of revolutions and grand visions that requires acceptance of common sense. It is rather *micro* political (Semetsky 2007, p. 3), staying at the level of the pure, original incommensurable particular. Every common sense is necessarily dogmatic and anti-political, so that the sense of the political is always a singular event that can never be made common.

Nevertheless, while education cannot make sense common, it can make sense *in* common. The educational encounter's effect does not have to be isolated or momentary, for sense can be communicated, resonating differently each time in a series of repetitions. Unlike knowledge attainment, which requires the subject to accept certain facts as true and to become coopted by the order of which they are part, Deleuzian apprenticeship requires the student to react to the world and to make a difference in it. The knowledgeable can apply what she has learned in the world, but the apprentice learns while acting and acts while learning. The Idea runs through her faculties, shattering their harmony, and then bounces back to the world to affect other people and problematize other things. When she learns to deal with a problem, she passes it on, thereby generating new ones: a key aspect of learning is being able to generate new problems – to swim farther in stormier waters, generating problems for the swimmer as well as for the teacher and others at the beach. Such education involves the exchange of sounds, gestures, and blows between the learner and the water, between her and the learner, and among her different cognitive faculties. Whenever the learner begins to think – at sea or on land, in school or on the street – thinking is not contained in her mind, as it is not limited to a single faculty, but necessarily affects how she speaks and acts, and thereby also affects others.

4.5 In Search of Lost Education

We can learn more about the process of apprenticeship and the way Deleuze ties it to thinking, communication and distribution of problems by turning to his *Proust and Signs*, in which he examines *In Search of Lost Time* not only as a search for memories of a time gone by, but as an educational journey. In this section, I show how Proust's work presents, according to Deleuze, thinking processes initiated by encountering signs demanding interpretation, and explain in what sense the Search involves education for thinking.

Proust's narrator searches for lost time, but Deleuze argues that "Proust's work is not oriented to the past and the discoveries of memory, but to the future and the progress of an apprenticeship" (2008b, p. 18): the entire Search, according to Deleuze, is "the narrative of an apprenticeship: more precisely, the apprenticeship of a man of letters" (p. 3). Like a classic *Bildungsroman*, the novel accompanies the narrator from childhood to maturity, describing the long transformative process he undergoes; this, however, is not a standard narrative formation that ends up accepting the social order and finding a place in it, nor is it about learning and attaining knowledge about the world. The narrator learns and gradually becomes a man of letters by interpreting signs he encounters: "Signs are the object of a temporal apprenticeship, not of an abstract knowledge. To learn is first of all to consider a substance, an object, a being as if it emitted signs to be deciphered, interpreted" (p. 4). Apprenticeship here means dealing with problems and interpreting signs; it has to do with learning truths of the world, but not by attaining them through the model of common sense and conventional philosophy; instead, Proust's work presents a different way of learning and thinking: "the Search is first of all a search for truth. Thereby is manifested the 'philosophical' bearing of Proust's work: it vies with philosophy. Proust sets up an image of thought in opposition to that of philosophy" (p. 60).

Deleuze stresses that for Proust the search for truth is not the given factor explaining processes of thinking and cognition, but rather the very thing in need of explaining:

> Proust does not believe that man, nor even a supposedly pure mind, has by nature a desire for truth, a will-to-truth. We search for truth only when we are determined to do so in terms of a concrete situation, when we undergo a kind of violence that impels us to such a search. Who searches for truth? The jealous man, under the pressure of the beloved's lies. There is always the violence of a sign that forces us into the search, that robs us of peace. The truth is not to be found by affinity, nor by goodwill, but is *betrayed* by involuntary signs. (p. 11, emphasis in the original)

Proust rejects therefore the common assumption that thought has a good, "upright" nature, automatically desiring truth. The search for truth does not get underway by some internal force like wonder or intellectual curiosity, but rather by "violent" encounters with signs: unlike qualities or attributes leading thought straight to recognizable objects, signs trouble and embarrass, set riddles and demand interpretation. They summon thought not to truth but to searching for it, namely to the creative activity of thinking: Deleuze writes that "What forces us to think is the sign. The sign is the object of an encounter, but it is precisely the contingency of the encounter that guarantees the necessity of what it leads us to think. The act of thinking does not proceed from a simple natural possibility; on the contrary, it is the only true creation. Creation is the genesis of the act of thinking within thought itself" (p. 62).[8] Deleuze finds various types of signs in the Search – such as the contradicting signs of love Albertine sends to the loving narrator, forcing him to desperately search for the truth behind them, with each sign generating an encounter that does not offer or reveal truth but rather demands interpretative work, namely thinking, without which truth remains out of reach: "To seek the truth is to interpret, decipher, explicate" (p. 12).

The ultimate example of such an encounter with a sign is the moment the narrator tastes the famous madeleine cake, from the first part of Proust's monumental work. I will cite it at length[9]:

> Many years had elapsed during which nothing of Combray, except what lay in the theatre and the drama of my going to bed there, had any existence for me, when one day in winter, on my return home, my mother, seeing that I was cold, offered me some tea, a thing I did not ordinarily take. I declined at first, and then, for no particular reason, changed my mind. She sent for one of those squat, plump little cakes called "petites madeleines," which look as though they had been moulded in the fluted valve of a scallop shell. And soon, mechanically, dispirited after a dreary day with the prospect of a depressing morrow, I raised to my lips a spoonful of the tea in which I had soaked a morsel of the cake. No sooner had the warm liquid mixed with the crumbs touched my palate than a shiver ran through me and I stopped, intent upon the extraordinary thing that was happening to me. An exquisite pleasure had invaded my senses, something isolated, detached, with no suggestion of its origin. And at once the vicissitudes of life had become indifferent to me, its disasters innocuous, its brevity illusory—this new sensation having had the effect, which love has, of filling me with a precious essence; or rather this essence was not in me, it was me. I had ceased now to feel mediocre, contingent, mortal. Whence could it have come to me, this all-powerful joy? I sensed that it was connected with the taste of the tea and the cake, but that it infinitely transcended those savours, could not, indeed, be of the same nature… I put down the cup and examine my own mind. It alone can discover the truth. But how? What an abyss of uncertainty, whenever the mind feels overtaken by itself; when it, the seeker, is at the same time the dark region through which it must go seeking and where all its equipment will avail it nothing. Seek? More than that: create. It is face to face with something which does not yet exist, which it alone can make actual, which it alone can bring into the light of day (Proust 1992a, pp. 60-1).

The taste of the madeleine is a sign demanding interpretation: the Proustian search for lost time and for the truth embedded in it gets underway not following some conscious decision or sentimental nostalgia, but rather due to an accidental,

---

[8] Proust writes, for example, that "as far back as at Combray, I was attempting to concentrate my mind on a compelling image, a cloud, a triangle, a belfry, a flower, a pebble, believing that there was perhaps something else under those symbols I ought to try to discover, a thought which these objects were expressing in the manner of hieroglyphic characters which one might imagine only represented material objects. Doubtless such deciphering was difficult, but it alone could yield some part of the truth. For the truths which the intelligence apprehends through direct and clear vision in the daylight world are less profound and less necessary than those which life has communicated to us unconsciously through an intuition which is material only in so far as it reaches us through our senses and the spirit of which we can elicit" (Proust 1992b, pp. 106–7).

[9] I am using two different translations of Proust to English, to remain as close as possible to the English translation of Deleuze's *Proust and Signs*.

unintentional encounter of the narrator's senses with this taste that awakens involuntary memories and thoughts about himself and his past. Similarly, encounters with signs take place in various other places in the novel. For example, a significant series of encounters with uneven paving stones, the noise of a knock of a spoon against a plate, and the touch of a napkin, in the last part of the Search, *Time Regained* (Proust 1992b, pp. 99–101)[10] – each time throwing the narrator, against his will to places and events from his past.

[10] Deleuze often refers to this series of encounters from the last part of the Search, and it is worth citing at full length: "But sometimes illumination comes to our rescue at the very moment when all seems lost; we have knocked at every door and they open on nothing until, at last, we stumble unconsciously against the only one through which we can enter the kingdom we have sought in vain a hundred years–and it opens. Reviewing the painful reflections of which I have just been speaking, I had entered the courtyard of the Guermantes' mansion and in my distraction I had not noticed an approaching carriage; at the call of the link-man I had barely time to draw quickly to one side, and in stepping backwards I stumbled against some unevenly placed paving stones behind which there was a coach-house. As I recovered myself, one of my feet stepped on a flagstone lower than the one next it. In that instant all my discouragement disappeared and I was possessed by the same felicity which at different moments of my life had given me the view of trees which seemed familiar to me during the drive round Balbec, the view of the belfries of Martinville, the savour of the madeleine dipped in my tea and so many other sensations of which I have spoken and which Vinteuil's last works had seemed to synthesise. As at the moment when I tasted the madeleine, all my apprehensions about the future, all my intellectual doubts, were dissipated. Those doubts which had assailed me just before, regarding the reality of my literary gifts and even regarding the reality of literature itself were dispersed as though by magic. This time I vowed that I should not resign myself to ignoring why, without any fresh reasoning, without any definite hypothesis, the insoluble difficulties of the previous instant had lost all importance as was the case when I tasted the madeleine. The felicity which I now experienced was undoubtedly the same as that I felt when I ate the madeleine, the cause of which I had then postponed seeking. There was a purely material difference in the images evoked. A deep azure intoxicated my eyes, a feeling of freshness, of dazzling light enveloped me and in my desire to capture the sensation, just as I had not dared to move when I tasted the madeleine because of trying to conjure back that of which it reminded me, I stood, doubtless an object of ridicule to the link-men, repeating the movement of a moment since, one foot upon the higher flagstone, the other on the lower one. Merely repeating the movement was useless; but if, oblivious of the Guermantes' reception, I succeeded in recapturing the sensation which accompanied the movement, again the intoxicating and elusive vision softly pervaded me as though it said "Grasp me as I float by you, if you can, and try to solve the enigma of happiness I offer you." And then, all at once, I recognised that Venice which my descriptive efforts and pretended snapshots of memory had failed to recall; the sensation I had once felt on two uneven slabs in the Baptistry of St. Mark had been given back to me and was linked with all the other sensations of that and other days which had lingered expectant in their place among the series of forgotten years from which a sudden chance had imperiously called them forth. So too the taste of the little madeleine had recalled Combray. But how was it that these visions of Combray and of Venice at one and at another moment had caused me a joyous certainty sufficient without other proofs to make death indifferent to me? Asking myself this and resolved to find the answer this very day, I entered the Guermantes' mansion, because we always allow our inner needs to give way to the part we are apparently called upon to play and that day mine was to be a guest. On reaching the first floor a footman requested me to enter a small boudoir-library adjoining a buffet until the piece then being played had come to an end, the Princesse having given orders that the doors should not be opened during the performance. At that very instant a second premonition occurred to reinforce the one which the uneven paving-stones had given me and to exhort me to persevere in

As the example of the madeleine indicates, the truth the sign "betrays" is different from the signified object. The taste of the madeleine is not simply a sign for some quality of the cake, although it would not have existed without it. Moreover, that truth is also not merely the subjective train of associations the sign may give rise to, for not any thought that may have occurred to the narrator following the taste of the madeleine would have been true in the same sense. The truth that demands to be interpreted through the taste of the madeleine is the truth of Combray, the narrator's childhood surrounding, no less than it is his own personal truth – in Deleuze's words, "Beyond designated objects, beyond intelligible and formulated truths, but also beyond subjective chains of association and resurrections by resemblance or contiguity, are the essences that are alogical or supralogical" (2008b, p. 25). Clearly, the thinking the Proustian sign generates does not adhere to the logical, commonsensical model of recognition, to the image Deleuze calls dogmatic – the object is only its starting point, and it does not try to identify or recognize it. This truth, therefore, cannot be found through the cooperation of the faculties, which is inherently limited to the act of recognition – the search for truth must involve independent, "transcendent" activity of the faculties, namely disruption of their commonsensical relation.

---

my task. The servant in his ineffectual efforts not to make a noise had knocked a spoon against a plate. The same sort of felicity which the uneven paving-stones had given me invaded my being; this time my sensation was quite different, being that of great heat accompanied by the smell of smoke tempered by the fresh air of a surrounding forest and I realised that what appeared so pleasant was the identical group of trees I had found so tiresome to observe and describe when I was uncorking a bottle of beer in the railway carriage and, in a sort of bewilderment, I believed for the moment, until I had collected myself, so similar was the sound of the spoon against the plate to that of the hammer of a railway employee who was doing something to the wheel of the carriage while the train was at a standstill facing the group of trees, that I was now actually there. One might have said that the portents which that day were to rescue me from my discouragement and give me back faith in literature, were determined to multiply themselves, for a servant, a long time in the service of the Prince de Guermantes, recognised me and, to save me going to the buffet, brought me some cakes and a glass of orangeade into the library. I wiped my mouth with the napkin he had given me and immediately, like the personage in the Thousand and One Nights who unknowingly accomplished the rite which caused the appearance before him of a docile genius, invisible to others, ready to transport him far away, a new azure vision passed before my eyes; but this time it was pure and saline and swelled into shapes like bluish udders. The impression was so strong that the moment I was living seemed to be one with the past and (more bewildered still than I was on the day when I wondered whether I was going to be welcomed by the Princesse de Guermantes or whether everything was going to melt away), I believed that the servant had just opened the window upon the shore and that everything invited me to go downstairs and walk along the sea-wall at high tide; the napkin upon which I was wiping my mouth had exactly the same kind of starchiness as that with which I had attempted with so much difficulty to dry myself before the window the first day of my arrival at Balbec and within the folds of which, now, in that library of the Guermantes mansion, a green-blue ocean spread its plumage like the tail of a peacock. And I did not merely rejoice in those colours, but in that whole instant which produced them, an instant towards which my whole life had doubtless aspired, which a feeling of fatigue or sadness had prevented my ever experiencing at Balbec but which now, pure, disincarnated and freed from the imperfections of exterior perceptions, filled me with joy" (Proust 1992b, pp. 99–101).

Proust's search is for "lost time", and the faculty that plays key role in it is naturally memory. But Proust's work is not a memoir, in which the narrator tries hard to remember and intentionally retrieves facts and events that seem worthy of commemoration and revitalization.[11] Deleuze writes that when memory is put to action by the will in a voluntary, deliberate way – which fits, of course, the commonsensical model in which the faculties cooperate with each other – it will necessarily miss the truth of the past it seeks to reconstruct:

> *Voluntary* memory proceeds from an actual present to a present that "has been," to something that was present and is so no longer. The past of voluntary memory is therefore doubly relative: relative to the present that it has been, but also to the present with regard to which it is now past. That is, this memory does not apprehend the past directly; it recomposes it with different *presents*... It is obvious that something essential escapes voluntary memory: the past's being *as past*. Voluntary memory proceeds as if the past were constituted as such after it has been present. It would therefore have to wait for a new present so that the preceding one could pass by, or become past. But in this way the essence of time escapes us. For if the present was not past at the same time as present, if the same moment did not coexist with itself as present *and* past, it would never pass, a new present would never come to replace this one. The past as it is in itself coexists with, and does not succeed, the present it has been (2008b, pp. 37-8, emphasis in the original).

That is to say, voluntary memory obeys the model of common and good sense, the model capable of recognizing objects only as beings, as a series of "snapshots" (p. 37). It therefore misses the way things are constantly becoming, namely the dimension of past (and future) in every moment of the present. To find the truth of becoming, to find the past as past, memory must act in a way unguided by the will, the understanding, or any other faculty – it must act involuntarily.

However, involuntary memory does not spontaneously awaken itself; it is not an autonomous, self-regulating activity. It is driven to action by sensibility, after the latter encounters a sign: the sign, Deleuze writes, "causes involuntary memory to intervene: an old sensation tries to superimpose itself, to unite with the present sensation, and extends it over several epochs at once" (2008b, p. 14). Following such an encounter, memory does not join in on a project of recognizing an object, but rather makes use of the compound made of the two overlapping sensations, the present and the old one,[12] as a kind of spell able to conjure up something uniquely its own:

> Flavor, the quality common to the two sensations, the sensation common to the two moments, is here only to recall something else: Combray. But upon this invocation, Combray rises up in a form that is absolutely new. Combray does not rise up as it was once present; Combray rises up as past, but this past is no longer relative to the present that it has been, it is no longer relative to the present in relation to which it is now past. This is no longer the Combray of perception nor of voluntary memory. Combray appears as it could not be experienced: not in reality, but in its truth. (pp. 60-1)

---

[11] "I understood but too well that the sensation the uneven paving-stones, the taste of the madeleine, had aroused in me, bore no relation to that which I had so often attempted to reconstruct of Venice, of Balbec and of Combray with the aid of a uniform memory" (Proust 1992b, p. 101).

[12] Proust writes that "there had been the irradiation of a small zone within and around myself, a sensation (taste of the dipped madeleine, metallic sound, feeling of the uneven steps) common to the place where I then was and also to the other place (my Aunt Léonie's room, the railway carriage, the Baptistry of St. Mark's)" (Proust 1992b, p. 104).

Memory is set in motion by sensibility without cooperating with it. Both faculties operate in an independent, transcendent, non-commonsensical manner. Sensibility transmits to memory what Deleuze calls "violence", namely the initial push experienced as shock because it cannot be recognized, understood and integrated into the familiar order of things. Only thus can involuntary memory save the past itself, the past that was never present, that was never qualified into a conscious present – the independent activity of memory is remembering something that was not present before, that did not go through the common mechanism of the faculties to become an object of consciousness.

Like Platonic remembrance, this activity of memory differs from overcoming what Deleuze calls "empirical forgiveness", namely recollecting something that has been conscious before but slipped away, waiting to be excavated and reactivated. Proustian memory does not restore lost truth, but rather creates it. The result of this creation is not phantasy or daydream but a new perspective through which something essential is revealed, something it was impossible to perceive while memory was operating in the dogmatic model of common sense: "Each subject expresses the world from a certain viewpoint… each subject therefore expresses an absolutely different world… Essence does not exist outside the subject expressing it, but it is expressed as the essence not of the subject but of Being, or of the region of Being that is revealed to the subject" (2008b, p. 28). This is a memory of what ontologically precedes common sense and the limitations it sets on the faculties – a past that is not interpreted in light of the present, which does not receive its meaning from the *doxa* that defines the present.[13] The truths that are thus created are tied to a subjective viewpoint but they are not to be reduced to it, as they are not to be reduced to the objects – they are events of encounters between reality and meaning, namely events making sense.

The Proustian Search, therefore, provides Deleuze with concrete examples of thinking not tied to the dogmatic commonsensical image: it describes the encounters with signs as events resulting in independent, "transcendent" activity of the faculties, starting with sensibility that violently awakens the others to their own independent activities. But in what sense do these encounters add up to a process of apprenticeship? Why does Deleuze think that by encountering signs and interpreting them the Proustian narrator is being educated as a man of letters?

To be sure, Proustian apprenticeship has nothing to do with acquiring a profession or accumulating knowledge. What the Proustian narrator learns, what makes him an apprentice, is not only the truths themselves but also the ability to create

[13] "let a sound, a scent already heard and breathed in the past be heard and breathed anew, simultaneously in the present and in the past, real without being actual, ideal without being abstract, then instantly the permanent and characteristic essence hidden in things is freed and our true being which has for long seemed dead but was not so in other ways awakes and revives, thanks to this celestial nourishment. An instant liberated from the order of time has recreated in us man liberated from the same order, so that he should be conscious of it. And indeed we understand his faith in his happiness even if the mere taste of a madeleine does not logically seem to justify it" (Proust 1992b, p. 103).

more truths, namely experience new encounters and interpret more signs: "To be sensitive to signs, to consider the world as an object to be deciphered, is doubtless a gift. But this gift risks remaining buried in us if we do not make the necessary encounters, and these encounters would remain ineffective if we failed to overcome certain stock notions" (Deleuze 2008b, p. 18). That is to say, although the interpretation of signs is not the result of voluntary, intentional exercise of the faculties, the encounters nevertheless do not happen by themselves, automatically: "One must be endowed for the signs, ready to encounter them, one must open oneself to their violence" (p. 64). Apprenticeship is therefore at one and the same time interpretation of signs and developing the sensitivity allowing the apprentice to encounter and interpret objects as signs: it is the ability to experience a madeleine cake soaked in tea, or uneven paving stones, as signs and problems – to encounter them in a way that makes sense and produces truths. The narrator becomes a man of letters, an artist, through a process of apprenticeship in which he learns how to think and make sense of the world as he encounters it.

Moreover, what the narrator learns when becoming an artist is not only how to make and experience truths, but also how to communicate them, namely how to make others think and make sense. An artwork involves the production of signs other people can in turn encounter and decipher: "the Search", Deleuze writes, "is not merely an instrument Proust uses at the same time that he fabricates it. It is an instrument for others and whose use others must learn" (2008b, p. 94). Proust's great achievement, for Deleuze, is his ability to make his work of art a conductor, a mediator, transmitting the truths the artist experiences while encountering signs, and translating then into new, different signs, which may generate in their turn more truths. This is what Deleuze means when he calls Proust's work "literary machine":

> What is new in Proust, what constitutes the eternal success and the eternal signification of the madeleine… is the fact that he produces them [the encounters] and that these moment become the effect of a literary machine… What is involved is no longer an extra literary experience that the man of letters reports or profits by, but an artistic experimentation produced by literature, a literary effect, in the sense in which we speak of an electric effect, or an electromagnetic effect. This is the supreme instance in which one can say: the machine works. That art is a machine for producing, and notably for producing certain effects, Proust is most intensely aware – effects on other people, because the readers or spectators will begin to discover, in themselves and outside of themselves, effects analogous to those that the work of art has been able to produce. (p. 99)

Proustian art, therefore, functions as a conductor passing on effects, violent influences, ideas arousing unexpected reactions in others – the narrator is like a spider, weaving a web of signs for others to encounter and get trapped in, communicating with them through the vibrations of the web (Deleuze 2008b, pp. 117–8; see Bray 2012). In other words, the literary machine produces opportunities for problematic, shocking and even dangerous encounters, forcing the faculties to act in a non-commonsensical way and generate thinking. It thereby allows what we have previously seen within the subject – the violence of an idea moving from one faculty to the other, raising each to transcendent activity – to happen also between different subjects.

Art, therefore, can connect different people and form various kinds of connections between them, but not through ordinary, everyday communication. The general lesson the literary machine teaches is that interaction and communication must not obey the commonsensical order. The latter dominates everyday interaction and communication, as well as the philosophy based on them: intelligence, namely commonsensical thought, "impels us to *conversation,* in which we exchange and communicate ideas. It incites us to *friendship,* based on the community of ideas and sentiments. It invites us to *philosophy,* a voluntary and premeditated exercise of thought by which we may determine the order and content of objective significations" Deleuze 2008b, p. 20). The Deleuzian-Proustian critique of traditional Western philosophy, therefore, applies not only to "Sophia", namely the element of wisdom and knowledge in philo-sophy, but also to "philia", the friendly connection between thinking beings implied by philosophy. This is a direct attack on the way the entire social or interpersonal sphere is organized:

> In the "philosopher" there is the "friend." It is important that Proust offers the same critique of philosophy as of friendship. Friends are, in relation to one another, like minds of goodwill who are in agreement as to the signification of things and words; they communicate under the effect of a mutual goodwill. Philosophy is like the expression of a Universal Mind that is in agreement with itself in order to determine explicit and communicable significations. Proust's critique touches the essential point: truths remain arbitrary and abstract so long as they are based on the goodwill of thinking. Only the conventional is explicit. This is because philosophy, like friendship, is ignorant of the dark regions in which are elaborated the effective forces that act on thought, the determinations that *force* us to think; a friend is not enough for us to approach the truth. Minds communicate to each other only the conventional. (pp. 60-1)

The dogmatic approach is valid so long as we are dealing with ordinary, "conventional" matters, but it is inherently conservative, rejecting the new for its difference from what is already known and accepting with friendly, democratic peace of mind the existing values and hierarchies.

Against this approach, Deleuze argues that Proust demonstrates how communication can be a rejection of "the dialectic as Conversation between Friends, in which all faculties are exercised voluntarily and collaborate under the leadership of the Intelligence, in order to unite the observation of Things, the discovery of Laws, the analysis of Ideas…" (2008b, p. 69). It can be based, rather, on "involuntary signs that resist the sovereign organization of language", the result of which "is no longer the world of speeches and of their vertical communications expressing a hierarchy of rules and positions, but the world of anarchic encounters, of violent accidents, with their aberrant transverse communications" (pp. 112–3). This sign language is not the ordinary language of everyday life, in which one has friendly conversations, writes articles and initiates political assemblies. It is a language in which "things or objects present themselves as involuntary signs turned against discourse, sometimes making speech go haywire, sometimes forming a counterlanguage that develops in the silence of encounters" (p. 115). This counterlanguage is not that of philosophy or politics of friendship, a friendly conversation in which the meanings of words and things are agreed upon, but rather what Deleuze and Guattari call "a philosophical language within language" (1996, p. 8): an interaction in which signs are transmitted, demanding to be interpreted, producing problems the sense of which does not stem from common sense but rather resides in the problems themselves, problems that are disseminated in an unexpected, uncontrolled way, like a virus undermining a system incapable of containing it.

To be sure, this sign language can also be a positive, affirmative basis on which new links and connections are constantly being formed – these would be unstable, non-hierarchical ones, unlike relations based on the commonsensical order of roles and positions. This applies also to educational relations: although thought-provoking education has been described in terms of master-apprentice or teacher-student relations, it does not necessarily involve a hierarchy whereby sense Ideas flow top-down: "We learn nothing from those who say: 'Do as I do'. Our only teachers are those who tell us to 'do with me'…" (1995, p. 23). Learning is therefore a mutual process in which the teacher also constantly learns from the student. Accordingly, the traditional roles of teacher and student are undermined and become dynamic, for despite being relative rare, thought-inspiring encounters do not occur only among the knowledgeable. Everyone, in fact, can teach others to swim, and awaken their thinking even against their will, and everyone can become students and start thinking – the Deleuzian thinker is a bona fide layperson, a child who assumes nothing in advance, even an idiot like Melville's Bartleby (Deleuze 1997) or Dostoevsky's Prince Myshkin (Deleuze and Guattari 1996, p. 62), as opposed to the Cartesian subject who thinks "naturally" like everyone else. When we make sense and make each other think, we are teachers, but not in the sense of knowledgeable experts: we are good teachers, in fact, because we are lay, idiot ones. Idiotism is not merely the learner's condition before plunging into the proverbial water, but her mode of existence: she is constantly transformed by learning and thinking, becoming different from herself, without ever becoming a privileged expert occupying a high position in a commonsensical, dogmatic order.

4.6 Conclusion

Deleuzian education that awakens thinking and makes sense is radically different from the mainstream education for thinking, and the type of relationships it envisions between thinkers and learners is radically different from the communities of inquiry commonly described in other discussions of education for thinking (Lipman 2003). The type of thinking addressed almost exclusively by contemporary education for thinking is rational and argumentative, grounded in the *dis*junctive logic of the excluded third, rather than in the Deleuzian *con*junctive logic that acknowledges the plurality of differences (Semetsky 2013, p. 220) and that consequently understands thinking as the independent operation of various cognitive faculties. Whereas communities of inquiry are designed for democratic deliberation and exchange of ideas in order to solve a common problem (Semetsky 2007, p. 10), Deleuze's education for thinking involves involuntary, violent interactions between learners that force them into thinking processes that not only do not construct inter-thinker collaboration, but deconstruct each thinker into a plurality of independent cognitive faculties. The links formed in Deleuze's education for thinking are temporary, and do not cohere around a single point such as collaboration or mutual support. Students and teachers who awaken thinking in one another do not necessarily have much in common, not even the same problems. Theirs is not a "dialogue of perfect equals", but rather they interact through the way they "converge and diverge according to disjunctive syntheses", through the way they are drawn together by things they lack and things they have in excess (Williams 2008, p. 166). Theirs is not a community of preserving or sharing common sense, but a free interaction of thinkers, an assemblage that makes sense.

References

Aristotle. (1957). *On the Soul, Parva Naturalia, on Breath* (W. S. Hett, Trans.). Cambridge, MA: Harvard University Press.

Bogue, R. (2004). Search, swim and see: Deleuze's apprenticeship in signs and pedagogy of the image. *Educational Philosophy and Theory, 36*(3), 327–342.

Bogue, R. (2013). The master apprentice. In I. Semetsky & D. Masny (Eds.), *Deleuze and education* (pp. 21–36). Edinburgh: Edinburgh University Press.

Bolaños, P. A. (2006). Deleuze's sense of "sense" and Nietzsche's nomadic thinking. *Unitas, 79*(3), 569–580.

Bray, P. M. (2012). Deleuze's Spider, Proust's Narrator. *Contemporary French and Francophone Studies, 16*(5), 703–710.

Carol, L. (1984 [1865]). *Alice's adventures in wonderland and through the looking-glass*. New York: Bantam Classics.

Cole, D. R. (2017). Deleuze and learning. In M. A. Peters (Ed.), *In Encyclopedia of educational philosophy and theory*. Singapore: Springer.

Colebrook, C. (2008). Leading out, leading on: The soul of education. In I. Semetsky (Ed.), *Nomadic education: Variations on a theme by Deleuze and Guattari* (pp. 35–42). Rotterdam: Sense Publishers.

Deleuze, G. (1986 [1983]). *Cinema 1: The movement-image* (H. Tomlinson & B. Habberjam, Trans.). Minneapolis: University of Minnesota Press.

Deleuze, G. (1989 [1985]). *Cinema 2: The time-image* (H. Tomlinson & R. Galeta, Trans.). Minneapolis: University of Minnesota Press.

Deleuze, G. (1990 [1969]). *The logic of sense* (M. Lester, & C. Stivale, Trans.). New York: Columbia University Press.

Deleuze, G. (1995 [1968]). *Difference and repetition* (P. Patton, Trans.). New York: Columbia University Press.

Deleuze, G. (1997 [1993]). Bartleby; or, the formula. In *Essays critical and clinical* (D. W. Smith, & M. A. Greco, Trans.). (pp. 68–90). Minneapolis: University of Minnesota Press.

Deleuze, G. (1998 [1988]). *Bergsonism* (H. Tomlinson, & B. Habberjam, Trans.). New York: Zone Books.

Deleuze, G. (2006 [1962]). *Nietzsche and philosophy* (H. Tomlinson, Trans.). New York: Continuum.

Deleuze, G. (2008a [1967]). *Kant's critical philosophy: The doctrine of the faculties* (H. Tomlinson, & B. Habberjam, Trans.). New York: Continuum.

Deleuze, G. (2008b [1964]). *Proust and signs* (R. Howard, Trans.). New York: Continuum.

Deleuze, G., & Guattari, F. (1987 [1980]). *A thousand plateaus: Capitalism and schizophrenia* (B. Massumi, Trans.). Minneapolis: University of Minnesota Press.

Deleuze, G., & Guattari, F. (1996 [1991]). *What is philosophy?* (H. Tomlinson, & G. Burchell, Trans.). New York: Columbia University Press.

Descartes, Renè. 1996 [1641]. *Meditations on first Philosophy*. Trans. John Cottingham. Cambridge: Cambridge University Press.

Dronsfield, J. (2012). Deleuze and the image of thought. *Philosophy Today, 56*(4), 404–414.

Gadamer, H. G. (2004 [1960]). *Truth and method*. (J. Weinsheimer, & D. G. Marshall, Trans.). New York: Continuum.

Gasparatou, R. (2017). On "the temptation to attack common sense". In M. A. Peters (Ed.), *Encyclopedia of educational philosophy and theory*. Singapore: Springer.

Gregoriou, Z. (2004). Commencing the rhizome: Towards a minor philosophy of education. *Educational Philosophy and Theory, 36*(3), 233–251.

Hwu, W.-S. (2004). Gilles Deleuze and Jacques Daignault: Understanding curriculum as difference and sense. In W. M. Reynolds & J. A. Webber (Eds.), *Expanding curriculum theory: Dis/positions and lines of flight* (pp. 181–202). New York: Routledge.

Kant, I. (2002 [1790]). *Critique of the power of judgment* (P. Guyer, & E. Matthews, Trans.). Cambridge: Cambridge University Press.

Kohan, W. O. (2011). Childhood, education and philosophy: Notes on deterritorialization. *Journal of Philosophy of Education, 45*(2), 339–357.

Kumashiro, K. K. (2004). *Against common sense: Teaching and learning toward social justice*. New York: RoutledgeFalmer.

Lecercle, J.-J. (2002). *Deleuze and language*. Basingstoke: Palgrave Macmillan.

Lipman, M. (2003 [1991]). *Thinking in education*. Cambridge: Cambridge University Press.

Masny, D. (2013). Multiple literacies theory: Exploring spaces. In I. Semetsky & D. Masny (Eds.), *Deleuze and education* (pp. 74–93). Edinburgh: Edinburgh University Press.

Masny, D., & Cole, D. R. (Eds.). (2015). *Education and the politics of becoming*. New York: Routledge.

Morss, J. R. (2000). The Passional pedagogy of Gilles Deleuze. *Educational Philosophy and Theory, 32*(2), 185–200.

Munday, I. (2012). Roots and rhizomes – Some reflections on contemporary pedagogy. *Journal of Philosophy of Education, 46*(1), 42–59.

Peirce, C. S. (2011). *Philosophical writings of Peirce* (J. Buchler, Ed.). New York: Dover Publications.

Plato. (1997a). Theaetetus. Trans. J.M. Levett and M. Burnyeat. In J. M. Cooper (Ed.), *Complete works* (pp. 157–234). Indianapolis: Hackett Publishing Company.

Plato. (1997b). Republic. Trans. G. M. A. Grube and C. D. C. Reeve. In J. M. Cooper (Ed.), *Complete works* (pp. 971–1223). Indianapolis: Hackett Publishing Company.

Proust, M. (1992a [1913]). *In search of lost time, Volume I: Swan's Way* (C. K. Scott Moncrieff & T. Kilmartin, Trans.). New York: The Modern Library.

Proust, M. (1992b [1927]). *In search of lost time, Volume VII: Time regained* (S. Hudson, Trans.). Paris: Feedbooks.

Rescher, N. (2005). *Common sense: A new look at an old philosophical tradition*. Milwaukee: Marquette University Press.

Reynolds, W. M., & Webber, J. A. (Eds.). (2004). *Expanding curriculum theory: Dis/positions and lines of flight*. New York: Routledge.

Roy, K. (2005). On sense and nonsense: Looking beyond the literacy wars. *Journal of Philosophy of Education, 39*(1), 99–111.

Semetsky, I. (2003). Deleuze's new image of thought, or Dewey revisited. *Educational Philosophy and Theory, 35*(1), 17–29.

Semetsky, I. (2004). The role of intuition in thinking and learning. *Educational Philosophy and Theory, 36*(4), 433–453.

Semetsky, I. (2007). *Deleuze, education and becoming*. Rotterdam: Sense Publishers.

Semetsky, I. (2013). Deleuze, *Edusemiotics*, and the logic of affects. In I. Semetsky & D. Masny (Eds.), *Deleuze and education* (pp. 215–234). Edinburgh: Edinburgh University Press.

Semetsky, I., & Masny, D. (Eds.). (2013). *Deleuze and education*. Edinburgh: Edinburgh University Press.

Snir, I. (2018). Making sense in education: Deleuze on thinking against common sense. *Studies in Philosophy and Education, 50*(3), 299–311.

Wallin, J. J. (2011). What is? Curriculum theorizing: For a people yet to come. *Studies in Philosophy and Education, 30*(3), 285–301.

Wallin, J. J. (2014). Education needs to get a grip on life. In M. Carlin & J. J. Wallin (Eds.), *Deleuze & Guattari, politics and education: For a people-yet-to-come* (pp. 117–139). London: Bloomsbury.

Williams, J. (2004). *Gilles Deleuze's difference and repetition: A critical introduction and guide*. Edinburgh: Edinburgh University Press.

Williams, J. (2008). *Gilles Deleuze's logic of sense: A critical introduction and guide*. Edinburgh: Edinburgh University Press.

Chapter 5
Jacques Derrida: Thinking Madness in Education

5.1 Introduction

At first glance, thinking occupies a rather marginal place in Jacques Derrida's broad and diverse oeuvre. Deconstruction indeed often deals with the notion of logos – or better, with *logocentrism*, namely the centrality of logos in Western philosophy – but it seems to be interested in it mainly as speech, language, text or even logic, not as thinking per se. Yet in a certain sense deconstruction is all about the rethinking of thinking: it challenges the classical image of the thinking subject and rejects the hierarchical dichotomy between reason and its absence, which narrows thinking down to rationality. Even when Derrida does not write explicitly about thinking, his works may be thought of as thinking about thinking, giving voice to thinking which in itself is a kind of writing. Thus, Derrida's writing, which is always already reading and thinking, is also an invitation to think, read, and write differently – it is a kind of education for thinking.

Education is a less implicit subject in Derrida's work. He was highly interested in questions concerning the teaching of philosophy in schools as well as the nature of the university, and was personally involved in public initiatives and campaigns in educational matters. Unlike his other writings, Derrida's texts on education often appeal to the notion of thinking: it is presented both as the university's most urgent task and as what is missing in the teaching of philosophy in schools. However, perhaps due to the pragmatic and political nature of most of Derrida's texts on education, they do not offer a detailed account of thinking, and this concept is not weaved into the rich texture forming Derrida's reevaluation of Western philosophy. This is perhaps why the notion of thinking is hardly discussed in scholarly work on Derrida and education (Trifonas and Peters 2004; Peters and Biesta 2009; Biesta and Egéa-Kuehne 2011). The present chapter aims at filling this lacuna by reconstructing Derrida's concept of thinking and analyzing its relations to education.

I. Snir, *Education and Thinking in Continental Philosophy*, Contemporary Philosophies and Theories in Education 17,
https://doi.org/10.1007/978-3-030-56526-8_5

The starting point for the discussion is "Cogito and the History of Madness", where Derrida argues against Foucault's reading of Descartes' reference to madness in the first chapter of his *Meditations on First Philosophy*. While Foucault claims that Descartes excludes madness from the *cogito*, constituting a dichotomous opposition between thought and madness, Derrida shows that madness finds its way into the Cartesian *cogito*, into the "I think" and into thought itself. This debate, I argue in the third section, has interesting educational implications: Derrida presents both Foucault and Descartes as teachers who not only provide their students with knowledge but also leave them with the madness required to break discursive boundaries and think for themselves. The fourth section broadens the perspective and examines Derrida's conception of thinking more generally. Following his critique of *phonocentrism*, namely of the superiority of speech over writing, I show that he understands thinking, like every system of signification, as a kind of writing – the thinking subject is in fact a writing subject who does not fully master the meanings of her thoughts. Finally, in the fifth and sixth sections I turn to Derrida's writings on education: I discuss his call for making room in schools for thinking against the predominant "philosophy of the state", and analyze his claim that the university should "blink", look at itself, and think of the conditions making thinking possible within its walls. Mad as these demands may seem, I argue that madness is integral to Derrida's conception of thinking in education.

5.2 Cogito, Reason and Madness

Derrida's text on Foucault and Descartes' *cogito*, originally presented in the form of a public lecture in 1963, is a rather rare appeal by the ultimate postmodern philosopher to both the founding father of modern philosophy and to his own contemporary who is no less famous for his critique of classical modernity. Nevertheless, Derrida chooses to discuss only a small part of Foucault's monumental 1961 book *History of Madness*: the three opening pages of the second chapter – which are no more than a prelude to the "archeological" work on madness, and were not even included in the 1964 abbreviated edition – where Foucault discusses one segment from the first chapter of Descartes' *Meditations*. Derrida addresses, therefore a seemingly marginal part of Foucault's book, in which a seemingly marginal part of Descartes' book is discussed. Yet much is at stake in these readings, which go to the heart of Derrida and Foucault's philosophies as well as their views on thinking.[1]

Foucault sees in Descartes a sign of a decisive moment in the history of madness, where it ceased to be integral to life, one of many possible forms of thinking and

[1] Although Foucault was present in Derrida' 1963 lecture, he did not respond to it until 1972, when he included in a new edition of his book an appendix titled "My Body, This Paper, This Fire" (2006b). Derrida, for his part, did not respond to this appendix until 1991, after Foucault's untimely death (Derrida 1994). The personal relationship between the two was renewed only in 1982, two years before Foucault's death (Macey 1995, pp. 142–5; Nass 1997, pp. 142–3).

being as it had been in the Renaissance; from then on, madness was expelled from rationality, from thought, and people defined as insane were forcefully incarcerated to protect society. When Montaigne, the ultimate Renaissance man, met the mad poet Torquato Tasso, Foucault writes, "there was nothing to assure him that all thought was not haunted by the ghost of unreason" (2006a, pp. 45–6). For the sixteenth century essayist, madness was still a viable possibility of thought, one bordering on genius, harboring secrets other people could not see; it was a different and unusual yet reasonable way to doubt the course of reason. The Renaissance man "was never sure that he was not mad" (p. 46).

Descartes, according to Foucault, marks the beginning of a completely different approach to madness. The possibility of madness is brought up in the *Meditations* shortly after the first skeptical argument, the one concerning sensory deceptions, when Descartes realizes that even if his senses may deceive him concerning distant perceptions this is not the case with close and immediate perceptions such as the existence of his own body:

> How could it be denied that these hands or this whole body are mine? Unless perhaps I were to liken myself to madmen, whose brains are so damaged by the persistent vapours of melancholia that they firmly maintain they are kings when they are paupers, or say they are dressed in purple when they are naked, or that their heads are made of earthenware or that they are pumpkins, or made of glass (1996, p. 13).

The mad, then, are wrong even concerning their own bodies, but Descartes, Foucault argues, does not use the possibility of madness to develop and radicalize doubt. Instead, he turns to the dream argument, using which he doubts the whole of his sense perceptions, leaving intact only the solid foundations dreams cannot create, "the inevitable marks of a truth that dreams themselves can never undo" (2006a, p. 45), namely logic and mathematics. That is to say, for Descartes even the dreamer is not mad, and some of his thoughts are true. Thus, the dream argument lies in the middle, further away from the one concerning sense perceptions but still sane, anchored in reality, containing true thoughts that can be doubted only through the deceiving God argument.

Foucault's analysis concerns the crucial difference he sees in Descartes between dream and madness. While the dream occupies a central place in the famous move of methodical doubt, the possibility of madness is suggested only to be dispensed with immediately: "such people are insane, and I would be thought equally mad if I took anything from them as a model for myself" (1996, p. 13). According to Foucault, therefore, madness is cast away from the stage of Cartesian thought not because some specific aspect of the madman's thought cannot be false, as in the case of the dream, but rather "because I, when I think, cannot be considered insane… it is an impossibility of being mad which is inherent in the thinking subject rather than the object of his thoughts… one cannot suppose that one is mad, even in thought, for madness is precisely a condition of impossibility for thought" (2006a, p. 45).

Unlike dreams, which are a constant, natural possibility of thought and hence capable of founding a rational argument, madness is excluded by the thinking subject. And unlike the age of Renaissance, in which madness penetrated the realm of thought and threatened subjectivity and truth, Descartes articulates a dichotomy between reason and thinking on the one hand and madness on the other. This is a gesture of purging thought of what will be labeled insane, confined, and examined by the science of psychiatry. From now on, "While *man* can still go mad, *thought*, as the sovereign exercise carried out by a subject seeking the truth, can no longer be devoid of reason" (Foucault 2006a, p. 47, emphasis in the original). Modern thought, Foucault says, cannot be mad.

Derrida challenges Foucault's reading of Descartes, or rather Foucault's challenge to the traditional readings of Descartes, which did not attach any significant importance to Descartes' treatment of madness (Derrida 2006b, p. 57). The movement of doubt at the first *Meditation*, according to Derrida, by no means excludes madness but rather embraces it in its two crucial moments, the one Derrida calls "natural" and the one he calls "metaphysical" for its reliance on supernatural hypotheses such as the deceiving God or evil genius.

Natural doubt is suspicion of sensual perceptions. According to Derrida, the possibility of dreaming is the apex of natural doubt, the ultimate radicalization of false perceptions, because the true elements in the dream – logic and mathematics – are not natural or sensory at all but rather "intelligible" (2006b, p. 59), namely founded on thought. Hence, while Foucault claims that Descartes renounces the possibility of madness and settles for the more moderate possibility of dreaming, Derrida argues that the dream in fact takes madness a decisive step forward. While the madman is wrong regarding *some* of his sense perceptions – he is delusional regarding his status, clothes or body – "In dreams, the *totality* of sensory images is illusory" (2006b, p. 58; emphasis in the original). The dream excludes any knowledge derived from the senses, while "madness is only a particular case, and, moreover, not the most serious one, of the sensory illusion" (p. 60). In other words, the dream is a "hyperbolical exasperation" of madness: "the dreamer is madder than the madman" (p. 61).

Furthermore, madness is to be found also in the stage of "metaphysical" doubt, in the skeptical argument directed not at sense perceptions but at the intelligible elements that are true even in a dream. This argument rests, as is well known, on the possibility of the existence of an evil genius or deceiving God able to make the thinker err even when making mathematical calculations or logical inferences. This God or genius, according to Derrida, evokes "the possibility of a *total madness*" (2006b, p. 63), a radical, complete disruption from which nothing escapes:

> [A] madness that is no longer a disorder of the body, of the object, the body-object outside the boundaries of the *res cogitans*, outside the boundaries of the policed city, secure in its existence as thinking subjectivity, but is a madness that will bring subversion to pure thought and to its purely intelligible objects, to the field of its clear and distinct ideas, to the realm of mathematical truths which escape natural doubt (p. 64).

Unlike the madness of the dream that exaggerates sensory madness while keeping pure thought safe and sane, the deceiving God represents the possibility of *total* madness because it is the madness of thought itself: "everything that was previously set aside as insanity is now welcomed into the most essential interiority of thought" (p. 64).

Hence, even the certainty of the *cogito* is not free of madness: "The certainty thus attained need not be sheltered from an emprisoned madness, for it is attained and ascertained within madness itself" (p. 67); thought can confirm its own existence to itself even from within the most extreme madness evoked by the genius, the *cogito* "is valid *even if* I *am mad*, even if my thoughts are completely mad" (p. 67; emphasis in the original). Thus, while Foucault interprets Descartes as saying "I think, therefore I am not mad", Derrida understands him as saying "Whether I am mad or not, *Cogito, sum*" (p. 68); according to Foucault, Descartes expels madness from thought, while according to Derrida in the cogito madness is "only one case of thought (within thought)" (p. 68).

In Derrida's reading the *cogito* is therefore a zero point in which reason and madness are intertwined as the distinction between them has not yet been determined – a moment preceding the split or uncoupling, as well as confinement and violence. This split, of the kind Foucault ascribed to the "classical" age of the seventeenth century and described in his unclassical reading of Descartes, has to take place nevertheless. For mad *cogito*, completely idiosyncratic in its madness, is necessarily prior to or beyond language and meaning: "if discourse and philosophical communication (that is, language itself) are to have an intelligible meaning, that is to say, if they are to conform to their essence and vocation as discourse, they must simultaneously in fact and in principle escape madness" (p. 65). Madness, which is not alien to thought, does have a voice, but one it is impossible to make sense of, understand and communicate to others. This voice, therefore, must be silenced for any communication to take place. Language, understanding and communication cannot bear the voice of madness, and they demand that thought be purified of it: "speech… is able to open the space for discourse only by emprisoning madness" (p. 74). Discursive, communicative space "carries normality within itself" (p. 65), namely obeys common rules of reasonableness. Language and meaning, in other words, are essentially common – at least potentially – and must be based on a "normality" excluding madness, excluding meaninglessness, forcing a split between sanity and its absence.

This is why the *cogito* on its own, in its madness, cannot be the foundation of subjectivity, of the *res cogitans* that continuously exists and thinks: "if the Cogito is valid even for the maddest madman, one must, in fact, not be mad if one is to reflect it and retain it, if one is to communicate it and its meaning" (p. 70). The thought of the *cogito* is (always also) mad and therefore cannot be part of a train of thought, a stream of consciousness or a dialogue between me and myself: "if the Cogito is valid even for the madman, [then] to be mad… is not to be able to reflect and to say the Cogito, that is, not to be able to make the Cogito appear as such for an other; an other who may be myself" (p. 71). In the *cogito*, who thinks itself without speaking to or reflecting on itself, thought can be mad, it *is* mad no less than it is reasonable; but for thought to have meaning, for it to be welcomed into language and discourse, into the rational subjectivity of the "I think", it must purge itself of madness.

Moreover, Derrida points out that the *cogito* is valid only at the very instant it is thought, when thought thinks itself (p. 70). It is out of time – for any past memory may be an illusion, a delusion caused by the evil genius – and out of history, of Foucault's "archeology", which is necessarily logos, assuming sane, rational discourse. Descartes cannot remain in this unstable, "hyperbolical" point not only because of the psychological anxiety it involves but primarily because it refuses all continuity and durability. For continuity to be possible and for memory to be valid, for there to be time and history, it is necessary to decide on reason and exclude madness. Descartes escapes this mad hyperbolical zero point with the aid of God – through the validity a benevolent God can grant his continuous existence in time, and no less important, through the rational argumentation used to prove God's existence (p. 71). God makes it possible for me to lock madness away and be a rational, stable subject: He guarantees that my reasoning is valid, that I do not delude myself when I remember my past arguments, and that the conclusions I draw are solid and meaningful. Madness is thereby excluded not only from discursive space, but also from time and history.

Hence, although Foucault is right to say that a confinement of madness took place, he is wrong in ascribing to Descartes and the seventeenth century a privileged status in this regard. The confinement of madness is not unique to Descartes and "the classical age", for "it belongs to the meaning of meaning" (p. 65). This does not mean, to be sure, that Foucault got the date wrong, that the confinement of madness took place in some earlier time, giving way to a sane, peaceful history of rational thought. For if the *cogito* is a zero point prior to history, obviously this priority cannot be temporal – the zero point cannot belong to a time before time. The confinement of madness that makes discourse and history possible must take place at every moment anew, and madness can rear its head at any moment. Even the *cogito* is not entirely unique to Descartes, and reappears in different times, for example in Augustin and Husserl. Each age, each discourse, has its own form of madness: madness has no single, fixed meaning, "it simply says the other of each determined form of the logos" (p. 71). Though confined, in other words, madness is never completely excluded, overcome, forgotten in some pre-historical past – it is rather internal to any discourse, including that of philosophy and science, inseparable from any subjectivity, including that of the rational thinker (Judovitz 1989, p. 46). It is present by way of being absent, opening the way for history and meaning without actually residing in them, an other that is part of any self.

Foucault's biggest mistake, from Derrida's perspective, is the assumption that a historical period – such as the classical age of the seventeenth century – is a total structure, a coherent whole the foundations of which mutually support each other. This assumption is evident, according to Derrida, in Foucault's inability to determine whether the confinement of madness he finds in Descartes is the *cause* for the medical and political developments described in *Madness and Civilization*, or merely their effect or symptom. In fact, this question should be meaningless for Foucault, for in a structural conception there are no causes and effects, only elements and relations (Derrida 2006b, p. 52). The major problem with this structuralist approach, according to Derrida, is the inability to account for changes, renewals and crises, such as those discussed by – and performed by – thinkers like Descartes and Husserl.

In Derrida's understanding, on the other hand, a structure or discourse is never entirely stable, for it is necessarily haunted by madness it can never fully master, which constantly challenges and unsettles it from within. But this constant struggle between discourse and madness, and the eternal return of confinement, are what allow for movement and change – madness keeps challenging discourse, pushing it forward, demanding action and reaction. Hence, philosophy "lives only by emprisoning madness, but… [it] would die as thought, and by a still worse violence, if a new speech did not at every instant liberated previous madness while enclosing within itself, in its present existence, the madman of the day" (2006b, p. 74). That is to say, madness is the productive element needed for the movement and renewal of any structure, philosophy and thought. Without madness, there would be no thinking, at least not living, moving, creative thinking.

There is no room here for a detailed discussion of Foucault's reply to Derrida in the 1973 appendix to *Madness and Civilization*, but its main point is worth mentioning, for it touches the heart of Derrida's view of thinking. According to Foucault, the biggest problem in Derrida's reading of Descartes, which is typical of Derrida's work in general, is that he focuses exclusively on the text, ignoring the fact that each text is a product of "discursive practices" that are not only linguistic utterances but rather a complex array of power relations, oppressive actions, exclusions and classifications (Gleitman 2006, p. 23). Derrida, in other words, overlooks the practical aspect of the text, namely the way it influences and is influenced by discursive events external to it. He thereby inherits what Foucault describes in "The Order of Discourse" as the dominant trend in Western philosophy since Socrates and Plato: concealing discourse by turning it into a set of signifiers. Ever since the sophists were muzzled by Socrates, argues Foucault (1982), "Western thought has taken care to ensure that discourse should occupy the smallest possible space between thought and speech" (p. 65). The philosophical tradition reduces discourse to a mediator between thinking and speech, a kind of neutral space through which thoughts smoothly pass on their way to becoming words. This approach turns discourse from a set of actions and events into nothing more than "a thought dressed in its signs and made visible by means of words" (p. 65). Foucault concludes:

> I am in agreement [with Derrida] on one fact at least: that it was not at all on account of their inattentiveness that classical scholars omitted, before Derrida and like him, this passage from Descartes. It is part of a system, a system of which Derrida is today the most decisive representative, in its waning light: a reduction of discursive practices to textual traces; the elision of events that are produced there, leaving only marks for a reading; the invention of voices behind the text, so as not to have to examine the modes of implication of the subject in discourses; the assignation of the originary as said and not-said in the text in order to avoid situating discursive practices in the field of transformation where they are carried out (2006b, p. 573).

Foucault, then, accuses Derrida of not seeing what is outside the text, of overlooking the dynamics of power that lies in the actual, material world beyond pure thought and language.

While various scholars took Foucault's reply to be convincing (Sprinker 1980), I believe that our discussion above already indicates that it may not do justice to

Derrida: indeed, Derrida is true to his saying that "there is no outside-text" (1997, p. 158). Rather, "text" for him is not a product of closed, stable linguistic system, but is constituted by a discourse that excludes whatever it considers to be mad, to be an "other" with whom it is impossible to think or speak; yet it never altogether dispenses with this other, with which it has a relationship that is all but purged of power and oppression. Is this enough to repel Foucault's critique? Does the unthought "other" of discourse, for Derrida, include the discursive practices and mechanisms of power Foucault claims he overlooks? I leave these questions open for the time being, only to return to them towards the end of this chapter.

5.3 Madness and Pedagogy

Although "Cogito and the History of Madness" is not about education, it addresses pedagogy – or rather, teacher-student relations – from the very beginning. Derrida opens his lecture by saying he "had the good fortune to study under Michel Foucault", referring to him as a "master" (*maître*) and to himself as "an admiring and grateful disciple" (2006b, p. 36). It is tempting to overlook this gesture, dismiss it as mere politeness or respectfulness (sincere or not). Proper respect for a colleague one is criticizing, however, does not necessarily involve considering him a master, and in fact, Derrida, who was four years younger than Foucault, was hardly his disciple. Derrida attended only one series of lectures Foucault gave at the École normale supérieure, and by 1963, the time of Derrida's lecture on the *cogito*, he was already a lecturer at the Sorbonne, enjoying an academic prestige not inferior to that of Foucault (Macey 1995, p. 56, pp. 142–3). It is possible, of course, that the lectures at the École normale had a significant influence on Derrida and that he indeed felt indebted to Foucault (Flaherty 1986, pp. 160–1). I suggest, however, that the teacher-student relation Derrida inscribes at the beginning of his text has a *philosophical* significance, namely that the pedagogical dimension is essential to the movement of thought Derrida describes and performs at the same time.[2]

The teacher-student relation appears several more times in Derrida's text, in a context very different from that of his personal relations with Foucault. One of the decisive philosophical moves Descartes makes in the first *Meditation* is described by Derrida as "pedagogical", namely one in which Descartes writes philosophy as if he was a teacher engaged in an educational dialogue with a non-philosopher

[2] Foucault also does not overlook Derrida's pedagogical gesture. He ends his 1972 response by describing Derrida's textual approach as "little pedagogy" that gives the master sovereignty over the text: "I shall say that what can be seen here [in Derrida] so visibly is a historically well determined little pedagogy. A pedagogy that teaches the pupil that there is nothing outside the text, but that in it, in its gaps, its blanks and its silences, there reigns the reserve of the origin; that it is therefore unnecessary to search elsewhere, but that here, not in the words, certainly, but in the words under erasure, in their *grid*, the "sense of being" is said. A pedagogy that gives conversely to the master's voice the limitless sovereignty that allows it to restate the text indefinitely" (2006b, p. 573).

student. I believe there are significant parallels between the two pedagogical relations Derrida portrays in his text – that between Foucault and himself, and that between Descartes and his imaginary student – and this pedagogy is not unrelated to the issue of thinking and madness. I examine first the pedagogical relations between Foucault and Derrida, and then turn to discuss Descartes as pedagogue.

The pedagogic relation between Foucault the teacher and Derrida the student is described in rather harsh terms. Despite the gratitude and debt he expresses to Foucault, Derrida writes that his master's text was for him "intimidating" (2006b, p. 36), and describes his own experience as a disciple as that of an infant who is an "unhappy consciousness" in face of the master's demands. The infant, Derrida writes, "cannot speak and above all must not answer back" (p. 37): the words of the admirable master sound authoritative, totalitarian, silencing; the disciple must listen and passively accept the discourse dictated from above. The master, as Michael Nass points out (1997, pp. 147–9), practices mastery, namely sovereignty and domination over his disciple. Moreover, the voice of the master is internalized, continuing to challenge and silence the disciple even when the pedagogical relations have allegedly ceased and the master is far away, absent, present only through the reproduction of his reflection in the student's consciousness. The tense relations with the master thus become an inseparable part of the disciple himself, an internal struggle he continues to wage until he is ready to break the maser's reflection and start speaking in his own voice (Derrida 2006b, p. 37).

The educational dialogue between master and disciple, therefore, can be read as a paradigmatic case in which an idiosyncratic madness is silenced and confined in order to create a discourse, a common language. Education here means letting the student into an already existing discourse, through the inculcation of some form of thought, some form of logos ("archeo*logy*"). Hence, educating a student involves silencing some of his voices, declaring some of his (actual or possible) thoughts mad to make him think properly. When Derrida tries to break away from the shadow of the teacher, to become a philosopher and a thinker with his own voice, he must set something of this confined madness free. The Derridean text, therefore, is made possible through a double relation to Foucault's teaching and Foucault the teacher: the teacher first educates the student, provides him with knowledge and a proper way of thinking, and then the student challenges the teacher, goes against him to develop his own unique voice, namely think by himself. A look at how Derrida thinks also of Descartes as a teacher will help us see that the master can be not only the authoritative figure against whom the student rises, but also the one providing the means for such act.

The Cartesian move Derrida describes as pedagogical appears in the very same paragraph in which madness is explicitly mentioned in the first *Meditation*: right after the argument saying that we cannot trust our senses, and before the dream argument. Foucault, as you may recall, argued that Descartes brought up the possibility of madness only to get rid of it, for unlike the man of the Renaissance the Cartesian *res cogitans* could not be mad. Against this, Derrida describes the example of madness as "a rhetorical and pedagogical movement" (2006b, p. 55) leading to the dream argument and making it possible. In this paragraph, Descartes writes:

> Yet although the senses occasionally deceive us with respect to objects which are very small or in the distance, there are many other beliefs about which doubt is quite impossible, even though they are derived from the senses – for example, that I am here, sitting by the fire, wearing a winter dressing-gown, holding this piece of paper in my hands, and so on (1996, pp. 12–13).

Doubting these and similar things is insane, "and I would be thought equally mad" (p. 13), to refuse to believe in them.

The key to understanding the pedagogical sense of this paragraph lies, according to Derrida, in its opening word, "Yet" (in the Latin original, *sed forte*, which Derrida points out that Descartes' contemporary French translator left untranslated). This word indicates that the paragraph that follows is a pretended objection to the Cartesian doubt, which Descartes puts in the mouth of an imaginary interlocutor who is not a philosopher and who finds the Cartesian doubt unnatural and insane:

> He [Descartes] pretends to put to himself the astonished objection of an imaginary nonphilosopher who is frightened by such audacity and says: no, not all sensory knowledge [is called into doubt], for then you would be mad and it would be unreasonable to follow the example of madmen, to put forth the ideas of madmen (2006b, p. 61).

The example of madness, in other words, is allegedly voiced by someone objecting to Descartes, refusing to accept the possibility that immediate sensory perceptions are false and reminding Descartes he is not mad to keep him on firm, natural ground. However, Descartes articulates this voice only to overcome it, to win over it in its own natural ground:

> Descartes *echoes* this objection: since I am here, writing, and you understand me, I am not mad, nor are you, and we are all sane… Descartes acquiesces to this natural point of view, or rather he feigns to rest in this natural comfort in order better, more radically and more definitively, to unsettle himself from it and to discomfort his interlocutor. So be it, he says, you think that I would be mad to doubt that I am sitting near the fire, etc., that I would be insane to follow the example of madmen. I will therefore propose a hypothesis which will seem much more natural to you, will not disorient you, because it concerns a more common, and more universal experience than that of madness: the experience of sleep and dreams (Derrida 2006b, p. 61).

This, then, is a pedagogical move in which the philosopher, namely Descartes, leads the non-philosopher, who is skeptic regarding skeptical arguments, to the desired conclusion, namely to accepting the possibility that all sense perceptions are false. Descartes puts on the textual stage a little pedagogical drama to educate the reader, who might also be a non-philosopher, and draw him into the Cartesian philosophical discourse. The uneducated disciple insists that madness be rejected only to find himself at the end of the lesson "madder than the madman", doubting all sense perceptions (and later also mathematics and logic) and not only some perceptions like the madman he summoned.

Descartes the teacher educates, therefore, in what seems to be a manipulative, oppressive manner, no less than Foucault the teacher: he leads his student to accept a certain conclusion, a certain discourse – the one we call Cartesian, perhaps even modern philosophy – despite his initial reluctance. The Cartesian educational manipulation is complex, however, as Descartes does not only exclude madness from the thought of his student but rather inscribes it at the heart of the discourse he establishes and teaches. Cartesian philosophy, we will be mad to forget, never overcomes madness, and it remains its source of vitality, an irreducible element within discourse that allows an individual to pave his own way within or outside of it. That is to say, in the educational act in which Descartes brings his student into discourse, imprisons his madness and gives him a form of rationality, he also leaves him with the gift of madness, or better – leaves madness in him, in the *cogito* that is the eternal zero point accompanying him wherever he thinks he goes. Thanks to this gift, which always already belonged to the student, Descartes the teacher does not turn his student into a rational subject identical in any way to all others, but rather leaves him with the possibility of breaking free at any moment in his own way, through his own madness – namely allows him also to think for himself. According to Derrida's reading, at least as I read it, the education offered by Descartes the teacher simultaneously closes down and opens up, introduces the student into a form of thought while making it possible for him to transcend or even change it.

Is this not what Foucault the teacher did as well? He let his student, Derrida, into a certain discourse while providing (or leaving) him with the mad possibility of thinking in his own way and breaking out of that discourse. When Derrida starts to think, to write and to speak for himself, he not only challenges Foucault but also makes use of what Foucault has given him, of the madness present within Foucauldian teaching – not only as an object of specific study, but as a refusal to formulate a logical, hermetically closed system of thought. The student breaks out by using what is already inside him, and inside what the teacher has taught or shared with him. Derrida's rebellion against the sovereign master appears to be also an act of loyalty, recognition that beneath the authoritative teaching there is also a seed that can grow on the student's own terms. The gratitude Derrida expresses to Foucault the teacher, according to this reading, is by no means empty politeness but an honest recognition of teaching which is at the same time instructive and enabling, confining and providing the means for breaking out.

Michal Gleitman (2006) suggests that Derrida's own style of writing can be understood as practicing such pedagogy, which not only teaches but also invites the students, namely the readers or listeners, to think for themselves. While Sprinker (1980, p. 77) argues that Derridean deconstruction has become an orthodoxy closing off avenues of thought, Gleitman writes that

> in its refusal to draw a clear, unequivocal line of argument and in maintaining vagueness and polysemy, Derrida's writing seems intuitively to be a very open one, allowing a plurality of avenues of thought, without forcing a single logic while oppressing other alternative forms… Derrida's style of writing opens various options and directions, and even if this writing form stems from some obsessive need for mastery and neutralization of the element of surprise, still one of its outcomes is a richness of possibilities. By doing so, Derrida poses a very different model of a teacher from the one he describes at the beginning of his lecture – one that opens to his students new possibilities from which the student is invited to choose as he likes and follow the lead of the teacher. (2006, pp. 96–7, my translation)

I suggest that this pedagogical pattern, embodied by these very different teachers – Descartes, Foucault and Derrida himself – reveals something essential about the way the latter thinks of education and thinking. Education should initiate into discourse but also provide the means for breaking out of it; let the student into a discipline while leaving the borderline between what within and outside it indeterminate. Thinking, for its part, is in need of such education because it needs both a discourse able to make it intelligible, meaningful and understandable, and madness allowing it to move by itself, in its own way.

5.4 Thinking as Writing

Derrida rarely formulates general theses, and his deconstruction is not a theory or philosophical system but rather a strategy, an approach to reading and writing philosophy. For this reason, deconstruction is almost never presented as an independent, abstract set of ideas and arguments. It prefers to be written through reading other texts, between theirs lines, parasitical on the concepts and arguments of others. Derrida's insights and arguments are by no means accidental, however; they are reiterated in each reading, each time challenging in a different way the fundamental presuppositions of Western metaphysics. The discussion of the Cartesian *cogito* is no exception: the deep connection between reason and madness within thought, formulated through the reading of Descartes (and Foucault) is traceable in other texts by Derrida, written through reading other texts and using different vocabularies.

Although the concept of thinking rarely surfaces in Derrida's writings, it is there even when it is absent, rethought through the deconstruction of the key hierarchical dichotomies organizing traditional philosophy. A brief look into some of the texts in which Derrida discusses the nature of language and the relations between speech and writing will allow us to understand Derrida's conception of thinking more generally, and examine its difference from the traditional conception of thinking. More specifically, I will show that for Derrida thinking, like language itself, is a kind of writing.

Emma Williams calls the prevailing understanding of thinking, anchored in the foundations of the Western metaphysical tradition, the "rationalistic" conception (2016, p. 3; see also Chap. 1). According to this conception, she explains, words are signs understood as "*representations* of preformed ideas that have come into the head as a result of sensory experience" (p. 131, emphasis in the original). That is to say, when the subject thinks, she forms ideas, which make present in her consciousness objects from the "real" world; then, in order to communicate her ideas to others, she dresses them up as words, which in turn allow the addressee to form the same ideas in her own mind, and think of the same objects. Language, therefore, is but a secondary, transparent mediator of meanings and ideal contents, namely of pre-linguistic thoughts.

Derrida is especially interested in the status of writing in this rationalistic or idealistic conception. Importantly, he argues that language is traditionally understood primarily as speech: it is not only a belated but also an unnecessary addendum to speech, unnecessary for linguistic communication; the written word is but a symbol of the spoken, living one, a secondary representation of a secondary representation, a symbol of a symbol. Writing, Derrida writes, was allegedly invented and put to use only thanks to the technical advantage it provides: "Meaning, the content of the semantic message, is thus transmitted, *communicated*, by different *means*, by technically more powerful meditations, over a much greater distance" (1984, p. 311, emphasis in the original). Writing, in other words, helps bridge over a distance or a gap, mediating between addressor and addressee when they are not present together.

This advantage of writing is also thought to be the origin of communication problems, however, which do not occur when speaking. The meanings writing communicates are more ambiguous and open to misinterpretations than in the case of spoken communication. To use Williams' example (2016, p. 139), when a friend tells me she had a bad day and I reply, "Tell me about it", did I mean to ask for more information, or did I say I knew how she felt? If we are talking face to face, most likely she would be able to figure out my intention from the context (prior knowledge, tone of voice, body language), or simply ask for clarification. But if this were a written communication, say on email or text messages, the addressor's absence makes misinterpretation much more likely. Writing, therefore, is not only secondary to but also "contaminates" the process of communication.

Thought appears in this rationalistic conception to be the ideal content in need of being communicated with minimum distortion. The process of thinking is accordingly understood as inner speech – whether in the form of interior monologue as in Husserl or dialogue as in Plato and Arendt (see Chap. 3) – in which the thinker/speaker is transparent to herself, namely in full control of and fully understanding what she means and thinks. Thinking, in other words is speaking made perfect. The spoken word, in this approach, "is the signifying substance *given to consciousness* as that which is most intimately tied to the thought of the signified concept. From this point of view, the voice is consciousness itself" (Derrida 1981, p. 22, emphasis in the original).

This simple, seemingly self-evident view characterizes all of Western philosophy, according to Derrida. He finds it in philosophers of various periods such as Plato, Condillac, Rousseau, de Saussure and Husserl, to name a few; in fact, he finds no exception. Deconstruction challenges this phonocentrism, namely the traditional precedence of speech over writing, of audible, temporal phoneme over visible, spatial grapheme. Derrida does not argue that writing is as good as speech, that there is enough presence in writing, but the opposite: that the absence characteristic of the structure of writing is generalizable, "valid not only for all the orders of 'signs' and for all languages in general, but even… for the entire field of what philosophy would call experience" (1984, pp. 316–7). To be sure, this does not mean that writing precedes speech in some temporal sense – that it was invented before speech or that we learn how to write before we learn how to speak – but rather that the characteristics traditionally ascribed to writing are in fact also attributable to speech, to experience, and as I will demonstrate also to thought.

As we have seen, while speech presupposes the co-presence of speaker and hearer, writing functions also in case of absence: the written sign bears meaning even if the addressor, the addressee or both are not there to breathe life into it. This absence, Derrida writes, "is not a continuous modification of presence; it is a break in presence, 'death'… inscribed in the structure of the mark" (1984, p. 316). That is to say, the absence characterizing writing is not merely a deferral in the functioning of the mediating sign transferring meanings from one consciousness to the other. Rather, writing functions also when absence is radical or complete, when addressor and addressee are "dead" or no longer relevant. To return to Williams' example, the written text message "Tell me about it" remains meaningful even if the one who wrote it and the one supposed to receive it are gone, even if the message is found on a device whose owner is unknown. In this case, it is impossible to trace an original meaning in the consciousness of the addressor, and still the marks bear meanings. In fact, the meaning of the message is open to countless interpretations, for we can graft it into various possible contexts.

Derrida's point is that such a seemingly unusual case in fact reveals the fundamental structure of writing, its ability to function without any present origin: "one can always lift a written syntagma from the interlocking chain in which it is caught or given without making it lose every possibility of functioning, if not every possibility of 'communicating', precisely. Eventually, one may recognize other such possibilities by inscribing or *grafting* it into other chains. No context can enclose it" (1984, p. 317, emphasis in the original). The written sign can have a life of its own; it can bear meanings irreducible to what the actual addressor meant. Derrida calls this characteristic of the written sign "iterability": iterability is "the possibility of being repeated in the absence not only of its referent, which goes without saying, but of a determined signified or current intention of signification, as of every present intention of communication" (p. 318). To be sure, this does not mean simply that misunderstandings or misinterpretations are always possible, but rather that the idea of one fixed meaning, of a stable original meaning, appears to be unfounded; "there can, in fact, be no 'origin' that founds language" (Williams 2016, p. 147).

Derrida's boldest claim, to reiterate, is that absence and iterability characterize *every* linguistic sign, not only written ones. Even the spoken word, allegedly characterized by full presence of speaker and hearer, is open to the same indeterminacy of meaning. Let us take one of Derrida's own examples this time, in which he analyses Husserl's discussion of agrammaticality, namely linguistic combinations that have no referent, like "green is or" (1984, p. 319). For Husserl, such word combinations that express no idea cannot be communicated and are no longer language. But even "green is or" can function and bear meaning when grafted in different contexts: in French, for example, "*le vert est ou*" may be heard as "*le vert est où?*", namely "where has the green (of the grass) gone?" – a possibility that is opened, interestingly, in spoken rather than written language – and it can also function as in Husserl himself, as an example of agrammaticality (p. 320). The possibility of such "citational grafting", of recording the sign and putting it to use in new contexts, Derrida explains, belongs to every sign, constitutes it as writing and makes the structure of writing the inner logic of all language and meaning.

The iterability inherent in language means that ambiguity, misinterpretations and failures are integral to every linguistic use. Contrary to common belief, however, this is also what allows language to function. Williams writes that "words function neither by virtue of an original inner idea nor because of the presence of some appropriate external context, but rather on account of their iterability, that is, the possibility of their being put to use in different circumstances" (2016, p. 184). Namely, that which makes language possible also makes it open, flexible and unstable: "the iterability that is the condition of possibility of language – that is, of our speaking and writing and doing all those things we ordinarily do with words – is at the same time the condition of its *impossibility* – that is, of its never functioning mechanistically, fully under our control, in the ways we are inclined to imagine" (p. 184; emphasis in the original).

This new, radical understanding of language necessarily changes how we understand the relation between language and thought as well as the nature of thought itself. While the rationalistic conception of language understands it as a medium communicating prefigured thoughts and ideas from one consciousness to the other, Derrida's attack on phonocentrism implies that language takes active part in any generation of meanings, that no thought or idea is independent of the context to which it is grafted and re-grafted. Hence, it is impossible to hold on to the conception separating thought from language, to think of pre-linguistic thought and neutral language. Language does not merely represent or communicate thought but rather constitutes it as meaningful: "Meaning must await being said or written in order to inhabit itself, and in order to become, by differing from itself, what it is: meaning" (Derrida 2006a, p. 11).

This means that thinking itself is a kind of writing: there is always an irreducible absence, a difference that is also deferral (*differance*) within thought or between thought and thinker – the thinker is not fully present when she thinks – she is not the ultimate source of her thoughts, not completely in control of their meaning. When I think, I do not say a monologue or engage in a dialogue with myself, but rather write signs the meaning of which I myself do not fully know in advance: "My own words take me by surprise and teach me what I think", in the words of Merleau-Ponty quoted by Derrida (Derrida 2006a, p. 11). Understood as writing, language is essentially "un-masterable", because it has "the potentiality to forge connections that we do not and cannot foresee" (Williams 2016, p. 184). Much like for Nietzsche (see Chap. 1), for Derrida language dictates thought for us; the point here, however, is not the structure of grammar but rather that of writing. Unlike the common image of a rational, self-conscious subject who controls his thoughts and stands behind the meanings he expresses, in Derrida we see a *writing subject* whose thoughts are determined by language and not only by her own will and consciousness. The meanings of that subject's thoughts depend on the context into which they are grafted no less than on her original intentions.

The absence in thought, in the consciousness of the writing subject, is exactly what we have seen in Descartes' concept of madness – an idiosyncratic, uncontrollable element, the other of thought that is inseparable from thought. As in the case of madness, the absence that does not allow the thinking subject to be fully present in thought does not only hinder thought and prevent it from flowing, but also keeps it from becoming petrified, from repeating itself endlessly. Absence pushes thought forward, allows it to be creative, to differ from itself: "only *pure absence*... can *inspire*, in other words, can *work*, and then make one work" (Derrida 2006a, p. 7, emphasis in the original). Gayatry Spivak writes that in Derrida's text "'penser' (to think) carries within itself and points at 'panser' (to dress a wound); for does not thinking seek forever to clamp a dressing over the gaping and violent wound of the impossibility of thought?" (1997, p. lxxxvi); thinking, which is writing, is possible only thanks to its conditions of *im*possibility, and rationality is possible only thanks to *ir*rationality, namely madness.

* * *

We have seen in Derrida's discussion of the *cogito* that discourse, communicated language, excludes madness without altogether getting rid of it. Madness remains part of thought, continues to haunt discourse, to undermine it and push it to transform and renew itself. This allows us to understand Derrida's view of writing: he does not write that communication is impossible, that meanings are impossible to share, or that people never understand each other. To a certain extent, linguistic communication and mutual understanding occur constantly, but what enables them is also what prevents them from functioning perfectly, and this is what allows discursive structures to change and be renewed.

Furthermore, Derrida's understanding of thinking as writing does not mean that thinking cannot be reflective or that critical thought is impossible. Thinking certainly can, and as we shall see, must look at itself and examine the power relations surrounding and inherent to it. It does mean that when thinking looks at itself, it might see the madness inscribed in it, and that it must also examine the linguistic and discursive power relations directing and making itself possible. In the following two sections, we will see how thinking is put to use by Derrida when discussing educational questions.

5.5 Teaching Philosophy and Thinking

The notion of thinking is central to both educational issues Derrida engages with: teaching philosophy in schools and the role of the university. Although the former is concerned with schoolchildren and the latter with adult students, they are not unrelated. Derrida's texts on these two issues from 1974–1990 were brought together in a two-volume book titled *Right to Philosophy*. As Derrida explains, this title refers not only to the right of the philosophical profession or to the right of every person to practice philosophy (Cahen 2001, p. 13), but also to whether it is possible to go "*straight* to it" (Derrida 2002a, p. 3, emphasis in the original) – to philosophize directly, without detours and without the mediation of some teaching or institution. Derrida's answer to this question, as we shall see, is negative: he argues that philosophy is *always* mediated, *necessarily* related to teachings and institutions, just as any institution or teaching necessarily inheres philosophy. The discussion of teaching philosophy in schools, we shall see, is tightly connected to the institutional question that is taken up in the discussion of the university.

In the case of both schools and the university, Derrida assigns thinking a key role vis-à-vis philosophy. Nevertheless, he almost never explicitly links these discussions to the challenge his thought poses to the traditional conception of thinking, namely to the connection between thinking and writing and to the place of madness in thinking. In what follows, I discuss these two issues one after the other, attempting to analyze the relations between thinking, education and philosophy, and point to the role of madness in school and university education. In each case, I do not go straight to thinking but rather present Derrida's discussion through the problematics on which he focuses, attempting to reveal the place of thinking and support my claim that thinking always involves madness.

Derrida's discussions of the teaching of philosophy in schools began as a reaction to government attempts in the early 1970s to reduce the teaching of philosophy in French schools. These attempts culminated in a reform by Minister of Education René Haby, calling to cancel the mandatory teaching of philosophy in the final year of school (the reform was never fully implemented, much thanks to the public critique it drew). Derrida took active part in the campaign against the Haby reform. He was a central co-founder of GREPh (French acronym for Group Investigating the Teaching of Philosophy) in January 1975, and often wrote and spoke publicly on the subject (Cahen 2001, p. 15). As shown below, Derrida's defense of the teaching of philosophy is in large part a call for educating *against* philosophy – or at least against traditional philosophy – which is why he phrases it also as a call for educating for deconstruction, or simply thinking.

The main arguments raised against the teaching of philosophy in schools (or more precisely – for its significant reduction), as Derrida presents them, can be divided in two. First, philosophy is not practical enough and therefore less important than other, more applicable sciences (Derrida 2002e, p. 159). Second, schoolchildren are not yet ready to study philosophy, namely, they are not emotionally and intellectually mature enough to deal with its challenges; moreover, philosophy is irrelevant to the twentieth century, and may even be dangerous to young minds. Both these arguments rely on distinctions that seem to be natural and self-evident: not only between practical and impractical knowledge or between relevant and irrelevant skills, but also between philosophical teaching and teaching without philosophy, and between those ready for philosophy and those who are not. Derrida challenges all of these distinctions, and points to their common root: they share the assumption of a clear line separating the philosophical from the non-philosophical, or the places proper and improper for philosophy. That is to say, the distinctions underlying the Haby reform and the public discourse it relied on assume that there is a "neutral" place untouched by philosophical speculations – be it non-philosophical scientific knowledge or natural, innocent childhood not yet committed to any specific philosophy – and that this place must be kept this way for the child's (and philosophy's) best interests.

Philosophy is usually thought of as a discipline not only containing some systematic, encyclopedic worldview, but also as one offering critique, the posing of difficult questions (Biesta and Stams 2001, p. 57). While the critical aspect is the one drawing most of the fire, those calling for reducing (or cancelling) philosophy instruction do not normally present themselves as objecting to the very idea of critique. They simply argue that the proper *time* for philosophical critique comes only after some fundamental, neutral, non-philosophical knowledge has been acquired, when the mind is no longer naïve and unexperienced but has been properly trained. Against this, Derrida argues that philosophical critique is never pure, never ex nihilo: each critical question necessarily presupposes something, rests on something. Philosophy always presupposes "traditions and the knowledge of questioning" (Derrida 2002a, p. 16), namely truths taken to be self-evident, guiding each question and critique (Biesta and Stams 2001, p. 65). "When I say I pose questions", Derrida writes, "I pretend to say nothing that would be a thesis. I pretend to pose or posit something that at bottom would not pose or posit itself… [But] Of course, even in the barest, most formal, most questioning form itself… there is no question that is not constrained by a program, informed by a system of forces, and invested with a battery of determining, selecting, sifting forms" (2002b, p. 87). Much like Deleuze (see Chap. 4), Derrida argues that presuppositions taken as self-evident are part of each philosophy no less than questions and critique; it is impossible to separate philosophy from "pre-philosophical" presuppositions. Moreover, such presuppositions, which are philosophical no less than pre-philosophical, are present not only in philosophy classes, namely in those bearing the explicit form and name of philosophy. They are interwoven into the foundations upon which other disciplines stand: "who can doubt in fact that a very specific philosophy is *already* being taught through French literature, the languages, history, and even the sciences?" (Derrida 2002e, p. 162).

This point is by no means merely theoretical, but also political: Derrida argues that the philosophy implicit in these disciplines is not politically "neutral" but is rather what he calls "the philosophy of the state", reflecting the existing, "imperialist" sociopolitical order of things (2002c, p. 101). This philosophy takes its presuppositions from the world as it is, thereby *making* it self-evident, transparent and immune to philosophical critique – it refrains from criticizing certain presuppositions that make it possible and guide its questions. Philosophical critique, as it is usually understood and practiced, only reproduces the authority and legitimacy of existing powers, as it naturalizes the presuppositions underlying the state as well as the global, colonial relations between states. Postponing the explicit teaching of philosophy, Derrida therefore writes, means that "the 'philosophy class' comes at a time when, empirically and implicitly, but very effectively, the 'philosophy' of the dominant social forces has already done its work through the other disciplines, notably those which in France are the usual preparation for philosophical training, namely the nonscientific disciplines" (2002e, p. 161). By the time the students get to study a class called "philosophy", the philosophy of the state already comes to guide their thoughts and dictate the "critical" questions they ask.

In fact, while much of the educational and philosophical debate revolved around the question of *who* has the right to philosophy (do children have a right to philosophy?), Derrida argued that the very notion of *a* "right to philosophy" and every application of this notion already presuppose philosophy. The paradigmatic case he appeals to in order to demonstrate his claim is the 1789 Universal Declaration of the Rights of Man, on which many rights in twentieth century French political discourse are founded, including the right to education from which the right to philosophy is supposed to be naturally derived (Derrida 2002a, p. 31). According to the Declaration, the Rights of Man are founded on nothing but "natural light", namely on what everybody are supposed to already know intuitively. But according to Derrida, what seems "natural" is always mediated by some preconceptions and understandings, conditioned by a certain language without which the "natural" would not have been self-evident at all; language, as we have seen, writes thought, taking active part in generating the possible meanings of what we think. The notion of human rights is not part of some natural, universal language – it has a history, a genealogy without which it has no right to exist, and this history shapes the philosophy written through this notion (Derrida and Montefiore 2001, p. 178; Egéa-Kuehne 2001, p. 190). Derrida writes that the declaration

> cannot posit and justify a right to instruction and in it, hypothetically, a right to philosophy, without already implying a philosophy, an instruction, in particular an intelligibility determined by its concepts and language. As speech act, such a declaration has always been a group of philosophical statements… [Hence] the access to the declaration, to the content of what it says, which gives the right to all rights, assumes instruction and the knowledge of language. Only instruction, and first of all instruction in language, can make one aware of right, and in particular of the right to instruction (2002a, pp. 32–3).

That is to say, there is no natural man able to intuitively recognize the "rights of man". It is not that the natural man constitutes the declaration, but rather the other way around: the declaration constitutes the natural man; each "natural man" has already undergone teaching, learned language and studied philosophy even if he has never attended a single class – let alone a philosophy class.

A similar argument is raised by Derrida to reject the claim that children under a certain age are not yet ready for philosophy, and should study only non-philosophical classes. The abovementioned preconceptions regarding the natural foundation of philosophy also underlie the image of the one who is ready to take on philosophical studies:

> [T]he figure of a young *man* who, virgin yet fully grown, ignorant and innocent, yet finally mature for philosophy, would begin to pose, without presupposing any knowledge, or rather begin to let be posed for him, the questions of all questions – between fifteen and eighteen years old, *after* puberty, *before* entering into society. Earlier would be perverse or, because of a natural stupidity, impossible. Later would be useless, ridiculous, or harmful (Derrida 2002e, p. 161, emphasis in the original).

Among other things,[3] the description of this figure expresses faith in that it is necessary to start philosophical instruction *before* some prejudices have become solidified in the young person's mind; *before* he has been corrupted by society and its preconceptions. It also highlights, however, that this young person is ready to take

[3] Among them, of course, the fact that the student of philosophy must be a young *man* rather than a woman.

up critical, unsettling philosophical questions only *after* he acquires non-philosophical education. Such general education is supposed to make sure the student does not enter philosophy out of either the follies of early childhood or the vulgar conceptions one learns before going to school. Hence this figure incorporates what Derrida calls "naturalistic mystification", according to which "once prejudices and 'ideologies' have been erased, what will be revealed is the bare truth of an 'infant' always already ready to philosophize and *naturally* capable of doing so" (2002d, p. 121, emphasis in the original).

Recognizing that there is no natural knowledge purged of philosophical presuppositions and hence of philosophy leads Derrida and his GREPh colleagues to argue that it is better to introduce the critical, skeptical dimension of philosophy as soon as possible, so as not to spare even what seems to be the most natural, simple truth. If there is no knowledge and education without philosophy, than "there is no natural age for the practice of philosophy" (2002f, p. 169), and it must be taught in the earliest classes (2002c, p. 111). Critical philosophy, in other words, must also be philosophy for children.

Furthermore, Derrida points out that restricting philosophy to a certain age in fact restricts it to a certain social class, the "social class of philosophy", the class whose young members have what it takes to become "natural", to succeed in the non-philosophical studies seen as conditional to the study of philosophy (2002c, p. 112). The class of philosophy is "a class for one class, bourgeois youth between puberty and their entrance into adult life, with an education that was more literary than scientific, led to consider as natural and eternal a very singular program that is apparently eclectic-baroque but also quite favorable to a particular ideological framework" (2002f, p. 167). It is therefore exclusive in a twofold sense: it excludes from philosophy *whatever* seems to be "unnatural", whatever contradicts (or is in tension with) the philosophy of the state (Derrida 2002a, p. 41), and it excludes from the class of philosophy *whoever* is not part of the philosophical class, the class that knows what should be accepted as natural. This is how the teaching of philosophy becomes – if it has not always been – a means for reproducing and preserving not only the state but also the class of philosophers, the Platonic social hierarchy keeping philosophy for the elites and the elites for philosophy.

It is clear, therefore, that Derrida and GREPh's call was not to preserve the existing condition of the teaching of philosophy against the Haby reform, nor an attempt merely to expand the reach of philosophical teaching to make it accessible to new audiences. The goal, rather, was nothing less than radical transformation of the teaching of philosophy, and with it a transformation of philosophy itself (Derrida 2002e, p. 163).

This is not only about a different method of teaching philosophy, be it anti-imperialist, de-colonial, anti-capitalist or other. In a sense, what is needed is teaching *against* philosophy, or at least against the philosophy of the state, although Derrida stresses that the point is not an attack on philosophy by some non-philosophy (2002f, p. 165). The important struggle is not for or against philosophy, but rather "between forces and their philosophical instances" (p. 172). The kind of philosophy Derrida positions vis-à-vis the philosophy of the state, this philosophy that is also anti-philosophy is sometimes called "deconstruction", and at other times simply "thinking": philosophical teaching that challenges rather than reproduces the philosophy of the state is education for thinking.

Derrida refrains from defining this thinking just as he does philosophy itself, but he insists that it goes further than traditional philosophy, the philosophy of the state, without altogether leaving the domain of philosophy. Such thinking is not committed to the content of any specific philosophy, nor even to the philosophical form of the question, but rather to what he calls "affirmation", the "yes" always already enveloped in each philosophical question, as critical as it may be: "the affirmation with no content than the other, to whom, precisely, a trace is addressed, even if in the dark" (Derrida 2002a, p. 13). That is to say, the thinking Derrida refers to is "attentive to otherness, to the alterity of the other" (Derrida and Montefiore 2001, p. 180). It is committed to the other of philosophy, to the non-philosophical that makes philosophy possible while still eluding it, remaining unthought by it: "Thinking is faithful to an affirmation whose responsibility places it *before* philosophy but also always before there *was* philosophy, thus short of and beyond philosophy, identifiable figures of philosophical identity, the philosophical question about the subject of philosophy, and even the question-form of thinking" (Derrida 2002a, p. 13, emphasis in the original). As Biesta and Stams (2001, p. 86) explain, "the deconstructive affirmation is not simply an affirmation of what is known to be excluded by the system. Deconstruction is an affirmation of what is wholly other (*tout autre*), of what is unforeseeable from the present".

We can see that the "other" that thinking affirms is in fact an expression of the madness discussed in the first two sections of this chapter: the madness inherent to the Cartesian *cogito*, which had to be confined for a space of rational discourse to be opened, but was never fully dispensed with. In an interview with François Ewald, Derrida makes this link between madness and the affirmation of the other explicit:

> For me, there is always, and I believe that there *must be more than one language*, mine and that of the other… and I must try to write in such a way that my language does not make the language of the other suffer [*souffrir*], that he/she puts up with me [*me souffre*] without suffering [*sans souffrir*] [because of it], receives the hospitality of my language without losing or integrating himself/herself in it. And reciprocally – but reciprocity is not symmetry… This is equivalent to saying that madness, a certain 'madness', *must* watch each and every step, and eventually must watch over thinking, just like reason also does (1995, pp. 290–1, emphasis in the original)

The language of the other, Derrida says, is the voice of madness, of whatever is not fully comprehensible in "my" language, in the language of rational discourse in which I am currently immersed. Hosting the other without assimilating him or her is here not only an ethical imperative, but also a vital need of thinking itself: without affirming the others, listening to their voices and responding to them, thinking only reproduces itself, does more of the same. Hence, madness does not threat thinking but rather looks after it by breathing new life into it.

Institutional philosophy, as the rational discursive space par excellence, cannot give room to madness, and does everything within its power to exclude it. This is exactly how it constructs the discourse regarding the teaching of philosophy in schools: is it not mad to teach philosophy to little children? Is it not clear to any sane person that some minimal liberal education must be acquired before taking on critical philosophical studies? This philosophy is deaf to the voices of the child, of the uneducated, of whoever is not part of the class of philosophy – it silences them to create a rational, coherent, sane discursive space. But madness, as we already know, not only refuses to be completely excluded from discourse, it is in fact essential to its vitality, to its movement, to the possibility of renewing it. It is thinking's responsibility, therefore, to affirm the mad voices, to listen to them and let them into the discourse, and no less important – to affirm the mad *bodies*, the physical presence in the class of philosophy of those figures it is apparently insane to let in there. It must do so, to be sure, not only for the good of the "mad" or the excluded, but rather for philosophy itself – without including the excluded, it will only reproduce itself and perish as thought.

This is precisely why affirming madness allows thinking to say "no" to what institutional philosophy, the philosophy of the state that is being taught in state schools, too often affirms uncritically, namely the authority of the state. Thinking's responsibility is to show "irresponsibility toward the state" (Derrida 2002a, p. 41), disrespect to the existing sociopolitical order. In other words, "'Thinking,' a word that entitles only the possibility of this 'no', must even, in the name of democracy still *to come* as the possibility of this 'thinking', unremittingly interrogate the de facto democracy, critique its current determinations, analyze its philosophical genealogy, in short, deconstruct it" (p. 42, emphasis in the original). Thinking should "break its contract with science or philosophy" (p, 41), as long as science and philosophy remain bound to the state as the source of their legitimacy and resources. Therefore, thinking is inherently political, striving to liberate whoever and whatever philosophy confines in the service of the state; and we must not forget, of course, that the moment the madness liberated by thinking is made present and receives a voice, it becomes part of a discourse, part of philosophy, thereby confining other forms of madness.

How can such thinking, which unlike the philosophy of the state has neither positive doctrine nor a solid foundation from which to take its questions, be taught? For Derrida there is no direct answer, one cannot go straight to the teaching of thinking. Deconstruction is not a philosophical technique and no thinking skills can be learned to practice it. Yet although thinking cannot be taught, it can still be called for; one can create a place for it to dwell in, where it can feel at home. Derrida addresses this question through thinking about the *institutions* in which deconstructive thinking can take place. He writes that we usually assume school walls to be "*external* to the act of philosophizing as publication, the press, the media" (2002a, p. 24), namely, that there is no essential link between philosophy and the institution hosting it – that philosophy can be practiced anywhere, unconditioned by any institution, and when it does enter an institution this need not affect its nature. But deconstruction, according to Derrida, implies also "the *exposure* of this institutional identity of the discipline of philosophy" (2002a, p. 9, emphasis in the original), namely, turning the spotlight to the inseparable link between philosophy and the institution that provides it not only with physical conditions but also with legitimation, with the authority to teach, grant titles, and decide what is included in and excluded from the "discipline". The importance of philosophy in schools notwithstanding, this institution, at least in the last 200 years or so, is undoubtedly the university. We turn now to Derrida's discussion of the place of philosophy and thinking – and consequently of madness – in the university.

5.6 Thinking at the University

Although philosophy can be practiced outside the university – and there have undoubtedly been (and perhaps still are) important philosophers operating outside any formal academic institution – every practice of philosophy in the last two centuries is related in countless ways to how the discipline is defined and taught at the university. Philosophy necessarily responds somehow to academic philosophy, at least by way of challenge and rejection. It is impossible, therefore, to understand what philosophy is – and consequently, how to teach philosophy and encourage philosophical thinking – without looking at the way it is practiced in the university.

Although the university, like any institution, presents itself as neutral, even as natural – an arena in which philosophy can thrive – Derrida argues that it necessarily harbors forces and interests (2002b, p. 69), excluding from its own class of philosophy whatever seems to contradict them. The university, in other words, is simultaneously the condition of possibility as well as the condition of impossibility of philosophy in the present time: it makes philosophy possible and provides it with prestige and legitimation and at the same time polices and confines it. The aim of deconstruction is therefore to think philosophically about whatever remains outside the scope of institutional, academic philosophy, including the academic institution itself and the way it influences philosophy and thinking.

In a 1983 text titled "The Principle of Reason: The University in the Eyes of its Pupils", Derrida asks whether the university today has a *raison d'être* (2004b, p. 129). The answer, if there is one, he argues, passes through the two words making up the French expression, namely reason and being: "the university's reason for being has always been reason itself, and some essential connection of reason to being" (p. 135). That is to say, the university applies reason to being, uses reason to understand what is. The philosophy at the bottom of the university is embodied, therefore in what Leibniz called "the principle of rendering reason", according to which for each true proposition, a reasoned account is possible and must be provided. The being of the university is reasoned by this principle: if there is reason for the university's being, it is that this institution looks for reasons for holding propositions as true.

Adherence to the principle of reason, Derrida argues however, means also turning it at itself, asking questions about this very principle (pp. 137–8): What is the reason for the principle of reason? What founds the foundation of the university? Such questions will not seem empty or tautological if we remember Derrida's claim that there is no natural or neutral place from which one can ask critical questions.

Applying this claim to reason itself means that reason too is never natural, neutral and unbiased: the voice of reason always comes from somewhere, from some philosophical, historical and political presuppositions that are all but necessary. To return to our discussion of the Cartesian cogito, reason always excludes madness, in fact many kinds of madness, in order to appear natural and universal; the excluded madness conditions rational discourse, influences the contingent presuppositions underlying it, and determines what makes sense in it. For this reason, "the eye of the university", looking with a questioning gaze and demanding reasons, must turn in toward itself – it must stop for a brief moment, for the blink of an eye, from looking outside, and blink: it must try to see vision itself (2004b, p. 154).

Derrida's point is that such an inner, reflexive gaze cannot be the task of institutional academic philosophy; some difference or distance is necessary for self-reflection to be possible. Critical self-reflection must be a task for thinking that cannot be reduced to institutional philosophy. Derrida calls, therefore, to turn the university into a site for thinking, opening within it space for a community of thinking "'at large' – rather than a community of research, of science, or of philosophy, since these values are most often subjected to the unquestioned authority of the principle of reason" (2004b, p. 148), namely to a specific configuration of reason. Thinking, then, needs to reflect on the principle of reason, submit it to critique, without altogether abandoning it: "'Thinking' requires *both* the principle of reason *and* what is beyond the principle of reason, the *arche* and an-archy" (2004b, p. 153, emphasis in the original). A community of thinking is a philosophical community that can – sometimes, for the blink of an eye – be anarchic and challenge the institution hosting it as well as its philosophy.

What does a community of thinking think about? What should thinking be concerned with if it refuses to adhere to the institutional understanding of reason and to accept its limits? Many answers to this question are to be found in Derrida's texts on the university, but I think that the three most important things Derridean thinking must think about are those already addressed here: reason, philosophy and the university.[4]

Thinking about *reason* is not the same as thinking about thinking, because thinking cannot be reduced to reason: "reason is only one species of thinking – which does not mean that thinking is 'irrational'. Such a community [a community of thinking] would interrogate the essence of reason and of the principle of reason, the values of the basic, of the principial, of radicality, of the *arche* in general, and it would attempt to draw out all the possible consequences of this questioning" (Derrida 2004b, p. 148, emphasis in the original). Without renouncing reason and giving in to some form of irrationalism, the community of thinking must interrogate the nature of reason, namely think of reason as anything but natural, and examine its history, sociology, politics, etc. As we know all too well, the history of reason can be seen as one of liberations and steps forward only at the price of exclusions,

[4] Derrida lists other themes about which the university and the human sciences in particular should think: the idea of man, democracy, sovereignty, the profession, literature, and others. (2002h, pp. 231–4).

confinements, labeling thoughts as mad and people as insane. Thinking about reason is thus also thinking about unreason, about the kinds of madness reason leaves unthought.

Such thinking about reason is not external to *philosophy*, and will necessarily affect it, demanding "to transform the modes of [philosophical] writing, the pedagogic scene, the procedures of academic exchange, the relation to languages, to other disciplines, to the institution in general, to its inside and its outside" (Derrida 2004b, p. 150). Opening philosophy up for thinking means, therefore, among other things, accepting new forms and styles of philosophical writing – ones not subjected to the prevailing standards of logical rigor, which are derived from the dominant form of reason – as well as subjects that traditionally fall outside the realm of philosophy, in disciplines such as literature, linguistics, history or political science. This thinking that is both philosophical and unphilosophical – in its style, contents, and refusal to separate style from content – clearly characterizes Derrida's own work: as John Willinsky (2009, p. 284) observes, Derrida's writings refuse the "best-seller tradition" of doing philosophy, giving his readers "a right of access to what is new, critical, controversial and experimental in philosophy".

The existing *university* seldom welcomes such radical thinking about reason and philosophy. Most if not all existing academic institutions are undoubtedly a set of organized – yet well-reasoned – limitations on thinking and philosophy in the service of the state and market. But it does not have to be this way, and if the right to dissident thinking is not given, it must be produced, executed, affirmed in practice. It is necessary to form "counter-institutions" (Willinsky 2009, p. 283), inside or alongside existing universities, where critical thinking can flourish. Such a "university without conditions", as Derrida sometimes calls it (2002h, p. 202), presupposes "a place of critical resistance, a form of dissidence" (Peters 2009, p. 117), and for this very reason it will be a truly educational site, one in which education and thinking are combined.

In the second section of this chapter, I extracted from Derrida's discussion of Foucault's reading of Descartes an educational model acknowledging the role of madness, namely one that is aware that education necessarily represses some kinds of madness and acknowledges the need to leave some room for them. Teachers such as Descartes and Foucault, each in his own way, have provided their real and imaginary students with bodies of knowledge containing madness, thereby allowing sensitive students like Derrida himself to make their own ways within and beyond the given discourse, namely to think for themselves. Such teaching is probably quite rare, but it is not exclusive to Descartes and Foucault. In fact, there is no reason to assume it can be practiced only by individual, unusual teachers. Why can such teaching not be institutional? Can we not think of an academic institution, a university, as educating in such a way as to leave room for madness? Is it impossible for a university to teach in such a way as to allow madness to break free in the thoughts of students, researchers, and whoever responds to the invitation to not only to teach and learn but think? Such a university will make use of what Derrida calls *mochlos* (2004a, p. 110), a kind of lever making it possible to break out by relying on what is already in, on madness that is always (also) inside and one only needs to look for it, listen to it or read it, use it rather than silence and confine it.

There is no one way to make such learning that invites thinking possible within the university, just as there is no single madness standard academic discourse excludes. The academic institution and the people in it should constantly think of ways of doing so. What is needed, in other words, is not going out of the university but rather thinking from within the university about the university. I have already mentioned the impossibility of detaching philosophy and thinking from the university, and the need to rethink even the university's *raison d'être*, namely the principle of reason. But if reason and institution are inseparable, then not only reason but also the institution has to be constantly under the critical gaze: Derrida writes that "Deconstruction is an institutional practice for which the concept of the institution remains a problem" (2002a, p. 53). Thus every publication or lesson can and should "problematize, that is, put forward, its own limits and conditions in order to draw attention to them, to make them a theme of research: What entitles us, what gives us the right to be here…?" (p. 6).

Forming such an academic institution – one that reflects upon its own institutional conditions, which philosophizes about its own philosophy – was an explicit goal of the International College for Philosophy (Ciph) founded in 1983 by Derrida and some of his colleagues. Despite or perhaps due to the commitment to philosophy expressed in the college's name it is by no means just another institution dedicated to philosophizing, the way it is practiced in university departments. In addition to its explicit internationality and lack of any regular positions and cathedrae, Derrida writes that the college is planned to be unique in that "priority should be given to directions in research, to themes and objects, that *currently* are still not *legitimated* in French and foreign institutions" (2002a, p. 10, emphasis in the original). The aim is to provide "capacity to access what is forbidden (repressed, made minor, marginalized, even unthought)" (p. 14). That is to say, the college will not try to define philosophy and mark its borders but rather to break them wherever they are set, and out of commitment to philosophy legitimize what it does not think, affirm in thinking what it leaves unthought. In a 1982 report to the French government, in which the rationale for the college is articulated, Derrida and his colleagues write:

> If we propose the creation of a college *of philosophy*, it is not first of all to signal that this institution belongs integrally to what we might believe we can determine in advance as the *philosophical* destination or essence. It is, *on the one hand*, to designate a place of thinking in which the *question of philosophy* would be deployed: the question *about* the meaning or destination of the philosophical, its origins, its future, its condition. In this regard, 'thinking' for the moment only designates an *interest for philosophy*, in philosophy, but an interest that is not philosophical first of all, completely and necessarily. It is, *on the other hand*, to affirm philosophy and define what it can be and do today in our society as regards new forms of knowledge in general, technique, culture, the arts, language, politics, law [*droit*], religion, medicine, power and the military strategy, police information, etc. The experience of thinking *on the subject of the philosophical*, no less than philosophical work, is what might be the task of the Collège (2002a, p. 19, emphasis in the original).

Philosophical thinking should be combined with thinking about (and beyond) philosophy, to allow the college community, the community of thinking, to practice philosophy and challenge it at the same time.

The founding of Ciph, an institution that maintained autonomy from the academic system despite government financial support, may seem like a step towards quitting the university, building a new home for philosophy that would allow it to bid farewell to the institution that has been its almost only abode for more than two centuries. But this is by no means Derrida's intention. He repeatedly says that philosophy must not abandon the university (2002d, p. 148), must not renounce what the university offers – or at least what it can offer. Notwithstanding the numerous defects of contemporary universities and the maladies of academic philosophy, Derrida writes that the university is still committed to critical evaluation, without which "the control, manipulation, diversion, or reappropriation of discourses will be that much easier outside the academy" (2002g, p. 183). Much more often than not, the philosophical publications outside the university rely on mass media and obey the powers of markets and politics, and thereby merely "reproduce outside the academy the most well-behaved scholarly models" (p. 184). Moreover, although the university professors seldom make use of the privileged conditions the institution provides them to become engaged public intellectuals, the figure of the professor is still worth protecting because, as Anne O'Byrne points out, it is "the opposite of the figure that we have in its absence, that is, the expert or, more particularly, the television expert" (2005, p. 403). That is to say, only the university, at least in the current sociopolitical reality, can demand in the name of academic freedom and immunity the right to think in the Derridean sense, namely to ask dissident, critical questions even about critique, to affirm and execute "The principle of unconditional resistance" (2002h, p. 204) to sovereign power.

To be sure, resistance to the conditions confining thinking at the university can take many forms. When speaking of the "university without condition", Derrida proposes to think about the university through the notion of work, namely to turn the gaze to the work done at the university. The paradigmatic workers of the university are of course the professors, whose profession is academic research and teaching. However, they are by no means the only ones working there: "in the university, among all those who in one way or another are supposed to be working there (teachers, staff or administration, researchers, students), some, notably students, as such, will not ordinarily be called *travailleurs* as long as salary (*merces*) does not regularly compensate, like a commodity in a market, the activity of a craft, trade, or profession" (2002h, p. 216). The work of students, adjunct teachers and administrators is often invisible, unrecognized, although it is an inseparable part of university activity and it is highly doubtful whether the professors could work without it. Moreover, many university workers work hard without the product of their work being recognized as a body of work (*oeuvre*): "It would often be difficult to identify and objectify the product of very hard work carried out by the most indispensable and devoted workers, the least well treated workers in society, the most invisible ones as well" (p. 216). The point, of course, is that the work of these workers is also embodied, among other things, in the visible product of the university, in the body of work signed by professors. Turning the gaze to these workers and these works, making them visible, is therefore one of the most urgent tasks of thinking that critically examines the relation between itself and the institution making it possible.

More generally, this means that thinking in the university should take upon itself the task of externalizing, making visible, and turning into an object of examination what seems to be furthest removed from philosophical thinking, from the classical image of thinking that thinks itself. Namely, the concrete, material conditions making possible the university and all thinking within it: funding and allocation of resources, student loans, working conditions of administration and services workers – all allegedly external to thinking, let alone to philosophy, but in fact constituting them and necessarily affecting them, infiltrating into them. If, at present, there is no philosophy without the university, and there is no university without such "external" conditions, ignoring them is true madness on the part of critical philosophy.

This brings us back to Foucault's reply to Derrida's critique of his reading of Descartes. Foucault, as I showed at the end of the first section, accused Derrida of ignoring what is outside the text, outside thought and language, namely of overlooking real power relations that are not necessarily textual. We can see now how far this claim is from Derrida's view, as it is expressed in what he says about thinking in the university: thinking, for Derrida, must think about its conditions of possibility, it must turn the mind's eye to the external conditions that are usually either unthought or thought to be external to thought. Put differently, thinking is never completely separate from the material conditions making it possible; hence, to be critical and reflective it cannot but take them into consideration and understand itself as conditioned by the power relations of which they are part. This insight may have been implied already in Derrida's discussion of Foucault's reading of Descartes, in which case Foucault's 1973 critique of Derrida was far off the mark. It may also be possible that Derrida formulated his views on thinking at the university, namely on thinking's need to reflect upon its own material conditions of possibility, *following* Foucault's critique. At least, it may be that this critique pushed him to develop this aspect of his thinking about thinking, to make it explicit. In this case, this is one more thing that Derrida, the teacher who is also a student, learned from his teacher Foucault.

5.7 Conclusion

Is what has been said about thinking at the university relevant also to thinking at school? I think the answer is positive. Indeed, these two institutions seem to be very different: the former focuses on research and the latter on teaching, the former targets adults and the latter children – but one of the main characteristics of deconstructive thinking is the challenging of simplistic dichotomies. Hence, although Derrida himself dedicates different texts to discussing the school and the university, his thought invites the deconstruction of the dichotomy according to which schools are for children to learn in and universities are for adults to do research. I will not pursue the claim that children can attend the university, nor that school does produce knowledge. I conclude by suggesting that if thinking, in the broad, affirmative sense Derrida ascribes to it, is essential to both school and university, then the two institutions are or rather should be placed along the same continuum, differing in degree but not in kind.

Discussing the importance of encouraging non-instrumental, resistant thinking in the university, O'Byrne writes that "if such resistance begins only in the university, it is far too late and the professor professing resistance will find herself in confrontation with students not just disposed but quite committed to non-critical modes of thought, students with an overwhelming tendency to regard themselves as informed, autonomous consumers of an educational product" (2005, p. 404). This is undoubtedly true from Derrida's perspective. But I think O'Byrne quite misses the point when she goes on to say (p. 405) that "The solution must be to give philosophy the right already possessed by every other discipline to have students work though a long and progressive curriculum beginning in the earliest classes". Derrida's point in demanding a place for thinking in education, as we have seen, is not a call for gradual progress, in which students move a step at a time to higher levels of critical thinking. Critical, deconstructive thinking, for Derrida, rather means openness to madness, to the "other" of conventional philosophical thinking. One can never be prepared for thinking madness, for letting madness generate thinking, which means that everyone is always already ready for such thinking.

Equally important, when thinking about school and the university being on the same continuum, is the need for thinking at school, just like at the university, to learn to blink – to look at itself and at the institution in which it takes place. This means that teaching philosophy at schools, which is according to Derrida a kind of education for thinking, necessarily includes thinking about the school and about the question what is school. In other words, philosophy in school is always also philosophy of education.

References

Biesta, G., & Egéa-Kuehne, D. (Eds.). (2011). *Derrida & education*. New York: Routledge.

Biesta, G., & Stams, G. J. (2001). Critical thinking and the question of critique: Some lessons from deconstruction. *Studies in Philosophy and Education, 20*, 57–74.

Cahen, D. (2001). Derrida and the question of education: A new space for philosophy. In G. Biesta & D. Egéa-Kuehne (Eds.), *Derrida and education* (pp. 12–31). London: Routledge.

Derrida, J. (1981 [1972]). *Positions* (A. Bass, Trans.). Chicago: The University of Chicago Press.

Derrida, J. (1984 [1971]). Signature, event, context. In *Margins of philosophy* (A. Bass, Trans., pp. 307–330). Chicago: The University of Chicago Press.

Derrida, J. (1994). "To do justice to Freud": The history of madness in the age of psychoanalysis. *Critical Inquiry, 20*, 227–266.

Derrida, J. (1997 [1967]). *Of grammatology* (G. Chakravorty Spivak, Trans.). Baltimore: The Johns Hopkins University Press.

Derrida, J. (2002a [1990]). Privilege: Justificatory title and introductory remarks. In *Who's afraid of philosophy? Right of philosophy 1* (J. Plug, Trans., pp. 1–66). Palo Alto: Stanford University Press.

Derrida, J. (2002b [1974]). Where a teaching body begins and where it ends. In *Who's afraid of philosophy? Right of philosophy 1* (J. Plug, Trans., pp. 67–98). Palo Alto: Stanford University Press.

Derrida, J. (2002c [1978]). The crisis in the teaching of philosophy. In *Who's afraid of philosophy? Right of philosophy 1* (J. Plug, Trans., pp. 99–116). Palo Alto: Stanford University Press.

Derrida, J. (2002d [1977]). The age of Hegel. In *Who's afraid of philosophy? Right of philosophy 1* (S. Winnett, Trans., pp. 117–157). Palo Alto: Stanford University Press.

Derrida, J. (2002e [1975]). Philosophy and its classes. In *Who's afraid of philosophy? Right of philosophy 1* (J. Plug, Trans., pp. 158–163). Palo Alto: Stanford University Press.

Derrida, J. (2002f [1975]). Divided bodies: Responses to *La Nouvelle Critique*. In *Who's afraid of philosophy? Right of philosophy 1* (J. Plug, Trans., pp. 164–172). Palo Alto: Stanford University Press.

Derrida, J. (2002g [1979]). Philosophy of the estates general. In *Who's afraid of philosophy? Right of philosophy 1* (J. Plug, Trans., pp. 173–192). Palo Alto: Stanford University Press.

Derrida, J. (2002h [1999]). The university without condition. In *Without alibi* (P. Kamuf, Trans., pp. 202–237). Palo Alto: Stanford University Press.

Derrida, J. (2004a [1980]). Mochlos, or the conflict of the faculties. In *Eyes of the university: Right to philosophy 2* (J. Plug, Trans., pp. 83–112). Palo Alto: Stanford University Press.

Derrida, J. (2004b [1983]). The principle of reason: The University in the eyes of its pupils. In *Eyes of the university: Right to philosophy 2* (J. Plug, Trans., pp. 129–155). Palo Alto: Stanford University Press.

Derrida, J. (2006a [1963]). Force and signification. In *Writing and difference* (A. Bass, Trans., pp. 1–35). London: Routledge.

Derrida, J. (2006b [1963]). Cogito and the history of madness. In *Writing and difference* (A. Bass, Trans., pp. 36–76. London: Routledge.

Derrida, J., & Ewald, F. (1995). "A certain madness must watch over thinking": Refusing to build a philosophical system, Derrida privileges experience and writes out of "compulsion". A dialogue around traces and deconstructions. In G. Biesta & D. Egéa-Kuehne (Eds.), *Derrida and education* (pp. 55–76). London: Routledge.

Derrida, J., & Montefiore, A. (2001). Talking liberties. In G. Biesta & D. Egéa-Kuehne (Eds.), *Derrida and education* (pp. 176–185). London: Routledge.

Descartes, R. (1996 [1641]). *Meditations on first philosophy* (J. Cottingham, Trans.). Cambridge: Cambridge University Press.

Egéa-Kuehne, D. (2001). Derrida's ethics of affirmation: The challenge of educational rights and responsibility. In G. Biesta & D. Egéa-Kuehne (Eds.), *Derrida and education* (pp. 186–208). London: Rourledge.

Flaherty, P. (1986). (Con)textual contest: Derrida and Foucault on madness and the Cartesian subject. *Philosophy of the Social Sciences, 16*, 157–175.

Foucault, M. (1982 [1971]). The order of discourse. In R. Young (Ed.), *Untying the text: A post-structuralist reader* (pp. 48–78). London: Routledge.

Foucault, M. (2006a [1961]). *History of madness* (J. Murphy & J. Khalfa, Trans.). London: Routledge.

Foucault, M. (2006b [1972]). My body, this paper, this fire. In *History of madness* (J. Murphy & J. Khalfa, Trans., pp. 550–574). London: Routledge.

Gleitman, M. (2006). *Alterity, mastery and dialogue in the debate between Foucault and Derrida regarding the Cartesian Cogito*. MA thesis. Tel Aviv: Tel Aviv University.

Judovitz, D. (1989). Derrida and Descartes: Economizing thought. In H. S. Silverman (Ed.), *Derrida and deconstruction* (pp. 40–58). London: Routledge.

Macey, D. (1995). *The lives of Michel Foucault*. New York: Vintage Books.

Naas, M. (1997). Derrida's watch/Foucault's pendulum. *Philosophy Today, 41*(1), 141–152.

O'Byrne, A. (2005). Pedagogy without a project: Arendt and Derrida on teaching, responsibility and revolution. *Studies in Philosophy and Education, 24*, 389–409.

Peters, M. A. (2009). The university and the future of the humanities. In M. A. Peters & G. Biesta (Eds.), *Derrida, deconstruction and the politics of pedagogy* (pp. 115–132). Bern: Peter Lang.

Peters, M. A., & Biesta, G. (2009). *Derrida, deconstruction, and the politics of pedagogy*. Bern: Peter Lang.

Spivak, G. C. (1997). Introduction. In J. Derrida (Ed.), *Of grammatology* (pp. ix–lxxxvii). Baltimore: The Johns Hopkins University Press.

Sprinker, M. (1980). Textual politics: Foucault and Derrida. *Boundary, 2*(8.1), 75–98.

Trifonas, P. P., & Peters, M. A. (2004). *Derrida, deconstruction and education: Ethics of pedagogy and research*. Hoboken: Wiley-Blackwell.

Williams, E. (2016). *The ways we think: From the stairs of reason to the possibilities of thought*. Hoboken: Wiley-Blackwell.

Willinsky, J. (2009). Derrida's right to philosophy, then and now. *Educational Theory, 59*(3), 279–296.

Chapter 6
Jacques Rancière: Thinking, Equality of Intelligence, and Political Subjectivity

6.1 Introduction

Jacques Rancière's thought has been of considerable influence in both educational theory and political philosophy. Ever since the 1980s, as he turned away from Althusserian Marxism (Althusser et al. 2016) to develop his own radical version of critical political theory, his thought has been challenging not only age-old philosophical conventions but also those of the progressive intellectuals of his own time. His work opens fresh and original ways of thinking about highly debated concepts such as teaching, intelligence, equality and democracy, weaving them into a unique comprehensive worldview.

Rancière's most significant contribution to educational thinking is to be found in his 1987 book *The Ignorant Schoolmaster* (1991). This book recounts the story of the "intellectual adventure" of Joseph Jacotot, a lecturer on French literature, upon arriving in 1818 to teach at the University of Leuven. Chance alone had set the adventure on course: Jacotot did not speak Flemish, while many of his students knew no French. To be able to work with them, he handed them a bilingual French-Flemish edition of François Fénelon's book *The Adventures of Telemachus*, and asked them, with the aid of a translator, to learn the French text by themselves by comparing it to the Flemish translation (Rancière 1991, p. 2). At the end of the term, when he asked the students to write in French what they thought of the book, he was surprised to see that they wrote in decent French, demonstrating that learning of that foreign language actually took place. His students had studied French all by themselves.

Jacotot, Rancière tells us, realized that this unexpected success contradicted the most fundamental pedagogical assumption, according to which learning requires the teacher to *explain* the subject matter to the students, to lead them through the difficult material and gradually transmit his knowledge to their ignorant minds. Contrary to this seemingly self-evident assumption, Jacotot's students learned

I. Snir, *Education and Thinking in Continental Philosophy*, Contemporary Philosophies and Theories in Education 17,
https://doi.org/10.1007/978-3-030-56526-8_6

without explanations. To account for this fact, Jacotot figured that the students who had learnt by themselves merely did what all children do when they learn to speak their mother tongue: "We speak to them and we speak around them. They hear and retain, imitate and repeat, make mistakes and correct themselves, succeed by chance and begin again methodically, and, at too young an age for explicators to begin instructing them, they are almost all… able to understand and speak the language of their parents" (Rancière 1991, p. 5).

Indeed, no infant learns to speak in isolation, but teaching plays no role in this process – a "language teacher" is not at all possible in infancy because the teacher would not have a common language with which to explain to the student. All the child can rely on is her own intelligence and this – in practically all cases – is enough. Moreover, children use their own intelligence not only to learn to speak: every child learns many things by herself, until being told at school that she cannot learn with the aid of her intelligence alone, that without explanations she will not be able to *understand* what she is trying to learn. This means that explaining something to someone amounts to telling her she cannot understand by herself, while in fact she has already learned by herself that which she knows best – the language without which there is no understanding. "The revelation that came to Joseph Jacotot", Rancière writes, "amounts to this: the logic of the explicative system had to be overturned. Explication is not necessary to remedy an incapacity to understand. On the contrary, that very incapacity provides the structuring fiction of the explicative conception of the world. It is the explicator who needs the incapable and not the other way around; it is he who constitutes the incapable as such" (1991, p. 6). Jacotot calls such a teacher-explicator, enlightened and well-intentioned as he may be, a "stultifying" master: he establishes a hierarchical difference between his own intelligence and the student's, positioning the latter and her intelligence in an inferior position.

When Jacotot demanded that his students learn by themselves, on the other hand, he explained nothing to them. His intelligence did not stultify theirs. To keep his intelligence and knowledge completely out of the picture, he started teaching things of which he was completely ignorant – painting, piano playing, litigation; he told his students nothing except that he had nothing to teach them, and they learned by themselves (Rancière 1991, p. 15). This does not mean, however, that Jacotot was superfluous in the process: as a teacher, a master, he had to stand at the door (Cornelissen 2010), forcing his students to learn and eventually to prove they have learnt. Rather than forcing his *intelligence* on theirs, he forced his *will* on theirs, making them use their own intelligence without subordinating it to that of another. And when they wanted to – their intelligence was all they needed to learn. This relation in which one will operates on another to make intelligence discover its own power and realize it is not inferior to any other, is called emancipation: an ignorant schoolmaster *emancipates* his students, not quite in line with the Rousseauvian paradox of forcing them to be free (Rousseau 1999, p. 58) as much as making them liberate themselves. Since such emancipatory teaching, unorthodox as it may be, merely mimics the most natural learning processes experienced by every child, Jacotot called it "universal teaching".

The Ignorant Schoolmaster is about a teacher, a university professor, but it is by no means a book only about education. Rancière argues that the stultifying principle of explanation operating at school is in fact the logic underlying the entire sociopolitical order: "We know, in fact, that explication is not only the stultifying weapon of pedagogues but the very bond of the social order. Whoever says order says distribution into ranks. Putting into ranks presupposes explication, the distributory, justificatory fiction of an inequality that has no other reason for being" (1991, p. 117). Every society expects its members to understand that it is founded on some logic, to believe that it is possible to explain the reasons behind the social hierarchies; in other words, they are asked to accept that some people occupy positions superior to others because their abilities are more suitable. But when one is emancipated, when one realizes he or she is intellectually inferior to no one, they see that all these explanations are false and that the sociopolitical order is nothing but arbitrary.

This basic insight, that all men are equal while the sociopolitical order establishes unjustifiable hierarchies between them, stands at the heart of Rancière's other writings, most of which do not concern education. Nevertheless, the political horizon of *The Ignorant Schoolmaster* is rather limited: following Jacotot, Rancière argues in that book that an egalitarian society, one that does not divide people into hierarchical ranks, is not at all possible, and that emancipatory intellectual adventures cannot really affect the sociopolitical order. This is an individual, not a collective or political emancipation: emancipatory education does not change the emancipated student's actual position in society – he is emancipated only in *thought*.

Yet the concept of thought is not central to Rancière's writings in education or politics. Even when describing his own work as elaborating the "radicalization of the question: What does it mean to think?" (Rancière 2011, p. 29), he does not press the question forward and fails to give an explicit answer. Indicatively, the secondary literature about his work, which has flourished in the last decade or so (May 2008, 2010; Biesta and Bingham 2010; Simons and Masschelein 2011a; Deranty and Ross 2012), has also neglected this concept (for a rare exception, see Larossa 2011). This should come as no surprise: Rancière constantly emphasizes the perceptible, visible aspects of sociopolitical existence, the sensible surface, rather than some hidden depth: people's "ways of being, ways of doing, and ways of saying" (Rancière 2004, p. 27) are at the heart of his discussions. Still, in this chapter, I argue that thinking can shed new light on Rancière's conception of emancipatory education, as well as on the relation between education and politics in his thought. I show that thinking embodies the dimensions of plurality and singularity in Rancière's politics, thereby playing a crucial role in the formation of political subjects. By thinking about thinking in Rancière, I demonstrate that universal teaching – understood as a unique kind of education for thinking – may indeed be political, and politics contains a necessary aspect of education for thinking.

I start by analyzing the importance of thinking for universal teaching. I argue that while stultifying education aims at confining thought to a single model, universal teaching emancipates thought and acknowledges a plurality of ways of thinking. This is elaborated in the third section by examining Jacotot's concept of thinking against the one prevalent in the age of enlightenment, so as to highlight the gap between singular thought and the sociopolitical order. Then, in the fourth section, I turn to Rancière's major political writings to argue that thinking plays an important role in his democratic politics, especially in the formation of collective political subjects out of a plurality of individuals. In the fifth section, I show that the formation of such political subjects involves educational activities that can also be seen as education for thinking, and that this educational aspect makes it possible to understand how political subjects can reproduce and generate each other. Finally, in the concluding section, I think of the possibility of a political subject acting in the name of children's equality.

6.2 Universal Education for Thinking

As seen in the introduction to this book, education for thinking is often presented as one of the cornerstones of progressive, critical education. Building on the foundations laid by Descartes and Kant, philosophers and educational thinkers from Dewey (1997) to our own time (Siegel 2017) argue that to be intellectually mature and enlightened one need not only dare think by oneself but also learn to think properly, according to the right method. Although Rancière does not directly address the notion of education for thinking, his critique of conventional school pedagogy, centered on the notions of explanation, understanding and intelligence, can be read as a fierce attack on such education.

Education, Rancière tells us, rests on the principle of explanation, according to which the student cannot understand the material on her own and is in need of a teacher, a "master explicator". This *differential principle*, in Rancière's terms, assumes the teacher and student's intelligence is unequal:

> The pedagogical myth divides the world into two. More precisely, it divides intelligence into two. It says that there is an inferior intelligence and a superior one. The former registers perceptions by chance, retains them, interprets and repeats them empirically, within the closed circle of habit and need. This is the intelligence of the young child and the common man. The superior intelligence knows things by reason, proceeds by method, from the simple to the complex, from the part to the whole (1991, p. 7).

As pointed out by previous commentators (May 2008, p. 57; Zipori 2011), this conceptualization differs from the one used in IQ or scholastic aptitude tests, the latter being a more or less natural, congenital ability to learn and perform academic tasks. The inequality of intelligences Rancière is talking about does not reflect differences in innate talents but rather a kind of acquired skill that is not only theoretical but also practical: knowing *how* to learn, read and understand. Instead of the vulgar intelligence of the child who wonders haphazardly according to the "nonmethod of chance" (Rancière 1991, p. 11), the superior intelligence is said to understand according to an order, allowing for reasonable, constructive progress of thought toward truth.

When stultifying education tells the student she cannot learn on her own, it in fact tells her she cannot think, and therefore has to listen to those who can. Yet as teaching, it recognizes the student has some *potential* to think, and that she must learn how to actualize it. For such education, learning is primarily learning how to think: it tells the student that her ordinary ways of thinking – with which she had learnt her mother tongue – are no longer enough to learn, and that she has to learn how to organize her thoughts and think methodically. That is to say, "superior" intelligence is nothing other than proper thinking: it is the ability to operate thought not through blind groping, but in an orderly, systematic manner. As the student advances and "acquires a new intelligence" (Rancière 1991, p. 8), a superior one, she learns how to think methodically.

The assumption underlying stultifying education – inequality of intelligence – is therefore that there is only *one* proper way to learn and to think. Narrowing the field of thought down to a single path implies inequality between individuals according to their progress along this path. The gap between the more and less progressed may be reduced by learning how to think, how to replace ignorance with knowledge, but it can never be completely closed: "At each stage the abyss of ignorance is dug again; the professor fills it in before digging another. The master always keeps a piece of learning— that is to say, a piece of the student's ignorance—up his sleeve" (Rancière 1991, p. 21). The path is infinite, and there will always be someone more advanced along the road. As the student becomes more intelligent, able to think and understand properly, he develops a sense of superiority towards others who he assumes unable to think the way he does. Thus, education for thinking *reproduces* inequality, and striving for equality requires that we renounce such education.

Universal teaching, on the other hand, rests on the assumption of *equality of intelligence*, according to which everyone can learn everything on their own, without need for explanation by someone of higher intelligence, namely better thinking skills. However, universal teaching is also an act on thought. The original task Jacotot gave to his Flemish-speaking students was "to write in French what they *thought* about what they had read (Rancière 1991, p. 2, my emphasis)". Later on, as Jacotot expanded the experiment and taught things he did not know, thinking stood at the heart of the tripartite question, "What do you see? What do you think about it? What do you make of it?" (Rancière 1991, p. 23), and Rancière explicitly states that "The whole practice of universal teaching is summed up in the question: What do you think about it?" (1991, p. 36). That is to say, when the teacher does not operate based on the student's assumed inferior intelligence but rather imposes his will on the student's, he forces the latter to think on her own. Equality of intelligence means that one does not need to learn in order to think, that anyone can think valuable, reasonable thoughts. Thinking, according to Jorge Larrosa's reading of Rancière, cannot be taught, and at the same time "it is always there, the thing that it is impossible not to learn as you read and write 'for real'" (Larrosa 2011, p. 173), that is, as the student becomes aware of her ability to learn. Universal teaching does not teach *how* to think, but rather teaches the student to think that she *is* able to think, that she is *already* a thinking being. This can be called "universal education for thinking".

The equality of intelligence does not mean that we all have the same *potential* for thinking which may or may not be developed. Similarly, it is not that everyone can learn on their own how to think methodically. Rather, it means that methodical thinking is not superior in any way to thinking which wonders around, which leaves room for chance and improvisation. To be sure, thinking never strays in total darkness, for no one is completely ignorant: "the one who is supposedly ignorant in fact already understands innumerable things" (Rancière 2010, p. 5), each of which can be a starting point for thinking, an object of comparison through which new things are learnt. Moreover, equality of intelligence also implies equality of the *products* of intelligence: the full power of human intelligence is equally manifested in every product of human thinking: "everything is in everything" (Rancière 1991, p. 19), as Jacotot put it. This means that every thinker can learn everything, just as children learn to speak: "by observing and retaining, repeating and verifying, by relating what they were trying to know to what they already knew, by doing and reflecting about what they had done" (Rancière 1991, p. 10). Unlike the single, pre-given path of superior intelligence, accepting the equality of intelligences implies "that you can start from any point and that there are multiple paths that can be constructed to get to another point and still another one that is not predictable. There is a multiplicity of paths, a multiplicity of ways of constructing one's intellectual adventure" (Rancière 2016, p. 139).

Accordingly, equality of intelligence by no means implies that everybody thinks the same way, or that differences between thinking beings dissolve (or should be dissolved) into a uniform mass. As we have seen, it is the assumption of *inequality* of intelligences that narrows thought down to a single model, and interprets the differences between thoughts as varying degrees along the single path to proper thinking. *Equality* of intelligence, on the other hand, has nothing to do with sameness. As Todd May makes clear, "If people are equally intelligent and are to act out of the presupposition of that equal intelligence… [it is not to say] that people are all the same… To put the point another way, it is not in the name of an identity or of a sameness that equality is acted out; it is… in the name of difference" (2008, p. 64). Equal intelligence does not mean dismissing all qualitative differences between thoughts to place them along the same line; it rather implies accepting the legitimacy of a *plurality* of ways of thinking. When we think, Rancière writes following Jacotot, we do not take a straight path to knowledge, to truth: "each one of us describes our parabola around the truth. No two orbits are alike" (Rancière 1991, p. 59). Thought orbits around and makes sense of the world in multiple paths. Thinking goes on journeys, intellectual adventures full of surprises and unexpected discoveries, just like the one Jacotot had. Equality of intelligence acknowledges the irreducible singularity of thought, the countless ways to do things with thoughts. It is an equality between many different singularities, an equality holding a plurality. Universal teaching, therefore, emancipates the student, who learns she can think as well as anyone else, and also emancipates thinking, which is no longer tied to a single model.

This seems to contradict what Rancière says about intelligence, bringing him close to Jacotot's opponents. In *The Ignorant Schoolmaster*, celebrating plurality and difference is ascribed to the adherents of *in*equality: "Look at the leaves falling from the tree. They seem exactly the same to you. Look more closely and disabuse yourself. Among the thousands of leaves, there are no two alike. Individuality is the law of the world" (Rancière 1991, p. 46). "Superior" minds advocate difference and individuality, for these are necessary for the intellectual hierarchy: they differentiate not only between manifestations of intelligence but also between human mental faculties, arguing that the student of the ignorant teacher only repeats and memorizes, without really understanding (Rancière 1991, p. 24). This claim echoes in the popular contemporary theory of "multiple intelligences" (Gardner 2006), which can only be evaluated using different tools and in different dimensions. However, such approaches, attempting to put the individual student at the center of the educational process, only split the dimensions of inequality, making the hierarchical ladder multidimensional without challenging the existence of hierarchical differences on each faculty or intelligence (Cornelissen 2010, p. 531).

In the name of equality, Rancière proclaims that all intelligences are "of the same nature" (1991, p. 9), manifesting one, indivisible power (p. 26). This by no means implies he believes everybody – or even all the emancipated – thinks the same way. Everyone can learn to paint, but not everyone can paint a masterpiece, just as not anyone who has learnt French on one's own can write like Racine or Hugo. The aim of universal teaching is to make the student able to say "me too, I'm a painter" (Rancière 1991, p. 67); namely, to give her a sense of "being able to" (Simons and Masschelein 2011b, p. 88), that there is nothing she cannot do or learn. Its aim is not to make all students think, write or paint the same way. This is the most important reason for insisting on the concept of thinking in Rancière: while the concept of intelligence emphasizes equality and absence of hierarchical differences, thinking stresses uniqueness, singularity and plurality. Eager to object to inequality and hierarchy, Rancière focuses on equality of intelligence, but the dimension of plurality, embodied by thinking, is no less important for his view.

Hence, acknowledging the diversity of ways of thinking does not mean all are equally effective, that no thought is "better" or closer to the truth than another is. People are often wrong, thinking false thoughts. But this does not necessarily testify to inequality of intelligence, of the power to think and learn, but rather to differences in the will and determination to think hard: "There is inequality in the *manifestations* of intelligence, according to the greater or lesser energy communicated to the intelligence by the will for discovering and combining new relations; but there is no hierarchy of *intellectual capacity*" (Rancière 1991, p. 27, emphasis in the original). Thinking indeed does not follow a method and is free to wander by chance, but this wandering is nevertheless highly demanding. Even while groping along her own way, the thinker must pay careful attention to details, retrace and recheck. The thinking being does not think naturally, automatically, by virtue of the mere fact of existing – thinking requires willpower, effort and attention. Even the genius whose works amaze the world does not have more thinking power than others do; he is nothing but a worker, who invests a lot of effort in what he does (Rancière 1991, p. 56). Whoever has not done a good job, on the other hand, "has not seen well because he hasn't looked well" (Rancière 1991, p. 50), and he has not looked well because he has not been paying enough attention.

To be sure, the will to pay attention, concentrate and put effort into thinking is not merely personal matter. What I want (or what I believe is reasonable of me to want) is influenced by the interaction between my will and that of others. When a teacher explains to me, tells me I cannot think and learn by myself, I cease willing to think hard – it does not seem to be worth the effort. Thus, stultified under the weight of inequality, convinced they cannot learn and understand without a master, most people just do not think hard enough. When the emancipating teacher imposes his will on the student, however, he compels her to think, although he does not impose a specific manner of thinking. When forced to, the student will blaze her own trail of thought, and find her own way of orbiting around the truth.

6.3 Education, Thinking, and the Age of Enlightenment

Jacotot's universal teaching is very different from the kind of education accepted in his time, the age of enlightenment and revolution that believed in progress, in teaching and instructing the masses. But the philosophers of the enlightenment also know that every social actor is at the same time able to think (Rancière 1991, p. 34); this rests on the Cartesian *cogito*, according to which every man is essentially a thinking being, who knows he exists because he thinks and thinks as long as he exists. Cartesianism has a clear egalitarian element for it acknowledges the ability of each person to think properly, according to the right method (see Chap. 1). As we have seen, however, by narrowing thought down to a method, it introduces *in*equality and leaves equality in the form of empty, abstract potential that merely conceals the unequal ability to fulfil that potential.

Rancière is fully aware of Jacotot's complex relation to Descartes. Like the founding father of modern philosophy, "he considered the fact of a mind at work, acting and conscious of its activity, to be more certain than any material thing" (1991, p. 9). But Jacotot takes the Cartesian formula *cogito ergo sum*, and turns it on its head: "I am a man, therefore I think" (Rancière 1991, p. 36); thought, Rancière reiterates, "is not an attribute of the thinking substance; it is an attribute of *humanity* (1991, p. 36, emphasis in the original). That is to say, thought is for the thinking being not only an abstract metaphysical characteristic through which he knows he exists. It is rather what he does as a man; and when he is fully aware of the fact he is thinking he verifies not only that he exists but also that he thinks no more and no less than any other man – thereby emancipating himself. "In place of the thinking subject who only knows himself by withdrawing from all the senses and from all bodies", Rancière further elaborates, "we have a new thinking subject who is aware of himself through the action he exerts on himself as on other bodies" (1991, p. 54). We are aware of our thought when it is active, executing whatever the will commands it. Far from being a rational animal, spirit trapped in a body of clay, the thinking being is "a will served by an intelligence" (1991, p. 55), whose thought obeys the commands of the will. The difference between Descartes and Jacotot (and Rancière), I suggest, is not only that between theoretical philosophy and emancipatory praxis, but also that between the one and the many – between thinking properly according to the one rational method and thinking according to individual will which is always also arbitrary. This, then, is a split, scattered Cartesianism, which accepts the claim that everyone is a thinking being while insisting on the plurality inherent to thought.

The irreducible plurality of thought is also evident in Jacotot's (and Rancière's) discussion of the gap between thought and language. Assuming the inequality of intelligences, conceiving thoughts as different in degree, implies they are common, commensurable and communicable – that they all speak the same language. Communicating thoughts through language is supposed to be a simple, smooth transition of meanings between homogeneous mediums; people differ in their ability to *use* language, not in their ability to comprehend and make sense of it. This view, popular among the enlightenment philosophers, is in keeping with the view that both thought and language operate according to the natural laws of rationality – or rather that the French language, as many French philosophers maintained, reflects the natural order of thought and reality and is therefore superior to others (Rancière 1991, p. 60).

However, like Diderot before him, Jacotot rejects the idea of a universal, natural language. There is nothing natural, rational or necessary in language, and all languages are equally artificial and arbitrary. He insists that uniting thought and (natural, superior) language implies *subordinating* thought to language, namely to social contingency, to the common public order that presents the social division into ranks and roles – as well as the hierarchies between different societies – as natural and unchangeable. In Rancière's words, "Man does not think *because* he speaks—this would precisely submit thought to the existing material order. Man thinks because he exists" (1991, p. 62).

Equality of intelligences, on the other hand, implies not only that language and its rules have no immediate connection to truth and reason, but also that thought precedes language and is independent of it. Intelligence is manifested in language, which is public, but while there is no private language (Wittgenstein 1973, §§243–271), thought is necessarily private, discrete, and independent of the public sphere and the norms and divisions characterizing it. Interestingly, Jacotot (and Rancière after him) does not reject the Platonic conceptualization of thinking as "the silent dialogue the soul has with itself" (Rancière 1991, p. 68), to which Arendt also appealed (see Chap. 3), but rather thinks of this dialogue as taking place in some emotional pre-linguistic level, which is utterly subjective. This results in an unbridgeable gap between thought and language: there is no "third level in between the individuality of that thought and common language" (Rancière 1991, p. 68), and every resemblance or proximity between thoughts can only be verified "by the long path of the dissimilar" (p. 67). The plurality of thoughts and thinkers is a plurality of singular worlds it is impossible to reduce to a common denominator; each is incommensurable with the others, mad from the point of view of language: mad like Jacotot, the ignorant schoolmaster (p. 19), mad like the *cogito* in Derrida's interpretation (see Chap. 5). Contrary to what Derrida said (1997, p. 158), there *is* an outside-text: pretextual thought does exist, although it is merely a singular point accessible only to its own subject, to the one thinking it.

However, unlike Adorno and Arendt (see Chaps. 2 and 3), Jacotot and Rancière do not think that thinking is an activity in its own right. Thinking has meaning only insofar as it is manifested, made public, namely, put into words and communicated to others: "The virtue of our intelligence is less in knowing than in doing… But this doing is fundamentally an act of communication" (Rancière 1991, p. 65). Hence, the thinker is constantly required to mediate between her singular thought and common language, to *translate* what is essentially untranslatable; the effort of thinking, therefore, also includes the attempt to translate thought to language and language to thought, to leap from the private to the public and make the singular common. What is important, in Rancière's words, is "the effort one brings every minute to translating and counter-translating thoughts into words and words into thoughts" (1991, p. 63). When thought is put into words and communicated, it is translated from the non-language of feeling into the language of the public; and when someone listens and tries to understand, that someone translates back to her own internal world of singular feelings.

Such translation is necessary and at the same time impossible: there is no one correct way of doing it. Translating thought to language involves improvisation, carving a unique path between distant, unrelated worlds. Hence, the act of putting singular feelings into words is a creative act of poetry, and everyone is a poet: "In the act of speaking, man doesn't transmit his knowledge, he makes poetry; he translates and invites others to do the same" (Rancière 1991, p. 65). Yet when one tries to understand words, one does not dive into some hidden abyss of wisdom, but rather translates a translation, deciphers indirectly someone else's thoughts that are inaccessible not because they express some superior intelligence but simply because they are thoughts: "Understanding is never more than translating, that is, giving the equivalent of a text, but in no way its reason" (Rancière 1991, p. 9). As translating the translation back to thought is never able to reproduce the prelinguistic thought, communication always fails. But we know for a fact that it also can work: meanings go through, and speaking beings understand each other well enough to coordinate their actions and lead a common life, namely to make up a hierarchical sociopolitical order made of the plurality of thinking beings who are all equal.

Paying attention to the dimension of thinking and to the plurality of equals it entails can shed new light on the link between Rancière's views of education and politics. Such a link is of crucial importance, for while stultifying pedagogy provides the logic upon which the hierarchical social order rests, universal teaching as presented by Jacotot cannot provide the model for political emancipation. As mentioned, the explicative principle is at work not only at school – it is the foundation of every social hierarchy, for people are expected to understand they have to obey their superiors, to assume the existence of an adequate explanation for the unequal order of things. This pedagogical logic becomes all the more relevant in the sociopolitical order that emerged in Jacotot's time, as the *Ancien Régime* in which hierarchy rested on tradition or divine power was replaced by a new, "organic" order (Rancière 2010, p. 6), in which inequality was supposed to be founded on reason, namely on maximal correlation between each person's intellectual abilities and social position.

According to Rancière, pedagogy is at the heart of this organic order also because it involves a plan for people's education: education aimed at removing the resentment toward the elites, establishing shared beliefs between the people and the elites, and allowing social mobility to a few gifted individuals without undermining the entire hierarchical structure (Rancière 2010, pp. 7–8). Hence, Rancière writes, "The school is not only the means towards this new progressive order. It is its very model: the model of an inequality which identifies itself with the visible difference between those who know and those who do not know and which devotes itself, visibly, to the task of teaching those who are ignorant that which they do not know, and thus reducing such inequality" (2010, p. 8). Society, he continues, "presents itself as a vast school, with its savages to civilize" (p. 13) – it promises to use education to close the gap between the people and the elites, but to that end relies on the knowledge only the former are supposed to have, thereby reproducing inequality in the very act that is supposed to end it.

While stultification in the field of education can find cure in universal teaching, Jacotot argues that freedom and equality cannot be institutionalized (Masschelein and Simons 2011, p. 150), and such teaching will never be able to emancipate the people and bring about free, egalitarian society. Unlike philosophers who argue that the political order introduces artificial equality among men who are by nature unequal (Pojman and Westmoreland 1997), Jacotot holds that "Society exists only through distinctions, and nature presents only equalities" (Rancière 1991, p. 88) – sociopolitical order necessarily involves divisions into roles and ranks, and will always remain irrational and unequal. This is evident from the singular nature of thought, which is essential for intellectual emancipation: only an individual can think, not a collective; as each individual's intelligence circles in its own unique orbit around the absent star of the truth, any attempt to bring emancipated thinkers together will necessarily make them yield to the law of gravitation, collapse into a uniform, immobile, unthinking mass (Rancière 1991, p. 77). Collectivity is opposed to the plurality of singular thinking beings without which there is no freedom: "There cannot be a class of the emancipated, an assembly or a society of the emancipated. But any individual can always, at any moment, be emancipated and emancipate someone else" (Rancière 1991, p. 98).

Hence, although one may argue that since emancipation is at the heart of universal teaching such education is "a fragment or moment of politics" (Simons and Masschelein 2011a, p. 5), in *The Ignorant Schoolmaster* Rancière stresses, following Jacotot, that universal teaching is *not* political, and "The act that emancipates an intelligence has, on its own, no effect on the social order" (2010, p. 14). It is rather limited to one individual emancipating another: "Universal teaching shouldn't be placed on the program of reformist parties, nor should intellectual emancipation be inscribed on the banners of sedition. Only a man can emancipate a man" (Rancière 1991, p. 102). In particular, no institution can emancipate, assume the role of an ignorant schoolmaster, since institutions – like society in general – are necessarily founded upon hierarchical divisions: "universal teaching isn't and cannot be a *social* method. It cannot be propagated in and by social institutions… Every institution is an *explication* in social act, a dramatization of inequality" (p. 105). No school, therefore, can emancipate, and no group of people or social class can be emancipated; the emancipated individual is emancipated in *thought*, not in actions – as a citizen she has to respect the sociopolitical order *as if* accepting its explanations (p. 105). Put differently, emancipated thought cannot be translated into the public, political sphere.

However, while in *The Ignorant Schoolmaster* Rancière weaves his own voice into Jacotot's, without keeping any critical distance from his protagonist, in a later reflection on that book he claims that "it is possible to correct this verdict, to consider the possibility of collective acts of equality. But, this possibility itself presupposes that we… refuse the idea of institutional mediation, of social mediation, between individual demonstrations of equality and collective ones" (Rancière 2010, p. 14). And: "it is possible to engage the social machine even as it runs, through the invention of individual and collective forms of egalitarian acts, but never to confuse these functions. It requires us to refuse to mediate equality" (p. 15). Unlike Jacotot, therefore, Rancière acknowledges the possibility of collective, political emancipating action, but separates it from individual emancipation; universal teaching is not political, and politics does not involve universal teaching. In what follows, I question this position, and appeal to the notion of thought to articulate a link between education and politics in Rancière's thought – a link his writings rarely make explicit, although they often orbit around it.

6.4 Thinking and Political Subjectification

Thinking is discussed in Rancière's major political writings even less than in his book on education. He focuses on aesthetics, on what lies on the surface, between people – in what is sensed and perceived, in speech and common visible objects. Thinking does surface from time to time, but never becomes the center of discussion, and its relation to other important concepts is never fully elaborated. The reason is not difficult to guess: just as in *The Ignorant Schoolmaster*, Rancière is reluctant to speak of hidden, invisible thought – this notion is associated with those arguing that there is some deep, concealed understanding behind ordinary meanings (Rancière 2004, p. 49), that there is a difference between those who understand words well enough only to obey and those who understand the full meaning behind them and are able to give orders (Rancière 2004, pp. 44–5). However, I believe that thinking, which as we have seen marks the dimension of plurality in equality, has an important place in Rancière's view of politics, and articulating it will contribute to understanding the relations between politics and education.

The title of Rancière's influential 1995 book *Disagreement* (*La Mésentente*) signifies a speech situation in which the interlocutors at the same time understand and do not understand each other: they use the same words to say different things because they use the same vocabulary to express completely different logics (2004, pp. x–xi). Rancière himself does precisely that in his book, as he redefines "politics" to give it a different meaning from the one it usually has. This is done through a distinction between *politics* and *police*: the police is "the set of procedures whereby the aggregation and consent of collectivities is achieved, the organization of powers, the distribution of places and roles, and the systems for legitimizing this distribution" (2004, p. 28), namely quite close to the allocation of shares that is usually called politics. The name politics, on the other hand, denotes "an extremely determined activity antagonistic to policing: whatever breaks with the tangible configuration whereby parties and parts or lack of them are defined by a presupposition that, by definition, has no place in that configuration – that of the part of those who have no part" (2004, pp. 29–30). Politics generates a conflict between the way the police "counts the lots of the parties" (p. 28), and those who are not even counted, who are not taken into account. The police is a hierarchical order, which politics exposes as contingent and as containing an inherent wrong, by applying a different logic – that of the equality of anyone with everyone. The police, then, is not only the "petty police", the armed forces responsible for enforcing law and order, for ensuring each part of society receives its proportional share; the police is this very proportion, this logic of distribution which counts the parts of the community and determines what and how much the legitimate share of each part is.

The police is also much more than official institutions, forms of government and legal systems. It includes the "distribution of the sensible",[1] the allegedly self-evident distinctions between the visible and the invisible, the audible and inaudible, what appears and what remains hidden from view (Lewis 2009). Thereby, it creates distinctions between those whose speech bears meaning and those who only make sounds, namely between whoever can reason and others who can only express pleasure and pain: this is the difference between man and animal in Aristotle's classic example (2017, 1253a), but also that between the master who can give orders and the slave who can understand only enough to obey, or between the man as a political actor and the woman who belongs at home. The distribution of the sensible determines, then, what is *sensed* as well as what *makes sense* – not only what is accessible to the senses but also what is meaningful thinking. In other words, while Rancière points to the double sense of *logos* – speech as well as count (2004, p. 26) – we must add a third one, namely logos as thought. The distribution of the sensible combines a form of sensual experience with the interpretation making sense of it (Rancière 2016, p. 136). Just as the political is inseparable from the aesthetic, so is the sensual inseparable from thought; the police is always also an order of thought legitimizing contingent inequality by making it appear natural and self-evident: "for a fact to be admitted, it must be thinkable; for it to be thinkable, it must belong to what its time makes thinkable…" (2004, p. 131).

[1] The French term *partage du sensible* is rendered differently in Rancière's books that have been translated into English. For example, "division of the perceptible" in *Disagreement* (2004), "distribution of sensibility" in *Staging the People* (2011), and "distribution of the sensible" in *Dissensus* (2015) and in *Recognition and Disagreement* (2016). I opt for the latter option, which stresses that what is being distributed and divided is what is being sensed and what makes sense.

Political philosophy, Rancière argues, is blind to politics, thinking only according to the logic of the police. The clear philosophical erasure of the difference between politics and the police, in which the ability to see politics and think about it is abolished, appears already at the starting point of political philosophy, namely in Plato. The *Republic* describes an order based on the community's essence, "in which all manifestations of the common stem from the same principle" (2004, p. 64), namely an *arkhê* – it is a city where "the superiority, the *kratos* of the best over the less good, does not signify any relationship of domination, no cracy in the political sense" (p. 65), for it distributes only according to natural entitlements; the social body realizes the cosmic geometrical order known (to some) in thought. The *arkhê*, Rancière writes, dictates a police with no exteriority, no reminder, which exhausts not only what exists but also what *can* exist and what can even be thought: it is an "archipolicing that grants ways of being and ways of doing, ways of feeling and ways of *thinking*, with nothing left over" (2004, p. 68, my emphasis). This is the reason education plays such a crucial role in the Platonic Republic and the philosophical tradition that follows it: it transforms the law from a dead letter to a living spirit, a spirit that animates thoughts and carries them along as they create it. In Rancière's words, "This republic is not so much based on law as a universal as on the education that constantly translates the law into its spirit" (2004, p. 68). Plato therefore lays the foundations for the kind of education for thinking which Jacotot criticizes, the one teaching students they are unable to study all by themselves, to think they are naturally inferior to others, incapable of thinking.

To be sure, arguing that the police determines the distribution of the sensible and the thinkable is not tantamount to the all too familiar claim that different ages and societies have different common senses, a different understanding of what makes sense and what is nonsense. Rancière argues that the unthinkable is not entirely erased but rather always present in the police, for it is the unperceivable equality between anyone and everyone that make the distribution of the sensible, and with it the unequal division into parts and parties, possible: "There is order in society because some people command and others obey, but in order to obey an order at least two things are required: you must understand the order and you must understand that you must obey it. And to do that, you must already be the equal of the person who is ordering you" (2004, p. 16). In other words, "the inferior has understood the superior's order because the inferior takes part in the same community of speaking beings and so is, in this sense, their equal. In short, we can deduce that the inequality of social ranks works only because of the very equality of speaking beings" (p. 49). That is to say, the fundamental, denied equality makes it possible for everybody to understand the common language, thereby making possible the contingent inequality of the police, the thought that some are entitled to certain shares while other are not. When political philosophy follows Plato in erasing politics, it erases, therefore, the very possibility of thinking equality. Not only is such a philosophy not the embodiment of superior thinking, it is in fact censorship of thinking, suppression of thought, anti-thinking.

This characterizes not only Platonic "archipolitics" but also contemporary political philosophy, that of "post-democratic" politics aiming at a consensus that harmonizes the parts of the community. The system of consensus is based on what Rancière calls "a regime of opinion" (2004, p. 103), in which the people and its logic of equality are repressed in the name of an undisturbed count presenting a totality of "public opinion", namely of counting of voices, votes and preferences, as identical to the people. Through the power of public opinion, the people become the population, an object of scientific knowledge observing and studying behavior according to statistical speculation (p. 105). This alleged reversal of Platonism, merging science and opinion and turning the people into a sociological category, in fact fulfils the heart of Platonic philosophy: "community governed by science that puts everyone in their place, with the right opinion to match" (p. 106). Opinion has turned from an expression of a unique viewpoint and independent thinking into the name of being at one's proper place, expressing one's natural share of the community. The identity between the distribution of the sensible and the determination of thought in the police reaches its peak, as everyone obeys the sweeping order of "not thinking anything, as part of the population, other than what this part of the population thinks when it expresses its share of opinion" (p. 106). The equality underlying the police, therefore, is not only unthinkable nonsense but also unscientific, a fact science cannot think and comprehend.

Politics, according to Rancière, consists of bringing forward the thought of equality, the egalitarian logic heteronomous to that of the police. It interferes with what is visible and sayable (Rancière 2015a, p. 37), operating a different distribution of the sensible (Corcoran 2015, p. 7). It thinks what is unthinkable, the equality of all speaking beings, in order to sense what is insensible – to make sounds hitherto inaudible (she does not only blather, she has an opinion!) and show the hitherto invisible (real work is being done at home!). Politics is not a discussion or debate between parties representing different interests or views, but rather an act of the part not even counted as party, as part of the police – "the part of those who have no part" (Rancière 2004, p. 9). The name of this part, according to Rancière, is the people, the *demos*, who are the supplement to every count of the population (2015a, p. 33). Democracy, accordingly, is not a name of a specific regime but rather politics' mode of existence (2004, p. 99): it is the act whereby the people engage in struggle in the name of the only thing they have – their equality with everyone else. In politics, the thinking of equality turns from an implicit, suppressed logic into an explicit, outspoken thought. Like the police itself, therefore, politics too is possible only because within the distribution of the sensible and the thinkable there is always the possibility of thinking nonsense, of thinking the unthinkable.

Politics, Rancière writes, occurs through "mechanisms of subjectification" (2004, p. 35), the formation of political subjects. Political subjects, that is, do not exist prior to the political conflict in which they confront the order of the police (p. 27). The political subject is always the people, but in the sense not of the whole population but of those who have no positive qualification (p. 8), of the part who has no part and yet demands to take part. In itself, the people is but the undifferentiated mass, but when it makes a concrete demand for equality it appears as something else entirely, that challenges the way the police is divided into parts. Political subjectification, therefore, is "the production through a series of actions of a body and a capacity for enunciation not previously identifiable within a given field of experience, whose identification is thus part of the reconfiguration of the field of experience" (p. 35). This series of actions has effects on the police, pushing forward the part of those who have no part and transforming the distribution of the sensible and thinkable; but these actions must also create and recreate the political subject itself, who is never a simple given. This means that many different people, the people making up the political subject, all have to learn to think equality, learn to think they are equal to anyone else and make this thought appear in public.

This is why Rancière points to the Cartesian *ego cogito* as the material of which political subjects are made: "Descartes's *ego sum, ego existo* is the prototype of such indissoluble subjects of a series of operations implying the production of a new field of experience. Any political subjectification holds to this formula. It is a *nos sumus, nos existimus*, which means the subject it causes to exist has neither more nor less than the consistency of such a set of operations and such a field of experience" (2004, pp. 35–6). In other words, the *cogito*, valid only in the first person singular, is at one and the same time the source for the demand of equality of anyone with everyone, and the basis upon which "we", the collective political subject, is founded: I think – I think just like everyone else; we, workers (or slaves, or women…) also think like everybody else – and we can do something about it.

Yet politics "does not create subjects ex nihilo" (Rancière 2004, p. 36), but rather uses aspects of the existing world of experience in an attempt to make them appear differently, to make a different world appear through them. The political subject, Rancière writes, is "an operator that connects and disconnects different areas, regions, identities, functions, and capacities existing in the configuration of a given experience – that is, in the nexus of distributions of the police order and whatever equality is already inscribed there, however fragile and fleeting such inscriptions may be" (2004, p. 40). The political subject is in need of a starting point, a visible object in and through which equality can be seen and thought – like the book in the case of Jacotot's students. For the French workers movement of the mid-nineteenth century, the obvious common egalitarian element was the 1789 Declaration of the Rights of the Man and the Citizen, which was recognized by employers and employees alike (2004, pp. 51–2). The republic of which the declaration was part did not *count* the workers, of course, did not see them as political subjects. But the point, according to Rancière, is not including hitherto excluded groups into the existing order of the police, nor exposing the gap between false ideology and true reality, but rather reinterpreting equality in a new way so as to transform the way it is understood in the police (p. 88). The workers appealed to the claim that all French people were equal before the law as the premise of a valid logical syllogism arguing a rather simple yet unthinkable thing: words must be taken seriously, consistently, so as to make the contradiction implied in negating the workers' equality apparent. The object of their thought was an existing common object – equality as formulated in the declaration and the consequent 1830 charter – but they thought it in a new way that had thus far been unthinkable, demonstrating that they were *already* equal (Rancière 2007, pp. 45–7).

The political subject is collective, but thinking is always in the first person singular, and no two thinkers are the same. The inherent dimension of the unthinkable thought of equality in politics means therefore that politics always concerns plurality – the plurality of thoughts and of thinkers. While the police is ordered according to a single principle, an *arkhê*, the subject who acts politically is made up of many singularities: the many different people who have no part in the police. This is not only a question of counting heads: there are countless ways of thinking the principle of equality, of putting content into the abstract equality of anyone with everyone. The generation of a political subject necessarily involves bridging over many different thoughts to form a concrete logic of equality against the logic of the police.

For the process of subjectification to put equality into action, to give it content and form, it also needs a *name*: political subjects do not act for abstract equality but for equality in the name of a *specific group* that has no part in the police. In the process of subjectification, individuals realize they are equal to all others and demand equality *as* part of a party that has no part. Naming makes the subject a concrete object through which to think and speak equality, through which to articulate the syllogisms demonstrating the equality of anyone with everyone. Creating a collective political subject, therefore, involves an act of self-naming: the prototype in this case are the Roman plebeians who broke the order of the city on the Aventine Hill in Pierre-Simon Ballanche's version of a tale told by Livy, who gave themselves names to demonstrate that they were speaking beings able to think and express intelligence equal to that of the patricians (Rancière 2004, pp. 23–4). The name opens a new world, one in which it is possible to see the denoted subject and hear his arguments. But the political subject, as we have seen, is not created ex nihilo. Politics uses names that are supposed to have natural, well-defined places in the order of the police, and transforms them into something else that did not exist before, into a name of a dispute.

That is to say, the name of the subject is not a neologism but rather a homonym – a word taken from the existing order of experience, from the common language, that receives a new meaning, which does not replace but rather adds to the original one. "Class" is a perfect example of such a homonym: this word was not invented with "class struggle", with the proletariat fighting to be part of the community. From the point of view of the police, this name simply designates a group of people with a specific status or rank, but at a certain moment this name receives political meaning, turns into a democratic subject, a specific occurrence of the demos (Rancière 2004, p. 90), namely an operator of conflict, "a name for counting the uncounted" (p. 83). The name of the subject – not only "class" but also "workers", "slaves", "women" etc. – unifies plurality and politicizes abstract equality through concrete, particular content.

To be sure, such subjectification, which moves bodies and identities from their natural places in the order of the police, is never final and stable, always fragile and contingent. The political subject does not become identifiable – that would blunt its political edge and make it part of the police. It remains an unstable structure, uniting in the name of the name different individuals for a political demonstration of equality: "There are political subjects or rather modes of subjectification only in the set of relationships that the *we* and its *name* maintain with the set of 'persons,' the complete play of identities and alterities implicated in the demonstration and the worlds – common or separate – where these are defined" (Rancière 2004, p. 59, emphasis in the original). Rancière calls this subject a "multiple" (p. 36) – a term that signifies, I suggest, not only the differentiation of the community from itself, namely the gap between the different counts of its parts, but also the need to constantly create and recreate the political subject out of a plurality of thinking individuals.

6.5 Education, Thinking and Politics

The mechanism of subjectification, of creating and recreating a political subject, involves two simultaneous processes: applying the logic of equality to the police (the process on which Rancière focuses), and applying it to individuals who are called to take part in the political subject. This second process is a kind of emancipatory education: an activity in which an individual is taught he or she is neither inferior nor superior to anyone else. The creation of a political subject involves educational processes that make individuals think of themselves as equal to everybody else. This sense of equality is indeed no subject matter one has to learn to become part of the political subject, but rather an effect of an educational process in which other things are learned – a process that can be seen, accordingly, as *emancipatory education for thinking* (which is not the same as what was referred to above as *universal* education for thinking). By highlighting the importance of education for thinking to processes of subjectification, this section establishes a link between the practice of the ignorant schoolmaster and that of emancipatory democracy, namely between education and politics.

The idea of political emancipation through education is of course not new. Intellectuals and social reformers have attempted since the dawn of enlightenment to liberate the masses by educating them, by teaching them the knowledge needed for equality and liberty. This traditional-progressive approach, according to Rancière, assumes that inequality is a result of a complex mechanism, and concludes that the oppressed need to be taught how it works because their subordinate place in the social hierarchy does not allow them to recognize it by themselves. This assumption, he argues, is circular: "On the one hand, it said: people get pinned down to their place in the system of exploitation and oppression, because they don't know about the law of that exploitation or oppression. But on the other hand, it said: they don't know about it because the place where they are confined hinders them from seeing the structure that allots them that place" (Rancière 2016, p. 134). This circle lies at the heart of what Rancière calls "the method of inequality", according to which knowledge "from above" is necessary to walk the path leading from the reality of inequality to a future equality. Ignorance appears here to be not accidental but rather structural; knowledge, accordingly, signifies not only the *possession* of science but also of the *place* of those who know (2016, p. 138). Thus the "science of inequality", the knowledge the oppressed have to be taught to make them equal, creates an *infinite spiral*, a continual reproduction of the hierarchical relations between those who know and those who do not: "the possessors of social science were always one step ahead, always discovering a new form of subjection and inequality" (p. 135), just like Jacotot's stultifying master.

Every social method, Rancière concludes, only verifies the assumption on which it is founded, reproduces its own starting point – assuming unequal intelligence will never be able to generate a political subject able to challenge the distribution of the sensible, but rather will duplicate the distinction by keeping the oppressed at the inferior place of the students. The political alternative, therefore, requires a different assumption, a different starting point, namely equality. Rather than thinking of equality as a goal to be pursued against the stubborn empirical reality, we must take it as a starting point to be verified in praxis (Pelletier 2009, pp. 141–2). This strategy or method, which Charles Bingham (2009) calls "presumptive tautology", means that assuming what needs to be proven is inevitable. To be sure, not all tautologies are equal, and one certainly has to propose the *right* tautology (Szkudlarek 2018, p. 6): to achieve equality one has to assume equality. This assumption was already at work in Jacotot's universal teaching, which refused to accept the commonsensical truism of inequality of intelligences. In the sociopolitical context, assuming equality means "the rupture of the inegalitarian belief or inegalitarian knowledge" (Rancière 2016, p. 139), namely refusing to accept not only the difference between knowers and ignoramuses, but also the very existence of knowledge required for emancipation. Emancipation, according to Rancière, means "that you must not wait to be taught about the mechanism of exploitation and domination" (2016, p. 140). This does not mean, however, that knowledge has nothing to do with the generation of political subjects, and that the method of equality can do without education. Rather, the assumption of equality needs to be verified, and intellectual emancipation has to spread through a kind of education much different from the one designed by the philosophers of the enlightenment, namely from stultifying education based on explication.

Rancière describes such processes of intellectual emancipation and political education among Jacotot's contemporaries, the French working class of 1830–1850, in his 1981 book *Proletarian Nights* (2012) as well as in the journal *Les Révoltes Logiques* published in 1975–1985 (Rancière 2011, p. 7). Unlike Jacotot's pessimistic view of the possibility of political change, Rancière describes the workers as attempting "to construct a world of equality within the world of inequality" (Rancière 2016, p. 140), to act according to the assumption that they already are thinking beings. Through reading materials written by the workers themselves, he recounts the proliferation among the workers – emerging as new political power – of "heretical knowledge" not subordinated to the traditional, well-established intellectual authorities: sciences such as magnetism and Mesmerism, which were spread by "eccentric theorists", industrialists, local grammarians and others who were by no means traditional intellectuals (Rancière 2011, p. 36). Although the truth-value of these theories was questionable already at the nineteenth century, engaging with them did not indicate any intellectual weakness on the part of the workers but rather the opposite: it was an act of *reclaiming science*, of taking active part in the intellectual universe. The workers imitated those who were supposed to be their superiors, thereby showing them (and themselves) that they are able to do the same. In so doing they disrupted the visible identities of the police order (Pelletier 2009, p. 145) as well as their own social category as workers (Simons and Masschelein 2011a, p. 2), thereby blurring the differences between those able to think properly and those capable only of doing and working (Mercieca 2012, p. 409). Engaging with heretical knowledge was an inseparable part of transforming the workers from a part having no part into a social power demanding its part. Social rehabilitation of the proletarians, Rancière writes, was "effected by the transformation of their material universe into a universe of intellectual determinations" (2011, p. 38). By acquiring that knowledge, the workers proved they could learn, that they too were literary animals, equal to any other speaking being; not knowledge itself but the appropriation of knowledge emancipated them, an appropriation demonstrating that they too could think.

When "semi-schooled proletarians" are being educated and emancipated by "semi-proletarian scholars" (Rancière 2011, p. 37), their interaction necessarily follows the Jacotist condition of one on one: it "is not a relationship of a single person to a multitude; it is the dialogue and promise of one individual to another" (p. 46); it generates "a chain of emancipation opposed to those 'flocks of emancipated' who are held in reins, according to Jacotot, by all the 'good methods'" (p. 50), namely the methods transmitting knowledge while reproducing hierarchy. Such dissemination of emancipation, such propaganda of equality, is not an education of the people but a form of popular education, as members of the people introduce others into the intellectual universe of readers and writers, knowers and thinkers. Looking at this shattering of the allegedly natural barrier separating the intellectually capable from the incapable one sees, in Rancière's words,

> The singular phenomenon of a production of meaning that is neither the consciousness of an avant-garde instructed by science nor the systemization of ideas born out of the practice of the masses; a pure product not of the activity of a group but rather of a network of individuals who, by various paths, found themselves in a position of spokesman, at the same time central and outside the game: not people who carried the word of the masses, but just people who carried the word (2011, pp. 27–8).

These people have turned into spokespersons not by carrying forward some message or theory in behalf of the masses, but rather "by taking speech *to the masses*" (p. 28, emphasis in the original), namely teaching the masses that they already can speak and write.

Unlike Jacotot's universal teaching, in which the emancipated individual who realizes she is equal is supposed to accept the social hierarchy as necessary despite being contingent, the kind of education we are discussing is clearly political: it not only concerns the thought of the emancipated individual but rather challenges the distinction underlying every distribution of the sensible: "the division between those whose lot is production and struggle, and those whose lot is discourse and ideology" (Rancière 2011, p. 30), namely that between those whose business does not require thinking and those who can and should think. Such education is at the same time political and philosophical, teaching "how to live the working-class condition philosophically" (p. 26) – how to be a proletarian differently, to change what it means to be a proletarian. Not, to be sure, by becoming conscious of some real knowledge regarding the workers and the forces oppressing them, but on the contrary, by "dizziness and loss of identity" (p. 26), turning the proletarian from a fixed identity into a destabilizing factor carrying the logic of equality. Paradoxically, such education makes the worker less aware of exploitation and its reasons (Rancière 2016, p. 142), but delivers a clear message to all those stultified into thinking they cannot think: "You must prepare to take command now" (Loick 2018, p. 3), there is no need for previous knowledge before doing what others are already doing, before acting politically. In such political education, even more than in the explicit educational context discussed by Jacotot, the object of study does not matter, whether it is "real" or "heretical" science; the very distinctions between more and less important scientific disciplines are first and foremost ways of saying who lacks the abilities needed to study and understand certain things (Rancière 2016, p. 149). What is important is that through study and the intellectual effort it involves the learner comes to think about her ability to learn and to think, realizing her ability is equal to anyone else's. This is why this is primarily a kind of *education for thinking*: it does not involve teaching or explaining a theory, not even one about the origins and causes of social inequality; it involves, rather, *intellectual indiscipline*: a situation in which one individual makes another realize he or she is a thinking being; in which he or she is forced to think hard, to make sense of oneself and one's world, to express oneself and translate one's thoughts into language, into the sphere of the visible and audible. What matters here is thought itself, the thought I think just like everybody else: not "me too, I'm a painter!" (Rancière 2004, p. 65), or even "me too, I'm a scientist!" but "me too, I'm a thinker!"

This education for thinking is political because it not only emancipates individuals but also forms a collective political subject, whose name ties the emancipated equals together and puts concrete content into the logic of equality. One's self-awareness that she thinks like anyone else involves also awareness of the fact that others like her –others occupying the same place in the order of the police, that of those not supposed to think and to know – are denied an ability they in fact have and a place they are able to occupy: "the idea of intellectual emancipation gave the idea of social emancipation its principle and model. The reflex of workers' self-emancipation was formed here, in the proletarian's effort to become aware of himself, to name himself, to give both himself and others the science needed by every free being" (Rancière 2011, pp. 45–6). That is to say, while social groups and institutions cannot be the emancipating agents, they can certainly play an important role in the emancipation of individuals as *members* of such collectives – a workers' party or organization, for example, cannot liberate a single individual, but an individual can be emancipated *as* a worker, and demand equality for *all* workers. Thus, while equality can be attributed to a collective – "we the workers (or the women) are equal" – only another worker (or woman) can emancipate a worker (or woman), not the party or a group. Political subjectification is composed, therefore, of countless episodes in which individuals are engaged in acts of emancipatory education with others, who emancipate them as parts of the political subject.

For this reason, although the student of politics is not taught *what* and *how* to think, she must realize she thinks not only as an individual but also as part of a party or group. On the one hand, she acknowledges the value of her singular way of thinking, which does not have to conform to any pre-given model to be meaningful; on the other, she thinks of equality in a specific way, as the equality of the political subject of which she is part. Her thinking is in constant tension between the particular and universal, between irreducible singularity and a collective demand for equality, between plurality and unity.

The discussion thus far has focused on the formation of a single political subject, a challenge to the police coming from a single group, having one name and acting democratically in the name of "the people". But Rancière also acknowledges that the anarchic foundation of politics means there is always *more than one possible subject*: "there is no single 'voice of the people'. There are broken, polemical voices, each time dividing the identity they present" (2011, p. 12). This not only means that political subjects replace each other in the course of history, like the oppressed classes in Marx's historical materialism. It means also that political subjects are born out of each other, and often exist simultaneously, in and against the same police: "the political process of subjectivation… continually creates 'newcomers', new subjects that enact the equal power of anyone and everyone and construct new words about community in the given common world" (Rancière 2015b, p. 59). I believe it is impossible to understand this plurality of political subjects, and especially the way one subject gives birth to another, without seeing its connection to the plurality of individuals composing every political subject – a plurality anchored in the irreducible singularity of each individual's thought.

To see this, let us first note that the logic of politics is not simply that of equality. It is the paradoxical logic of conflict between two heterogeneous logics, the police's logic of inequality, *and* the logic of equality. Politics does not replace one logic *with* another but rather superimposes one *over* the other (Rancière 2004, p. 35), namely holds on to both simultaneously: "if politics implements a logic entirely heterogeneous to that of the police, it is always bound up with the latter. The reason for this is simple: politics has no objects or issues of its own… What makes an action political is not its object or the place where it is carried out, but solely its form, the form in which confirmation of equality is inscribed in the setting up of a dispute, of a community existing solely through being divided" (pp. 31–2). That is to say, politics speaks equality through the common language, demonstrates its existence through objects already available in the unequal police order. It multiplies what already exists, generates a new perspective from which to look at an existing object, and gives new meanings to words hitherto spoken only in a certain way. This heterogeneous rationality is embodied in the political subject, but carried by the individuals composing it. Each of them thinks simultaneously through two heterogeneous logics: equality and the police. Each political individual is inherently split – a *dividual* (a term borrowed from Critchley 2007), an individual that is not one.

Rancière conceptualizes this split as that between man and citizen. Unlike the widespread view of citizenship as bringing artificial equality to the natural inequality between people (Arendt 2003; Pojman and Westmoreland 1997), in Rancière, the citizen is part of the police, of the world of inequality, while men are naturally equal:

> Citizenship means, on the one hand, the rule of equality among people who are inferior or superior as men, that is, as private individuals subordinate to the power of ownership and social domination. On the other, by contrast to all the restrictions of citizenship – from whose scope many categories of people are excluded, and which limits citizens by placing certain problems out of their reach – 'man' entails an affirmation of the equal capacity of everyone an anyone (2015b, p. 56).

To be sure, it is not the citizen who acts politically, but nor is it the natural, pre-political man; it is rather the political subject in-between the two. "Political subjects", Rancière makes clear, "exist in the interval *between* different identities, between *Man* and *citizen*" (2015b, p. 56, emphasis in the original). The subject gives a name and specific content to the abstract equality of all men, making it possible to confront the inequality of the citizen. Thus, the tension between the one and many exists not only between the collective political subject and the individuals composing it, but also within each of these individuals, each dividual who is at the same time subject, citizen and man.

The point Rancière does not think through, however, is that the dynamics of heterogeneous logics is necessarily different from one person to the other even within the same political subject. Thinking is by nature singular, unique, and acknowledging that the emancipated individual is in fact a dividual does not contradict but rather supports this singular dimension. Each dividual thinks at the same time using the logic of the police and the egalitarian logic of the political subject, and each does so *in her own unique way*. To bring this closer to Rancière's terms, her thought orbits in an elliptic cycle around two centers – police and equality – and no two orbits are alike.

This plurality of paths, each inhering tension between different centers of gravity, is productive. It allows the emancipated dividual to keep a distance from the collective political subject and consequently to think oneself equal not only as a member of a specific group or party but also of other groups: the one emancipated as a worker, for example, may think she is also equal as a woman, and the emancipated woman, that she is equal also as a black person or lesbian. Hence, politics, which according to Rancière is quite rare, also contains a mechanism of distribution and dissemination – understanding subjectification as education and paying attention to the dimension of thinking reveal a political potential that remains undeveloped in Rancière: namely, the ability of the thinking of equality to be translated into ever more contexts and demands.

Charles Bingham (2009) makes a parallel claim when discussing Rancière's method, which he dubs, as already mentioned, "presumptive tautology". After applying this method to discussing progressive education and critical education, he realizes the method he used was not exactly what he thought it was: "I noticed that this method itself has traces of Rancière's thought that cannot be so easily articulated under the literal name of 'Rancière's presumptive tautology' that I had given it" (p. 414). Rancière's method has been retranslated, reinterpreted in another's thought to become somewhat different from itself. It is still Rancière's method, part of his unique world of thought, but it is also part of a different world – Bingham's – in which its meaning is a bit different. The name the method is associated with – Rancière's, in this case – signifies its origin, but this name, according to Bingham, is not only literal but also metaphorical. That is to say, the name signifies both the way it was used "originally" by its author, and the necessarily different ways it is being used in other contexts: the metaphorical use is "the meaning of one person's method once it has been changed by another person's particular way of using that method. In my case, for example, there is not only my use of Rancière's method, but there is also a sense in which my use of Rancière's method can never be precisely the same as another person's use of the 'same' method" (p. 416). This is precisely how, according to Bingham, Rancière uses Jacotot's method: he leaves it the name of the "founder" but also turns it into a metaphor, into something different that is part of his own thought no less than of that of the nineteenth century French lecturer. Every use of a method or a name, in fact, is a translation that includes a unique interpretation, thinking from a singular point of view that applies the origin – if indeed there is one – in new contexts, giving it new meanings.

This is also the relation between the name of the political subject and the many thinking individuals – or rather dividuals – composing it. They use an existing name – the people, workers, women, etc. – in a way that is not only literal but also metaphorical. When each of them thinks equality according to the name of the political subject, he or she translates this equality in his or her unique way. Each translator stamps on equality her own name, the stamp of her singular thought, next to the name it already has. Hence, each political action is metaphorical, poetic and creative, making it possible to generate new subjects out of the old names. What Bingham seems to miss is not only the connection between the thinking processes he describes and the formation of political subjects, but also the educational dimension of the metaphorical use of the name: a name is used in language, in public, and whoever acts in the name of the name, whether that of a philosophical method or a political subject, also performs a translation, demonstrates that translation is possible. Others might become upset with the translation, condemn it as an illegitimate distortion; or they may follow its example, namely embrace the new translation and offer their own – in the political context, this means thinking about equality with everyone else in terms of other political subjects.

Let us now examine this point through Rancière's discussion of the formation of feminist politics at the time of the French revolution (Rancière 2015c, p. 68). At that time, women were not considered full citizens because republican citizenship was understood to be the sphere of universality, while women were seen as belonging to the private, domestic sphere. Against this logic, Olympe de Gouges argued that since women were qualified to mount the scaffold, they were equally qualified to mount the platform of the assembly: "Her argumentation blurred the boundaries separating these two realms by setting up a universality entailed in the so-called particularity of bare life… On the scaffold, everyone was equal: women were 'as men'. The universality of the death sentence undermined the 'self-evident' distinction between political life and domestic life" (Rancière 2015b, p. 57). De Gouges held on to a certain egalitarian element already inscribed in the young republican police, and reinterpreted it from the point of view of women, thereby giving birth to a feminist political subject. This means that her struggle against the order of the police relied on previous and parallel struggle, that of a different political subject, namely the French people or third estate who overturned the *Ancien Régime* and constituted the republic. The revolutionary democratic action left its egalitarian inscription within the – necessarily non-egalitarian – republican police, one it was possible to reactivate, to use as a starting point for a new intellectual and political adventure. De Gogues had to think equality at the same time as part of the people and as a woman, to take the people's thinking of equality and think it also as a woman.

However, de Gogues' political task did not end here. For her, being emancipated also meant emancipating others, forming a collective political subject. To form a collective subject who thinks the equality of women to anyone else she had to carry the word forward, be a spokesperson, an *educator*. She had to read the egalitarian foundations of the republic, the Declaration of the Rights of the Man and the Citizen, with other women who knew the people's demand for equality but did not take part in it, and retranslate equality with them into the language of the feminist subject. To be sure, this was no "science of inequality" de Gogues was teaching. She did not transmit knowledge of the mechanisms oppressing women or a theory of their possible liberation. She taught by *performing* her ability to think, to take part *as a woman* in the intellectual universe she was not supposed to take part in, thereby making other women think they could also find a place in this universe, think of themselves as thinking beings just like everybody else. Consequently, each of these women was able think both the non-egalitarian logic of the republican police and the egalitarian logic of the feminist political subject, in her own unique way. This uniqueness, this distance from the collective political subject, made it possible for each in turn to think equality as part of yet another political subject – as a black woman or lesbian, for example – and spread her own word.

6.6 Conclusion

We have seen that despite Jacotot's refusal to politicize universal teaching, for Rancière emancipatory education, which is education for thinking that one is a thinking being like anyone else, is an essential aspect of the formation of the political subject as well as the axis on which the possibility for multiplying political subjects turns. Now, by way of conclusion, let us revisit school. Although Rancière's writing in the political context is aimed in large part against traditional school education, his challenge of every hierarchy of knowledge and knowers implies that emancipatory political education can take place everywhere – even at school. Of course, it will not be school as an institution that will emancipate and form the political subject; rather, as a place in which a plurality of people is gathered regularly, where questions about possession and appropriation of knowledge are always at stake, school can be more than a site in which hierarchies are (re)produced. Masschelein and Simons (2011, p. 150) suggest that in *On the Shores of Politics* and elsewhere, Rancière describes school as a site of equality thanks to the separation of school logic from the police's productive logic (Rancière 2007, p. 55). School, accordingly, can be a bedrock for countless encounters in which heretical knowledge is produced and taught, in which (younger or older) people demonstrate their being part of the intellectual universe and become part of a political subject.

However, I think that if school has a political added value, if it can become a political site of special importance, it is because it can be the site in which a new political subject, one hitherto unknown to political history, can emerge – namely, the children. Children clearly have no part in contemporary police – their voices are not heard as expressing intelligence, their bodies do not seem to belong wherever serious discussions take place and decisions are taken. "Go away, kid, you have nothing to do here!" is the sentence through which the distribution of the sensible repeatedly places them on the side of those capable of understanding and obeying orders, yet incapable of giving them. Still, the capacity to understand, to take part in common language, indicates that the child has no less intelligence than the adult, just like the slave compared to the master, the woman compared to the man etc. The child too, according to Rancière's logic, is a thinking being.

It is possible, therefore, to emancipate the child as a child, to make him or her think they think just like anyone else, just like any adult. This can be done not by the teacher as a teacher, but rather by anyone, even another child – a child clinging to egalitarian aspects from the existing reality and translating them so as to express her equality as a child and make other children think the same in their own way. While school is by no means necessary for the formation of such political subject, for such education for thinking, I think it can host this subject, or rather the conflict the childish subject generates between the logic of equality and the distribution of the sensible that denies equality of children. Children dream and imagine, but children also always already think. If only children learn to think they think…

These thoughts go beyond mere interpretation of Rancière's thought, to carve a new path from and around him. What is important, in any case, is that by reading Rancière this way, we learn something important regarding the nature of thinking and its relation to politics and education. We learn that thought, when emancipated and political, is much different from the systematic, coherent chain of reasoning it is often assumed to be. On the contrary, emancipated thought is a heterogeneous plurality – it involves more than one thinker and more than a single train of thought. It takes the thinker on unexpected journeys along twisted paths, which intersect with each other and with those of others in unexpected ways. When it starts with "I think, therefore I am equal", thought can multiply and take on countless forms, inspire new thoughts, incite new political conflicts and generate new thoughts in others, who are different yet equal.

References

Althusser, L., Balibar, É., Establet, R., Macherey, P., & Rancière, J. (2016 [1965]). *Reading capital*. New York: Verso.

Arendt, H. (2003 [1959]). Reflections on Little Rock. In J. Kohn (Ed.), *Responsibility and judgment* (pp. 193–213). New York: Schocken Books.

Aristotle. (2017). *Politics* (C. D. C. Reeve, Trans.). Indianapolis: Hackett Publishing Company.

Biesta, G., & Bingham, C. (2010). *Jacques Rancière: Education, truth, emancipation*. New York: Continuum.

Bingham, C. (2009). Under the name of method: On Jacques Rancière's presumptive tautology. *Journal of Philosophy of Education, 43*(3), 405–420.

Corcoran, S. (2015). Introduction. In *Dissensus: On politics and aesthetics* (S. Corcoran, Ed., and Trans., pp. 1–33). London: Bloomsbury Academic.

Cornelissen, G. (2010). The public role of teaching: To keep the door closed. *Educational Philosophy and Theory, 42*(5–6), 523–539.

Critchley, S. (2007). *Infinitely demanding: Ethics of commitment, politics of resistance*. New York: Verso.

Deranty, J.-P., & Ross, A. (Eds.). (2012). *Jacques Rancière and the contemporary scene: The philosophy of radical equality*. New York: Continuum.

Derrida, J. (1997 [1967]). *Of grammatology* (G. Chakravorty Spivak, Trans.). Baltimore: The Johns Hopkins University Press.

Dewey, J. (1997 [1910]). *How we think*. Mineola/New York: Dover Publishing.

Gardner, H. E. (2006). *Multiple intelligences: New horizons in theory and practice*. New York: Basic Books.

Larossa, J. (2011). Endgame: Reading, writing, talking (and perhaps thinking) in a faculty of education. In M. Simons & J. Masschelein (Eds.), *Rancière, public education and the taming of democracy* (pp. 166–186). Hoboken: Wiley-Blackwell.

Lewis, T. E. (2009). Education in the realm of the senses: Understanding Paulo Freire's aesthetic unconscious through Jacques Rancière. *Journal of Philosophy of Education, 43*(2), 285–299.

Loick, D. (2018). If You're a critical theorist, how come you work for a university? *Critical Horizons, A Journal of Philosophy and Social Theory, 19*(3), 233–245.

Masschelein, J., & Simons, M. (2011). The hatred of public schooling: The school as the *mark* of democracy. In M. Simons & J. Masschelein (Eds.), *Rancière, public education and the taming of democracy* (pp. 150–165). Hoboken: Wiley-Blackwell.

May, T. (2008). *The political thought of Jacques Rancière: Creating equality*. Edinburgh: Edinburgh University Press.

May, T. (2010). *Contemporary political movements and the thought of Jacques Rancière: Equality in action*. Edinburgh: Edinburgh University Press.

Mercieca, D. P. (2012). Initiating 'the methodology of Jacques Rancière': How does it all start? *Studies in Philosophy and Education, 31*, 407–417.

Pelletier, C. (2009). Emancipation, equality and education: Rancière's critique of Bourdieu and the question of performativity. *Discourse: Studies in the Cultural Politics of Education, 30*(2), 137–150.

Pojman, L. P., &Westmoreland, R. (1997). Introduction: The nature and value of equality. In L. P. Pojman, & R. Westmoreland (Eds.), *Equality: Selected readings* (pp. 1–14). Oxford: Oxford University Press.

Rancière, J. (1991 [1987]). *The ignorant schoolmaster: Five lessons in intellectual emancipation* (K. Ross, Trans.). Palo Alto: Stanford University Press.

Rancière, J. (2004 [1999]). *Disagreement: Politics and philosophy* (J. Rose, Trans.). Minneapolis: University of Minnesota Press.

Rancière, J. (2007 [1990]). The uses of democracy. In *On the shores of politics* (L. Heron, Trans., pp. 39–61).

Rancière, J. (2010). On ignorant schoolmasters. In G. Biesta & C. Bingham (Eds.), *Jacques Rancière: Education, truth, emancipation* (pp. 1–24). New York: Continuum.
Ranciere, J. (2011). *Staging the people: The proletarian and his double* (D. Fernbach, Trans.).New York: Verso.
Rancière, J. (2012 [1989]). *Proletarian nights: The workers' dream in nineteenth-century France* (J. Drury, Trans.). New York: Verso.
Rancière, J. (2015a [2001]). Ten theses on politics. In *Dissensus: On politics and aesthetics* (S. Corcoran, Ed., & Trans., pp. 35–52). London: Bloomsbury Academic.
Rancière, J. (2015b [2005]). Does democracy mean something? In *Dissensus: On politics and aesthetics* (S. Corcoran, Ed., Trans., pp. 53–69). London: Bloomsbury Academic.
Rancière, J. (2015c [2004]). Who is the subject of the rights of man? In *Dissensus: On politics and aesthetics* (S. Corcoran, Ed., and Trans., pp. 70–83). London: Bloomsbury Academic.
Rancière, J. (2016). The method of equality. In K. Genel & J.-P. Deranty (Eds.), *Recognition or disagreement: A critical encounter on the politics of freedom, equality, and identity* (pp. 133–155). New York: Columbia University Press.
Rousseau, J-J.. (1999 [1762]). *The social contract* (C. Betts, Trans.). Oxford: Oxford University Press.
Siegel, H. (2017). *Education's epistemology: Rationality, diversity, and critical thinking*. Oxford: Oxford University Press.
Simons, M., & Masschelein, J. (2011a). Introduction: Hatred of democracy… and of the public role of education? In M. Simons & J. Masschelein (Eds.), *Rancière, public education and the taming of democracy* (pp. 1–14). Hoboken: Wiley-Blackwell.
Simons, M., & Masschelein, J. (2011b). Governmental, political and pedagogic Subjectivation: Foucault *with* Rancière. In M. Simons & J. Masschelein (Eds.), *Rancière, public education and the taming of democracy* (pp. 76–92). Hoboken: Wiley-Blackwell.
Szkudlarek, T. (2018). Postulational rhetoric and presumptive tautologies: The genre of the pedagogical, negativity, and the political. *Studies in Philosophy and Education, 38*(4), 427–437.
Wittgenstein, L. (1973 [1953]). *Philosophical investigations* (G. E. M. Anscombe, Trans.). London: Pearson.
Zipori, O. (2011). Intelligence. *Mafte'akh: Lexical Review of Political Thought, 3*, 21–51.

Chapter 7
Conclusion

7.1 The Splitting Paths of Thinking about Thinking

In Hebrew, the words for thinking and importance are derived from the same root: something becomes important when it is thought about, when it is made an object of reflection; thinking is inherently important. This book attempted to think about thinking and explore its importance. It demonstrated that in education – an important subject in its own right – thinking is of special importance, and it is important to think about the conception of thinking used in education. Without detracting from the importance of the traditional Cartesian conception of thinking and the existing field of education for thinking, it pointed from various directions to their problematics and incompleteness, offering alternatives ways of thinking about thinking and its relation to education.

The book made no attempt to present a comprehensive theory of thinking or a coherent system of education for thinking based on the continental instead of the analytic tradition. Its five chapters opened up five splitting paths, which occasionally intersected but rarely referred to each other or attempted to merge. They did not chart a roadmap of education (f)or thinking. Each chapter presented a different view, with unique characteristics, in which education, thinking and politics appeared in very different light. The reason for that approach, as should be clear by now, is not only the tendency of the continental philosophers discussed to develop their own philosophical worldviews instead of debating aspects of a relatively consensual frame of thought. It is also the result of the subject at issue, namely of thinking itself, or rather the deep connection between thinking and philosophy. Philosophy is a kind of thinking – perhaps the most exalted, demanding and strenuous one; hence, philosophizing about thinking is at the same time philosophizing about philosophy, thinking about thinking. Evidently, philosophizing about thinking is somewhat tautological: when philosophy searches for thinking is finds itself, discovering the very same presuppositions that have led it throughout the investigation. Every

I. Snir, *Education and Thinking in Continental Philosophy*, Contemporary Philosophies and Theories in Education 17,
https://doi.org/10.1007/978-3-030-56526-8_7

philosopher conceives of thinking in a way that suits his or her philosophical style. This does not mean philosophical conceptions of thinking are invalid or that they have to leave the stage for other, more objective or scientific investigations. The opposite is true: it means there is no one exhaustive way – philosophical, scientific, or other – to understand the complex phenomenon of thinking, and we had better look at it from several perspectives. In other words, the evasive nature of thinking calls for a plurality of ways of thinking about it, objecting to any reduction of thinking into a single model or theory.

In this concluding chapter, I do not attempt the impossible by articulating a unified theory that encompasses the five philosophers discussed in the book. I also refrain from criticizing some of the views and praising others, as I find all five equally worthy of positive consideration by educational scholars and practitioners. Instead, I try to shed new light on the differences and similarities between the five approaches, so as to allow them to appear more clearly. To that end, I examine the views of Adorno, Arendt, Deleuze, Derrida, and Rancière along the three main axes around which the book revolves: the conception of thinking, the relations between thinking and politics, and the possibility of education for thinking. The first is approached through examining the relations to the Cartesian *cogito* and to language, the second through focusing on the question what politics is, and the third through asking whether education for thinking can find place at school. In each case, the comparison reveals agreements and overlaps between some philosophers, but also indicates the lack of common ground on which to build a comprehensive theory of education for thinking based on all. Finally, I use the meta-analysis to draw some general conclusions and attempt to think about the relations between the continental conceptions of thinking and concrete educational practice.

7.2 *Cogito*, Language, and the Nature of Thinking

All five philosophers refer in different ways to the traditional conception of thinking, whose most characteristic expression is the Cartesian *cogito*, although its roots stretch much deeper into the history of Western philosophy. While not always wholly rejecting the Cartesian understanding of thinking, they all find it limited and unsatisfactory.

The four main characteristics of this understanding, presented in the introductory chapter are: (1) man is essentially a thinking being, and each of his mental activities is a mode of thought; (2) thought involves ideas which are mental representations of objects, and knowledge is correct correspondence between representation and object; (3) as all men are by nature thinking beings, differences in their thinking result not from variations in their ability to think but from the uses they make of this ability, namely their success in applying rational methods of thinking; and (4) the Cartesian dualism of mind and matter implies that the thinking subject is autonomous, and thinking is independent of the external – historical, social or political – world. None of the philosophers discussed in this book accepts all four. In fact, most reject all, but do so in very different ways and for different reasons, and naturally, the alternatives they offer are far from identical. Examining their relations to Descartes will be the groundwork for comparing their different conceptions of thinking.

Arendt, discussed in Chap. 3, is a proper starting point. Despite or perhaps because of her relation to Heidegger, for whom Descartes was one of the main targets of attack (see Chap. 1), her critique of Descartes is rather benign. The point of departure for her discussion of thinking is the distinction between thinking and knowledge, which means she rejects the claim that all mental activities are modes of thought. She does not object to the representational nature of scientific knowledge, only to its exclusivity and objectivity – she puts it in historical context, and examines it against other ways of looking at and experiencing the world. Unlike representational, scientific knowledge, pure thought is interested not in the existence of things but in their meaning. In much the same way, although Arendt does not accept Descartes' metaphysical dualism, she also does not utterly deny the independence of the thinking subject from the material world – the thinker does leave the world behind and thought is not conditioned by it, but this is only a temporary situation that ends when the demands of the real world reassert themselves. In other words, Arendt does not only argue against Descartes, but also learns from him: the solitude characteristic of the Cartesian cogito is for her clear indication not only of modernity's alienation from the world but also of man's need to withdraw from the world from time to time and engage in silent, inner dialogue.

Derrida, the subject of Chap. 5, also looks at Descartes with a sympathetic eye. Unlike Foucault's reading, which understands the *cogito* as violently excluding and confining madness, Derrida argues that madness is inseparable from the *cogito*, accompanying it wherever it goes. Still, he rejects Descartes' identification of thought with ideas or representations, which is a clear expression of the "metaphysics of presence", which takes representation to be literally a kind of reenactment of the origin's presence, unaware of the writing-structure of every sign. Moreover, Derrida objects to the independence of the thinking subject, presenting it – much like Nietzsche and Heidegger – as being led by his thoughts, rather than having control of their meanings. Recognizing the madness inherent to the *cogito*, Derrida also rejects the universality of rational, scientific method: every rational discourse, he argues, necessarily excludes madness, and each discourse is shaped by the madness against which it has constituted itself. Hence, the task of thinking is the Cartesian task of the *cogito*, namely self-examination of its own nature and of the conditions of its possibility and impossibility.

A sympathetic relation to Descartes can be found also in Rancière (Chap. 6). The moment of the *cogito*, of the "I think!", is the paradigm of Rancièrian subjectification: it is a performative moment of self-affirmation, of recognizing that I am a thinking being. To be sure, Rancière is interested not in the ontological existence of the thinking substance, which is not really in doubt, but in its ability to think, which is doubted by the sociopolitical order he calls "the police". In the *cogito* the subject does not discover its existence but rather becomes a subject, namely announces its ability to think and demand the place of a thinker in the social order. That is to say,

Rancière adopts the egalitarian moment implied by Cartesian philosophy – the ability of each subject to realize s/he is a thinking being. However, he vehemently objects to the idea of a rational method intelligent thinking must follow – such method acts against equality, differentiating between those who think properly and those who need to learn how to do so. Thinking can take countless routes; all it needs is strong will, hard work, and careful attention. Rancière also accepts a version of the Cartesian dualism, insisting that inequality in the material world proves nothing about the mental one. However, he does reject the independence of mind from matter, arguing that the distribution of the sensible in the police determines what is reasonable to think in it. Finally, the split between mind and matter, politics and the police, is also adopted by Rancière, arguing that every person can think both political equality and the hierarchical thought demanded by the police: the thinker thereby becomes a "dividual", able to think at one and the same time in various incompatible ways.

Although rarely referring explicitly to Descartes, Adorno's critique of the Cartesian conception of thinking, discussed in Chap. 2, is clear. He understands the rational, scientific method as instrumental rationality's attempt to rule over nature. Similarly, Descartes' theory of ideas, according to which thinking involves representations, is seen as an expression of "identity thinking" which eradicates differences between individual objects to better manipulate them. Thinking, for Adorno, must reflect on the non-identical as such, be led by the object rather than forcing some preexisting conceptual frame on it. For this reason, Adorno strongly objects to the claim that every mental action is a mode of thought, arguing that reasoning according to the identity principle is no thinking at all. Still, it seems that the most significant controversy Adorno has with Descartes concerns the independence of the thinking subject from the material world. Despite his differences from orthodox Marxism, Adorno maintains the understanding that thinking is never separated from sociohistorical reality – whether giving itself over to the logic of domination or transcending it toward the non-identical, it is always conditioned by the actual world, influenced by the way it experiences it.

Finally, in Chap. 4, Deleuze's critique of Descartes goes even further than Adorno's, in presenting the seventeenth-century philosopher as the embodiment of the dogmatic image of thought: even as Descartes presumes to doubt every unfounded belief, Deleuze argues, he still assumes we all know what thinking is – a natural faculty striving toward the truth. Much like Adorno, Deleuze objects to reducing thinking to representations, which miss difference itself – that which is singular and becoming in everything. But he ties representations also to the concept of common sense, which in philosophers like Aristotle and Kant refers to the cooperation of senses or faculties needed to recognize and represent an object. Such cooperation, Deleuze argues, misses the differences between the individual faculties, forcing them into a unifying, emasculating model. The Deleuzian version of objecting to the inclusive conception of thinking is the distinction between thought and thinking: while the former stands for the dogmatic, commonsensical use of representations, the latter is the independent activity of the faculties, as each operates in its own unique way. Such activity cannot begin voluntarily but only as a result of a violent shock that starts in sensibility and is carried on to the other faculties, awakening each to its unique activity. The Deleuzian thinker, therefore, is as far removed as possible from the Cartesian subject – a thinker who thinks with sensibility, memory, and imagination, without dominating them or dominating others through them.

Before moving on to examine the five philosophers' conceptions of politics, let us look at another important aspect of their conceptions of thinking, which did not play a significant role in Descartes: the relation to language.

For Arendt, following Plato, thinking is engaging in silent dialogue with oneself. This clearly implies that thinking makes use of language, and that pre-linguistic thought is impossible. An important aspect of Arendt's own thought, accordingly, is studying the precise meanings of words and concepts such as freedom and authority, labor, work and action – she seems to believe that everyday language is often limited and inaccurate, and that thorough examination is needed to reveal the correct meanings of words and trace their changes throughout history.

Rancière also views thinking as involving inner dialogue, but unlike Arendt (and Plato) he argues that the silent conversation of between me and myself is not linguistic but rather takes place in an emotional, pre-linguistic level. Since language is not natural but a social construction, it reflects the distribution of the sensible accepted in the police, namely the social hierarchies presented as natural ones. Thinking, on the other hand, is essentially singular and subjective – translating it to common, understandable language is therefore a creative, poetic act, evidence of the intellectual capacities of every speaking being.

The distinction between thought and language is close to Derrida's view, as he recognizes the madness inherent to the Cartesian *cogito* and argues that to enter discourse – which can also come in the form of inner dialogue – this madness must be excluded and confined. Much like Rancière, Derrida argues that the excluded does not disappear but is rather an inseparable part of the excluding order, making it possible for it to change and develop. Unlike Rancière, however, he does not identify the excluded with certain thoughts or thinkers. Rather, the madness that is constantly being excluded is the gap that separates thinker and thoughts, frustrating the former's attempts to be in full control of the latter's meanings; like language itself, thinking is a form of writing.

The connection between thinking and writing is present also in my reading of Adorno. Adorno does not think there is prelinguistic thinking, but that thinking operates through indirect linguistic articulation of the non-identical, which is more suitable for writing than for speaking. While writing takes time, speech demands quick reactions, leaving the thinker no time to choose his words carefully; it therefore tends to become mere wrangling, an attempt to win the debate and dominate the interlocutor, rather than providing yet another opportunity to think. Although the temporal dimension is important also for Derrida, Adorno's view is very different from his. While Derrida applies the structure of writing to thought and language in general, for Adorno spoken thought is not altogether impossible, only more difficult and rare; he does not understand the delay characteristic of writing in terms of *non*-presence but rather of *over*-presence of the thinker, helping him approach the non-identical object.

Deleuze's view seems unique also in this respect. Genuine thinking, for him, makes sense, and there is no sense without language. But sense cannot be common, expressed offhandedly in ordinary language. It is an independent dimension of language, an effect created at the encounter between language and things; an event in which language *does* something to things, unlike most linguistic uses in which words are exchanged but nothing really happens. Thus, sense inheres not in nouns or in adjectives but in verbs and it is often articulated in the form of questions generating problems and forcing thinking to begin. To be sure, these questions are not part of any dialogue or conversation, either with oneself or with others – they arise in surprising, unusual ways, encountering others in the most unexpected places. They can be spoken like the instructions of a swimming teacher or written like Proust's narrator's search – what is important is that thinking is not only reacting to problems in a non-commonsensical way but also passing them on, making sense to others.

This brief review clearly indicates that although confronting similar questions and circling around the same issues, there are substantial differences between the conceptions of thinking offered by the five philosophers. They all share the desire to take significant steps beyond the Cartesian *cogito* and problematize the relation between thought and language, but they do so in very different ways and by maintaining different levels of proximity to Descartes and to everyday language. This also characterizes their relation to politics.

7.3 Thinking and Politics

For Arendt, politics involves speech and action in the common, public world, appearing in front of others in an attempt to make a new beginning in the world inhabited by a plurality of men and women. Thinking moves in the opposite direction: to think one must temporarily withdraw from the common world to engage in silent dialogue with oneself. Thought can be politically – or rather morally – relevant only in extreme historical situations in which the political space is eradicated and crime becomes the norm, when only solitary thinking about meanings can tell the thinker what she ought *not* to do. While leaving the world behind to engage in solitary thinking can be politically dangerous, judging – which is not identical to thinking but involves what Arendt calls, following Kant, "thinking in enlarged mentality" – is of the highest political importance: looking at the world from other people's perspectives contributes to making the world common, namely to the very possibility of political action.

Rancière also praises political action, and much like Arendt distinguishes it from the sociopolitical order – a distinction he terms as that between politics and the police. Both politics and the police are tightly connected to thinking. While the latter is a hierarchical order determining who is qualified to think and who is not – and accordingly, who gets to make decisions and who merely executes – the former challenges this order in the name of the thinking capacity of those who are not supposed to be able to think. Thinking is political, therefore, when it reaches beyond the divisions which seem self-evident in the police, that is when it thinks itself: when a thinker understands that he or she is able to think no less (and no more) than anybody else, when "I think" becomes a performative action demonstrating the equal thinking capacities of each thinker.

For Adorno the important distinction is not between political and non-political thinking, but between political thinking and mental activities that are not worthy of the name thinking: genuine thinking is inherently political, in the sense of challenging the very foundation of existing social reality, namely the principle of domination. Unlike cognitive processes that conform to the identity principle and cooperate with domination, thinking the non-identical offers an alternative relation between subject and object, and at the same time exposes the falseness of reality, the all-embracing presence of domination. To be sure, this politics of thinking the non-identical is much different from that of Rancière, which aims at overturning the police order and the division of the sensible. It is a minor, minimal kind of politics – a letter in a bottle impossible to predict how and whom it will affect.

Despite the differences between their conceptions of thinking, Deleuze and Adorno's conceptions of politics are relatively close, as are their views regarding the political nature of thinking. Deleuze also thinks politics cannot be an activity within the existing order, and genuine thinking necessarily undermines that order. Unlike thought, which conforms to the dogmatic image and merely reproduces the hierarchical relations in society as well as between each subject's faculties, thinking is a deregulated, independent activity of each faculty, transcending common sense as both recognition and *doxa*. Such thinking does not solve problems, bringing harmony back into the world, but rather reacts to them in a way that spreads them further, problematizing or rather deterritorializing more aspects of reality. This, then, is also a minimal, minor kind of politics, which does not aim at comprehensive political change but only at minor, singular subversion of the existing order.

Of all philosophers discussed in this book, it seems that the political dimension is the least explicit in Derrida's work. But even in his writings, the shadow of politics always looms over the philosophical discussions, including when thinking is on the line. Thus, while politics is not an explicit aspect of Derrida's reading of the *cogito*, it is in fact no less political than Foucault's. Although Foucault stresses the confinement of mad *people* at the classic age whereas Derrida focuses on the exclusion of mad *thoughts*, the latter also has severe political implications: madness, which is inseparable from the *cogito*, namely the zero point of all thinking, is expelled every time the thinker enters into discourse, into the common, public sphere that cannot tolerate it. As such, it is at one and the same time the condition of possibility and impossibility of politics – its spectral presence in every discourse, which stems from the inability to utterly get rid of it, destabilizes every sociopolitical order and makes unorthodox, subversive thoughts possible. This political dimension is made more explicit in Derrida's discussions of the teaching of philosophy at schools and the university: in both these cases what is at stake are not only academic and pedagogic concerns but also thinking's responsibility to examine the social and political conditions making it possible. At school as well as the university, thinking is assigned with the political task of questioning what Derrida calls "the philosophy of the state", namely the philosophical presuppositions upon which rests the hierarchical order of the state.

These are undoubtedly very different conceptions of politics and of its relation to thinking, but they do have something important in common. Much like their relation to Descartes' conception of thinking, what they all share can only be articulated negatively: they all challenge the established model of capitalist, liberal democracy, pointing to its limitations and offering alternative ways of thinking about politics. For all of them – Arendt being somewhat of an exception – thinking is no form of intelligently contributing to the existing political game but of exposing its faults and undermining it. Education for thinking, therefore, appears in each case to be a way of going against the political current, fostering the prospects of political resistance.

7.4 Education, Thinking and Institutions

While all philosophers discussed in this book refuse to reduce thinking to method and object to the idea that it is a kind of skill or technique with a simple set of rules that can be learned, they do believe it possible to educate for thinking or at least create the conditions that encourage students to think. Education plays significant role in their engagement with thinking – in some, to be sure, more than others – and they all consider the question of how to engage others, whether children or adults, in the activity of thinking.

At first sight, it may seem that education for thinking against the current, for thinking that criticizes the sociopolitical order, would be unwelcome at school and more welcome in other settings: the family, the community, the playground or the sea. However, while some of the philosophers discussed above do criticize the school, arguing that it might hamper education for thinking, they all believe that such education can take place also in there, and some even see it as an especially hospitable setting for fostering thinking.

Rancière holds that emancipatory education – which as I see it is also a kind of education for thinking in which the student learns he is already capable of thinking and learning – cannot be mediated by an institution. Indeed Jacotot, the so-called ignorant schoolmaster, was teaching at a university, but went against its most fundamental logic, and his success was thwarted as his followers attempted to institutionalize his method. Every institution implies hierarchical division into roles and positions and cannot be the source of emancipation and equality. Even when education for thinking is part of the formation of a collective political subject, as in the case of nineteenth-century French workers, it operates through teaching esoteric knowledge by uncertified teachers, outside formal institutions. Yet even Rancière does not totally deny the possibility of universal education for thinking, for political subjectivity, taking place at school – not, to be sure, as part of the official curriculum, but thanks to schools' ability to bring together different people, young and old, who are unlikely to spend time together elsewhere.

Deleuze's approach to institutional education is also highly reluctant. Although he does not dedicate much space to criticizing school, his direct attack on every sociopolitical order and common sense leaves little room for doubt regarding his relation to traditional education. Both his examples for what I interpret as education for thinking – learning to swim and the apprenticeship of a man of letters in Proust's *Search* – are not taken from the school context, and the latter case even lacks a teacher or instructor. In both, the student or apprentice confronts problems or signs shaking up his senses and producing involuntary reactions that are not translated into cooperation between the faculties but push each faculty to its limit, thereby passing the problem on to others. The teacher may not be necessary – perhaps one can even learn to swim all by oneself – but can help approach problems or signs in a way that does not attempt to solve and make them disappear in the abyss of accepted knowledge. But even here, it is argued, education for thinking in an institution such as a school or university is not impossible: a teacher can indeed ignite thinking not by transmitting knowledge or skills but rather by performing thinking in action – as Deleuze himself used to do, according to testimonies – or when the formal constrains of the lesson create the conditions in which the senses encounter a problem and thinking begins involuntarily.

Unlike Deleuze, Derrida often writes about educational institutions, analyzing the ways the school and university make possible and at the same time limit thinking. He shows how these institutions thwart certain people from thinking and certain subjects from being thought, and struggles to broaden the possibilities of thinking – to allow more (and younger) students to study philosophy at school, and more questions to be asked at the university. That is to say, despite being aware of the inherent limitations of educational institutions, Derrida insists on thinking in and about them, protecting the right to learn and be learnt in them as well as their duty to allow more thinking to take place: the (relative) freedom granted by the university and (relative) public nature of school make them irreplaceable sites for free, critical thinking. This does not mean, of course, that Derrida thinks critical, "deconstructive" thinking can take place only in formal institutions: the relations between Descartes and his (real or imaginary) interlocutors, as well as between Foucault and Derrida, are related but not confined to institutions. At the very least, they indicate that educational interactions between teachers and students can confine as much as liberate madness always and everywhere.

Adorno too criticizes the educational institutions of his time, which fail to educate for maturity and responsibility, and like Derrida, he insists on struggling to improve them, namely making them more hospitable for genuine thinking. For him public education has a crucial role not only in rebuilding Germany after the horrors of Nazism but also in the larger context of struggling against capitalism and preventing another regression to Fascism – a danger perhaps even more acute today than in Adorno's time. Although genuine thinking cannot really be taught and school is by no means a necessary condition for it, school can provide it with appropriate conditions, assist and direct it: teachers can ask students to write essays, demand thoughtful writing that experiences its object as non-identical, and allow essays to be read and commented on by others. Hence, despite the authority and discipline that are inseparable aspects of school education, it can nevertheless become hospitable to genuine thinking activities.

Finally, Arendt, who barely wrote about school and education, also implicitly recognizes, in my reading, the importance of school for fostering thinking. Whereas Arendt insists that everyone can think almost everywhere, and that people have thought even in the most difficult and darkest of times, she also argues that just as it is possible to make thinking difficult and dangerous, so it is possible to create hospitable conditions for it. Thinking, for Arendt, requires withdrawing from everyday life, and although it would seem that the private sphere is optimal for such withdrawal, it is in fact school that can suspend the demands of society and politics. Moreover, since withdrawing from the world can put not only the thinker but also the world itself in danger, it is important to allow it to take place where it can be balanced with judgment, namely thinking in enlarged mentality. Such mentality requires thinking from the point of view of others, for which not only imagination but also actual interactions with them are necessary. Thoughtful exchanges of perspectives, therefore, are an important task of the Arendtian school, next to providing time for each student to engage in inner dialogue with him or herself.

7.5 Concluding Thoughts

Comparison requires brevity, which necessarily comes at the expense of the detailed account that gives each philosophical position its full meaning and depth. But the above comparison not only sheds light on the similarities and dissimilarities of the five paths presented in this book. It also allows for a brief exploration of the relation of the philosophical views to educational practice, as well as to the field of education for thinking.

It must be said at once that despite its relative complexity and radicalism, I believe continental philosophy has much to convey to teachers and parents, curriculum designers and educational policy makers, no less than to fellow philosophers and educational theorists. It does not have to remain on the level of abstract theory, but may be relevant to the actual world of educational practice in various ways, as suggested below.

Some of this book's philosophical conclusions are relatively easy to implement in school settings. Writing essays, as suggested by Adorno, and giving students time to engage in inner dialogues as proposed by Arendt, and even broadening the scope of philosophy teaching as demanded by Derrida, are undoubtedly highly difficult tasks under contemporary conditions, but are nonetheless concrete goals worthy of struggle. Even the philosophies of Deleuze and Rancière, which seem to refuse being incorporated into school curricula, are not irrelevant to school. Deleuze has taught us that when the teacher thinks in class he can ignite unexpected, non-commonsensical thoughts in students, while Rancière has shown that an educational institution can not only be a site where students learn they cannot think by themselves but also one where they realize they are thinking beings just like anybody else.

However, implementing the continental conceptions of thinking requires serious consideration of the underlying philosophical views. Writing essays or giving students time to think about meanings, for example, are of little value if detached from the complex philosophical approaches of Adorno and Arendt. There are no short cuts in continental philosophy, and executive summaries are of no help here. There is no way to continental education for thinking that does not pass through the dense forest of the philosophical texts; to educate in the spirit of continental philosophy one has to carefully read the relevant philosophers and be acquainted with their views.

Furthermore, while this book attempted to give room to five different philosophical perspectives that belong to the continental tradition, it is highly doubtful whether they can all be applied simultaneously. The five approaches pull in very different directions, and although they do not logically contradict each other, it is obviously unreasonable to ask students at the same time to write essays, talk to themselves about meanings, be open to involuntary interpretation of signs, and think about the conditions making their thought possible. At the end of the day, even if all paths are tempting, it is impossible to take them all at the same time. Each requires full attention, as well as sincere commitment. Unlike a scholar writing an academic book, the educational practitioner has to make a choice. In writing this book, I chose not to choose, to remain in the position of the scholar or academic who shows the paths and clears them of obstacles and misunderstandings rather than actually takes them.

For this reason, despite the stark critiques made by the five philosophers of the prevailing conception of thought and the implied rejection of the prevailing approaches to education for thinking, this book should not be read as an attack on the existing field and a call for doing away with it. As I attempted to pave five different paths without privileging any, so I wish to think of them as adding up to the existing ones rather than taking their place. Nevertheless I do hope that after reading this book taking the familiar path would not be the same; at the very least, it would be more hesitant, less automatic.

Even if the five philosophical approaches discussed in this book cannot be directly applied to concrete educational practice – and I am by no means convinced that this is the case – the effect of philosophical ideas, as that of thinking itself, need not be measured strictly in terms of applicability. There are other possible ways of thinking about the relations between philosophy and everyday life, or between the worlds of thought and action. Philosophical thoughts can motivate, ignite, encourage, and inspire without being fully translated into the language of praxis. Unlike the way we usually think of application, inspiration is unpredictable. We can never know in advance whose thoughts will be inspired and how. Thinking works in mysterious ways. If there is one thing I hope, it is that this book would inspire its readers to think new thoughts that I could never have imagined.